Capt.

The Last White Hunter

Reminiscences of a Colonial Shikari

The Last
White Hunter

Reminiscences of a Colonial Shikari

Donald Anderson
With
Joshua Mathew

Indus Source Books

Indian Spirit, Universal Wisdom

Indus Source Books
PO Box 6194
Malabar Hill PO
Mumbai 400 006
INDIA
Email: info@indussource.com
www.indussource.com

THE LAST WHITE HUNTER:
Reminiscences of a Colonial Shikari

First published in 2018

ISBN: 978-93-85509-12-4

Cover design: Sethu Subramaniyan SS

Printed at Thomson Press (I) Ltd., Delhi

For
my wife Riya and my sons Mathew & Joseph

Contents

Acknowledgements

I would like to thank

- My mother for encouraging my reading habit, and my father for familiarising me with the works of Kenneth Anderson

- Naveen Sathyanand for looking after Donald while I wrote the book

- Don's sister June and her children in Australia

- Don's friends – Darryl Ross, Sudhir Christopher, Jimmy Job, Meru Sal, Noel Peacock, Nader Mirza, 'Poochi' Christopher, Mark Davidar, Suresh Raj, Udhank Raj, Sunita Dhairyam, Victor and James D'Souza, Gordon Thompson, Maria Vinda and Lincoln for being his support system over the years

- Those who gave their time and money to help Don – Gauri Lankesh, Philip Wollen, K.M Srinivas Murthy, Ashok Tendolkar, Kakarla Jayaraman, Prashant Sethi, Sherry Khan, Ajit St John, Harsha, Dheeraj, Raghu, Siddharth Reddy, Mrs. Marie Ross and many more

- Dr. Kenneth D'Cruz, Don's last doctor

- Nair, Lord and the boys from the Richmond Road Baptist Church who did their bit to make Don's life comfortable during his last days

~~~

• Ruskin Bond, Dr. Ullas Karanth, Jeremy Wade and T.N.A. Perumal for their contributions

• Sonavi Desai at Indus Source Books for having faith in the book

• Annu Kurien my first editor

• Sethu Subramaniyan SS for designing the book cover

• Jenny Mallin – author of *A Grandmother's Legacy – a memoir of five generations who lived through the days of the Raj*

• Lakshminarayan and Joseph who helped record Don's stories

• Theodore Baskaran, Mahesh Rangarajan and Dr. Divyabanusinh Chavda for guidance on the construct of the book

• Hugh & Colleen Gantzer, Romulus Whitaker, Michael Ludgrove and Keerti Ramachandra for their incredible generosity

• S Muthiah – historian & journalist and Harry Maclure of *Anglos in the Wind* for promoting the book long before it was published

• Verghese Jacob and Sunita for helping me with my research in Hyderabad

• For going out of their way to help me – Roger Binny, G Shaheed, Raza Kazmi, Aloysius P. Fernandez, Aditya Sondhi, James Champion, Andrew Poots, 'Bird' Suresh, 'Rags' Raghavan, Bhanuprakash, Lavanya Kukrety, Akhila Vijaykumar, Michelle Wadhwani, Shinie Antony, Patrick Michael, Sandhya Chandrashekar, Don Caswell, Susan Robertson, Jerry Jaleel, Barney Berlinger, Iain Burr, Rodney Galiffe, Pranay Gupte, Diego Guiaro, Coral Edge and Faye Hinge, Stanley Carvalho, Janice Payne, Len Boesinger, Ryan Lobo, Vinod Kantamneni, Ananda Teertha Pyati, Kerry Edwards, Ludo Wurfbain, PM Sukumar, Oliver Gunaseelan and many others

And of course Google, who made my effort infinitely easier

Foreword

I WAS BORN IN 1932, TWO YEARS BEFORE DON, AND CAME from a completely different background. He was the son of the famous hunter and author Kenneth Anderson, and lived on Kasturbha Road, near the Cubbon Park police station, within the Bangalore Cantonment, while I grew up in a traditional Indian environment in Bangalore. From our younger days, we were both enamoured by shikar—while he got to experience it first hand, accompanying his father, I had to be content with just reading books. And that instilled in me a love for the outdoors and wildlife. I couldn't afford a gun but I was bitten by the romance of the jungle and would never miss an opportunity to visit one.

However, as I grew older, I realised that getting a gun wasn't so difficult and for a short period of time I did my fair share of shooting and was also a member of the Mysore state rifle association. There were many cliques in Bangalore at that time, and on a couple of occasions I've had the privilege of hunting with Don. I was simply amazed at his skill, not just as a crack shot, but also at jungle craft. He had an unnerving eye for understanding signs and patterns in the jungles—developed over the years he spent with his father. However, unlike Don, I soon realised that while hunting gave me a tremendous adrenalin rush, I was soon filled with remorse and regret. The culmination was my chance meeting with O.C Edwards, a teacher at Bishop Cotton's school at Bannerghatta. Those days Bannerghatta was a pucca forest that held plenty of game and I had a gun in one hand and a bird I had shot in the other, when I met him—clearly my first impression was not exactly the best! I had heard of Mr. Edwards and his photography but I had never given it much thought till that day. I met him on many more occasions and he instilled in me the belief that photography was a far nobler pastime than hunting. He also taught me scientific names and animal behaviour and it's interesting to note that Don was his pupil at Bishop Cotton's school and underwent the same training. While we were both naturalists, Don and I chose different paths—I chose the camera while the gun continued to be his favourite weapon. We met each other on a few occasions and I soon realised that to be a good hunter or wildlife photographer, you need to understand the environment that your subject is in, the season, the time of day, and, of course, the behaviour of your subject and what influences it. Even when it comes to the equipment there are a lot of similarities—having a steady hand, aiming through the aperture, ensuring that your breath is steady and knowing the exact moment when to squeeze the trigger. Don was a master at all this and my experience with the rifle helped make my transition to the camera that much easier.

At that time, there was no concept called wildlife, creatures were classified into "big game" or "small game" and Donald Anderson was the quintessential big game hunter. With his khakhi clothes, slicked back hair and a cigarette, he always reminded me of the white hunters from East Africa whom I had read about. It wasn't a façade, he was often seen in Bangalore with a dead panther on his motorcycle and was admired equally by both men and women. Retrospection will always find faults at any point in time; most people today will castigate the actions of the hunters from the British Raj but it's easy to forget that that was the norm and an integral part of the social fabric in those days. Over time our concept and understanding of the creatures of the forest has changed for the better, but it didn't start suddenly one day. People like Kenneth and Donald Anderson didn't just hunt animals when they visited the jungles; they observed animals and were a source of information that people benefitted from. The world has all kinds of people, and Don Anderson is one unique individual who rightfully holds a place in history.

—T.N.A. Perumal
(A pioneer in wildlife photography in India)

Introduction

THIS IS A STORY OF PEOPLE AND PLACES LONG BURIED with the memories that complement the passage of time. These are anecdotes and memories of a time when life was not hurried; when moments seemed to last twice as long and people probably not as much. A time of freedom and infinite possibilities, of innocence and rectitude, and yet a time of ignorance and profligacy.

As I conjure out of the distant past, incidents in my rather colourful life, to narrate them to my friend, my memory often fails me. If I knew that things would no longer be the way they were during those times, perhaps I might have held on to those moments more dearly, but that is life.

Unlike my father, who was equally good with the gun and the pen, my skill has been only with the former, and hence I always dismissed the notion of putting together my memories in written form, when my friends and well-wishers suggested that I do. In my younger days, my attempts to be a raconteur would fall flat as the words I had typed on a page would stare back at me unflinchingly, reminding me of how poor a writer I was. I soon realised that I could not introduce the reader to the mystery and the magic of the Indian jungle through my writings, and I never attempted that again. Until now. My friend has convinced me that the bits and pieces of my gossamer-like memories, bound together, will make an interesting read for some people and so I have decided to humour him.

Deep within, I know that I don't have much longer to live, so I try to enjoy every full moon night surrounded by a million twinkling stars that shine brightly in the night sky. Today, I'm on the banks of the Moyar river in the Nilgiris and listening to the water rippling over the boulders. I can never understand people who say that they could not do without city life, when here, in a place akin to paradise, there are a million things that are so breathtaking to watch and observe. The sun begins to set, the jungle quietens down, and I know it is time to go to my abode a mile away before it gets too dark. As I get up gingerly and walk a few hundred yards, there is a distant "*dhank*" from the hill on my left. A sambar! Yes, a tiger or panther is afoot. I can imagine him strutting along, muscles rippling with every step, mouth half open, just waiting to quench his thirst after a hot day's wait. It's a clear night and he will hunt to satiate his hunger. I switch on my torch and walk as noiselessly as I can, watching the last struggle between light and darkness on display on the horizon. After reaching my hut, I put my cot outside and sit on it, while the fire I have lit crackles and pops, its flames dancing to the tune of the breeze that caresses the valley. I listen. Yes, just listen. You probably will ask, "Listen to what?" Well, my answer would be, "everything". There are various things one could listen to in the jungle. The soft cries of the night birds, the "*ponk*" of the sambar, the harsh bark of the jungle sheep, the shrill cry of the spotted deer, the sawing of the panther, the moan of a tiger. Yes, there are hundreds more. In my younger days, some of these sounds would get my adrenalin pumping and I would be up on my feet, rifle in hand, but now I think differently and I suppose all hunters go through this stage. When one is young and full of adventure, every trip to the jungle has to be replete with a kill. But when a shikari gets old, he is quite content to sit back, watch and listen.

I'm trying to relive my halcyon days... when my brow was not creased with worry or pain, when my hair was not tinged with grey, a time when I did not have to think where my next meal was coming from or how much suffering I would have to endure. Those were the days when I did exactly what I wanted to without a care in the world for another living creature.

It is no exaggeration to say that my life has been dictated by my love for hunting, and though I may not have profited financially, I have lived a life as fulfilling as I could have envisioned. Many people have asked me whether I regret shooting so many animals, and it is perhaps the toughest question I have been asked in my life. Considering the risks I took in the jungle, and the lifestyle I led, I never expected to live to this day and was sure, perhaps even hopeful, that my last drops of my blood would be soaked by the grass in one of my favourite jungles. I never thought I would live long enough to feel compunction. But Providence had other plans. I attended the funerals of all my close friends or came to hear of their passing away in places like Australia and England, and every time I did, I thought that I would be the next to go. Well, I did not die; I just grew old.

Although I am an educated man and have had almost no belief in God or even karma, I've come to terms with the fact that someone wanted me to live this long, to remind me of my acts, and perhaps seek retribution for the lives I had taken. My parents passed away thirty years ago and my sister migrated to Australia soon after Independence, so I have not had any real family to speak of for the past so many years. While I've always enjoyed the company of friends and like-minded people, in the end, I am alone.

And I am the last one.

I am the last male heir of the Anderson family. I am possibly the last living Scot from British India who chose to stay on after Independence. And I am the last of the white hunters for whom the forests of India have provided unimaginable adventure and excitement.

—**Donald Malcolm Stuart Anderson**

Chapter One

Growing Up in Bangalore

BEGINNINGS ARE OFTEN HERALDED WITH OPTIMISM and good cheer.

Sunday, 18 February 1934, was no exception. Even the brief showers couldn't dampen the mood, for an heir was born to the Anderson bloodline. Though the family lived within the cantonment at that time, we were partially shielded from the political cauldron that the country was simmering in. "Freedom" and "Independence" were just words spoken in hushed tones by the locals and not taken too seriously. Yes, there was a certain order and discipline. There was tranquility and happiness. And nothing exemplified all this better than the hundred-year-old house I was born in.

"Prospect House" was a resplendent red bungalow at No. 3 Sydney Road, Bangalore, built on twelve acres of land teeming with trees. Queen's flowers, rain trees, exquisite cork, trumpet and coral trees, lilac jacaranda, yellow cassia, bright orange spathodea and red *gulmohar* trees brightened the garden, while mango, jackfruit, guava, *chikoo*, avocado, sweet lime, custard apple, lemon, and pomegranate trees bore fruit depending on the season. Though this exotic garden existed before my parents were even married, my dad added his own touch by introducing wild orchids, *borum, mohua,* and different species of cacti gathered from his forest jaunts. He would even supply plants to the horticulturist at Lalbagh, with whom he shared a great friendship. In addition to the native animal life such as monkeys and squirrels that the grounds of Prospect House

4

were home to, my dad kept a menagerie of mammals, birds, and reptiles which created a backyard jungle of sorts. If that wasn't enough, flocks of parakeets, mynas, barbets, owls, and other birds filled the air with song.

Prospect House, Sydney Road

For a house that did not have a second floor, the first thing you would notice is how tall it was. Of course, it had huge attics, but the thick double-layered wooden ceiling still towered above us, and all the rooms had awning windows at the top, the architectural norm those days. There were three capacious bedrooms and two bathrooms on each side of the house, and curving around the house was a massive wrap-around verandah. The living room held trophies of animal heads mounted on walls, army shields, family photographs in rosewood frames, elegant Victorian furniture and a grand fireplace at one end.

A long mahogany table occupied the centre of the dining room and at an angle above the table was a very cleverly constructed skylight. Its design ensured that in the morning, the table would be suffused with soft light, while by noon it was protected from the harsh sun. This room had several glass cupboards filled with expensive crockery and playing in this room was absolutely forbidden. Right at the back were two large pantries, which were the most interesting rooms as far as my sister June and I were concerned, for it was filled with wire-meshed meat-safes and locked wooden almirahs that held jams, jellies, pickles, biscuit tins, sweet boxes and endless gastronomical possibilities. The kitchen was a separate building at the back, identified by the continuous stream of blue-grey smoke that wafted out of the chimney from wood fires; gas burners were decades away. Food was brought from the kitchen into the pantry, and during the cold months, there was a small area where food was kept warm over hot coals before it finally made its way into the dining room. Unlike in other parts of India where families, especially women and children, were sent to the hills during the summer to escape the heat of the plains, Bangalore enjoyed wonderful weather all year round. We wore sweaters and used quilts throughout the year and we never had fans or fridges.

For many years, Mum, Dad and I used two of the three rooms on one side of the house, while my grandparents and June used rooms on the other side. The bed rooms were so big that in addition to the large four-poster beds covered with mosquito nets in the middle of the room, there were wooden almirahs, dressing tables, chests of drawers and quaint elephant footstools. The sprawling bathrooms had two doors— one provided access from the inside and the other opened out. Servants dispensed water into small cisterns placed on the outside walls, and this filled giant brass containers inside, under which fires were lit, ensuring that we had piping hot water whenever it was needed. However, the bathrooms were so big that even with all the heat, in the farthest corner, it would be freezing cold!

My grandfather and I were given special privileges, for we had a room each to ourselves, while June shared one with our grandmother. Of course, that meant that every other room was fair game for our exploration and play. The attic, full of old and extremely dusty things, was usually off limits, as my grandmother feared that it held snakes and spiders. Nevertheless, June and I often spent a lot of time there, hopeful that we would find hidden treasure or at least a map to one.

Apart from the main building, there were a couple of small cottages on the premises which were used for storage or as outhouses that served as living quarters for the hired help, and a big garage filled with automobiles. As my grandfather was in the army, I grew up seeing a lot of cars and would spend time talking to the drivers, often begging them to let me sit behind the wheel.

We had a large number of domestic helpers, and all of them were Tamilians. In 1831, when the capital of Mysore state was moved from Mysore city to Bangalore, two distinct geographic sections already existed. The Bangalore cantonment was one, created in 1806, and at one point covered more than thirteen square miles, perhaps the largest British cantonment in south India. Our house stood on the border of Cubbon Park, the last bastion of the cantonment in that direction. Beyond this was the *pettah*, the second area, home to the local Kannadiga population. For some reason, hiring Kannadigas as domestic help was unheard of. As a result of this segregation, I grew up speaking Tamil from an early age. I presume that this tradition of having Tamil helpers existed for generations, because both my grandfather and my father knew Tamil; in fact, my father could also read the language, while my grandfather, having been in the army, knew Hindustani and Telugu in addition. It was very peculiar and perhaps it was not needed, but we did not speak Kannada while we were growing up. Well, maybe not completely, for I did pick up the choicest of expletives necessary for daily subsistence!

Though we were a fairly small family, a large house and the upkeep of all the animals we owned required a battalion of sorts to keep things in order. Two of my favourite people were Kanikam and Catherine ayah (nanny). Kanikam's only responsibility was to look after our dogs. At any given point in time, in addition to the menagerie of wild animals that my dad cared for, we had at least ten or twelve dogs of all breeds, shapes and sizes. Kanikam took his job a bit too seriously, for his dogs meant the world to him, and that meant ignoring pleas, commands or threats from anyone to get anything else done. Catherine, my ayah, was similar in this respect, because her world revolved around me. Although she was hired to look after both June and me, I was her unequivocal pet. The first bond for a child in those days was not with his parents, but his ayah, and the Anderson children had our Catherine ayah. She was short, of dark complexion, and obviously had very little education. She loved us, and if I have the license to exaggerate I would say that she, rather than Mum, brought us up during our early years. "Donald *baba* (little one)" was her favourite, and the two of us were quite inseparable. I would insist on sleeping with her and developed a habit of putting two fingers under her armpit before I would fall asleep. God only knew the hygiene of our ayah, but this habit seemed to induce my soundest sleep. No talcum powder, no deodorants, no concept of shaved armpits, and as for baths—well, once a week was good enough—and thus it was no wonder I was knocked senseless! Despite my tender age I was selective about the armpit I chose; I always chose the right one, the more potent one—sleep was then just minutes away.

I started my schooling when I was about four years old. There were no separate nursery schools, and at home, there was no particular hurry to give my illustrious career a head start. My first school was Bishop Cotton Girls' School, where my sister June went. Back then, all young boys studied in Bishop Cotton Girls' till the first standard and then went to the boys' school, which was on different premises. As I refused to go to school without my beloved ayah, my parents requested that she be allowed to stay in class with me. The school considered this a harmless request and agreed. The world was a simpler place back then. So, that year, my kindergarten class had about fifteen children and one very excited ayah. She and I shared the same desk and bench for a whole year. I was not exactly the most communicative child back then, and my mother's questions on what I learnt during the day were mostly answered by Catherine ayah. Needless to say, she aced the first year, while I failed miserably and had to repeat lower kindergarten. She was unfortunately not given a chance to prove her mettle with the upper kindergarten syllabus and retired to full-time household duty. So, I took three long years to traverse the perilous kindergarten classes, clearly the formative years in any young boy's life.

Once I had to go to school without my ayah, as she was ill, and only bribes of chocolates and toys managed to change my stubborn resolve. However, after I had been dropped off, I vociferously insisted that I was willing to give up all those bribes in return for her, but it was too late. So, I ran from one class to the next screaming June's name, the only person who would understand my plight, and following me was a bevy of the best, from Bishop Cotton's girls' school. Luckily, June's class was not too far away, and I managed to find her easily. I then dived at her feet, grabbed her legs and held on for dear life. People at school got an idea of the strength I possessed even at that age, because it took at least three of them to pry me loose, while I shouted, kicked, punched, and bit anything that looked remotely human. Poor Catherine ayah was so distraught at what I had been subjected to, and, despite her illness, she accompanied me to school the next day and normalcy was restored.

As June and I got a little older, we were gifted a pony each; Judy was

June's, while mine was called Nelson. We never rode them on our own, but had two chokras (young boy helpers), who looked after them, to hold the reins and guide them as we sat atop, looking pleased as punch when we arrived at school. I am sure it was my dad's idea, and we were looked upon with admiration by many of our friends. As we got bigger, we got Raleigh cycles, a popular brand back then, and as there were hardly any motorcars at that time, there was no danger in riding to school. A unique feature of these cycles was that the chain used to run in a metal casing filled with oil, and this made cycling very easy. If you were an adult, you had to have a license to ride a bicycle, and if you were riding it after dusk, you had to have a small kerosene lamp in front; dynamos were years away. As I got older, a fad among young boys was to have a plastic card placed against the spokes of the bicycle so that it made a sound like a motorcycle when we pedalled very fast, or so we thought! This became our preferred mode of transport wherever we wanted to go, even going all the way to Devarabetta, which lay thirty-five miles away, no small feat even for those days.

Occasionally, we would take some of our domestic helpers to the jungles, and for some time, Catherine ayah was a foregone inclusion. Having done many of these trips, she began to consider herself a veteran, and like *dorai* (the master), cut out for such adventures. Back home, she would embellish some of her stories to her peers, who listened with awe. This went on for a while until we went to a place called Muttur on one of these trips. Catherine ayah, June, and I stayed at camp while Mum and Dad had gone exploring. Soon, the sun started to set and we were getting a bit uneasy looking at the lengthening shadows. Our imaginations were working overtime, and suddenly June saw something and shouted "*puli, puli*" (tiger, tiger)! She was not alarmed and was just pointing out the obvious. While I was excited, our poor ayah reacted as if she had been shot, and fell on her back, pole-axed, as we laughed our heads off.

The next incident with our ayah was far from amusing. We had gone to Muttur again, and this time, Dad went "*ghooming*" (wandering) on his own, while Mum, June, Catherine ayah, and I stayed behind at camp. After waiting a long while for his return, we decided that we had had enough and would try to find him, relying on our proficient jungle craft. Mum tended to overlook details, and after a while, we realised that the torch we were carrying did not have any batteries. So, we felt then that discretion was perhaps the greater part of valour and decided to return to the camp. Catherine ayah volunteered to lead the way, laying claim to this arduous task because of her experience in the jungles. Needless to say, we lost our way, and in the semi-darkness, instead of sticking to the game path, we veered off. Suddenly, our pack leader started to scream that she had been caught by a *minispuram* (evil spirit), who was choking her and trying to drink her blood. We froze in our tracks, concerned only about our own safety. Meanwhile our ayah managed to escape her tormentor—a wait-a-bit-thorn bush, but had her face and hands badly scratched in the process. She started screaming again, fearing the next attack and ran straight into us. It was minor consolation because then all of us collectively started to scream for help. Luckily, our camp was next to a river, and a woman from the *Poojaree* tribe who was living near the river bank heard our cries and came to our rescue. There was no real risk, of course, but the *Poojaree* woman did not know that. All she knew was that some people were in trouble, and in complete darkness, armed with nothing more than a sickle, she found us and helped us get back to camp. The next day, she showed us where she was when she had heard our cries, and it was indeed a rather long way off. We were amazed and truly grateful, wondering what made her respond the way she did. That was true bravery.

Blossom, Donald, June and Catherine ayah – Botanical Gardens, Ooty

Trips to the jungles with June were few and infrequent because she often suffered from asthma. There were no inhalers in our days, and my parents did not want to run the risk of her getting an attack away from the city. Hence, she was not allowed on trips to cold places and had to stay at home with our grandmother. To compensate for those times, Dad would occasionally set up tents in our garden, which was great fun. Of course, we would stock our tents with lots of food, warm blankets, and torches, and spend the entire night there. It was very exciting. We would be less than a hundred yards from the house, but it felt as if we were in the jungle, which made June very happy. June and I were totally spoilt by our dad. Despite his notoriety as a skinflint, during our early years, he was an over-indulgent father and I realised how lucky I had been as a child only when I became an adult.

I was a terribly naughty child, and I don't mean it in a precocious or endearing way. Dad never believed in corporal punishment, but my Mum clearly did not believe in spoiling the child by sparing the rod, coat hanger, ladle or anything she could get her hands on. I remember, one day when I was about five or so, I had been particularly mischievous and was caught red-handed. My mum did not have any armament within reasonable distance, so she felt that one of her slippers was good enough to wreak carnage. I knew that it wouldn't really hurt me, but she looked so furious and the odds didn't seem particularly in my favour, so I decided to make a run for it. I sprinted out of the back gate and into Cubbon Park. For some distance, she ran with a slipper on one foot, while the other was bare. This gave her a slightly ungainly gait and made me laugh uncontrollably. As most kids know, laughing at a furious mother never ends well, so she called in reinforcements and a comical sight ensued. I was being chased by Mum, who was followed by Catherine ayah pleading that I be spared, and running after her was the mali (gardener) and the cook, who apparently had some free time to join in the foray. From the corner of my eye, I could see June, who was watching the melee and laughing so hard that she was on her knees with tears streaming down her face. It must have been a comical sight for the neutrals who were having a stroll in Cubbon Park, and it became a much talked about story for years to come. Puncturing a hole in my theory that I could outrun anyone, I was caught and dragged back to the house and given a walloping that hurt my poor ayah more than me.

Despite our age difference, June and I used to fight a lot when we were children. I hated anything to do with studying, usually because I was not any good. June, on the other hand, was brilliant at everything she attempted. Academics, sports, music, arts—she excelled in everything she did. She was also sweet and kind and everyone loved her. I hated her for all these reasons, and I used to bully her to do my homework and other chores for me. If she refused, twisting her arm and hitting her were my primary methods to get her to change her mind. While she was strong, I was stronger and would hurt her quite a bit. She, however, never told on me, and would just go away and spend time with our grandmother who doted on her.

I do not recall the reason, but at some point, June moved out of her grandmother's bedroom and into mine, and though I resisted it at first, I eventually came to accept the unwelcome intrusion. June was petrified of ghosts and our house had enough enthusiasts to seed those thoughts in her head. It was not just our father who tried to convince us in every possible way that there were ghosts amongst us, but the servants did one better with their repertoire of stories of *pisach* (devil) and other spirits who loved nothing better than to eat the flesh of small children. Every once in a while, June would drag her mattress and blanket under my bed and sleep there. Many years later, the explanation she offered for her behaviour was that the one on top of the cot was the first to be spotted and devoured by these spirits who were looking for the easiest prey. Once satiated they would never think of actually looking under the bed! Her fear at times was so acute that when she had to go to the bathroom in the middle of the night, she would wake me and drag me along. I was not as scared as she was, but I could be most obstinate about getting up from the comfort of my bed and leaving behind my hot-water bottle. She would then bribe me with pin money or sweets. Once we reached the bathroom, she would make me either talk to her or sing quite loudly, to assure herself that I had not been captured while she did her deed.

All his life, my dad was obsessed with the occult and we were witness to an ever-increasing intensity he had towards this hobby. At Prospect House, he had a room that was dedicated to his research. Ever since we could remember, this room was dark and full of scary things, and it even had an odd smell. If we were on our own, we avoided it at all costs. While I was braver than June, I still would not venture inside alone. This room lay between our bedroom and the bathroom, which complicated matters for us. Going to the bathroom at night was something we dreaded and only considered if it was a real emergency. Even then it was a most scary affair—there was no question of switching on a light those days, so we would light a candle and tiptoe our way past the spooky room. It was a fine balancing act, trying not to look directly at the room, yet nervously glancing at the dancing shadows in the flickering light, all the while holding on till we reached our destination! Of course, we would never admit to being scared to our parents, but one day, June blurted out her fears. The next morning, Dad called us into his occult room to prove that there was nothing to be frightened of. Of course, he never said "there are no such things as ghosts"—it would have been against his very nature to utter those words, but he wanted to convince us that we had nothing to fear. After much persuasion, June and I were seated next to each other on two chairs in front of a crystal ball placed on a low table. Sitting on the other side of the table was Dad conducting our initiation into the world of the supernatural. I remember staring hard into the crystal ball, and to my horror, I could make out a moving shape in it. Without wasting a moment, I let out a scream and burst out of that room, past the dining room and out of the front door. June, seeing this, shrieked and ran as well, following me. It was a close finish, but I remember that Dad beat us all to the garden! Once nerves were calmed, we asked each other why the other ran. June mentioned that she had not really seen anything, but had run because I had. Dad sheepishly admitted that he ran on seeing us run. Since it was I who had seen something in the crystal ball, I proceeded to describe what I saw. It was daytime, and after hearing the details of the spectre, feeling quite brave, the three of us headed back to the room to have another look at the ball. We then discovered that what I had seen was just a rolled-up Persian carpet through the crystal ball! The irony of the situation was that my dad who had spent so many years trying to see a ghost had run the fastest when the moment of truth had arrived! That ended the mystery of the ghost in the crystal ball, but our fear of the room continued for many years to come.

Another weapon in his arsenal was a planchette. A planchette is a flat piece of wood with an apparatus to hold a pencil or pen. People such as my dad believed that the presence of spirits or their energy moved the planchette, and we would have amateur sessions trying to contact people who had passed away. We were always in awe of how letters would appear, and it was left to each of us to interpret them, although we took our dad's interpretation as the final word. Sometimes the spirits would not express themselves by the written word, but would simply answer questions by tapping. One tap meant a Yes while two taps meant a No. While that captured our attention during those years, when we grew up we lost interest. My dad, however, upgraded to the Ouija board and attended séance sessions that were common at the house of a Mrs.

Lazaar. She would talk in tongues and was quite famous for contacting dead people who had unfinished business in this world. She was much sought after, especially among the Anglo-Indians. In the old days, there was room for ghosts, but looking at the population now, I doubt people have the time for ghosts, while ghosts probably have no space to live in!

Dad was always interested in new things and ideas, and he instilled a sense of curiosity in us as well. Unlike today, my parents were not overly protective of us and Dad treated us like little adults, giving us the freedom to try things, take responsibility and learn through our mistakes. He would even create situations for us to enhance our sense of adventure, such as taking us to explore "Bumble-Bumble Elves cave". The cave was a routine stop for us when we travelled on Bannerghatta Road. We would stop by the tenth mile stone and walk for two furlongs to come across this mysterious place on the left side of the road. As the entrance to the cave faced away from the road, typically, one would not even notice this place. You would have to walk past it, and then climb down to reach the entrance. Inside was a shrine and the cave was home to hundreds of bats. It was not very deep as caves go, but somehow the sun never shone directly inside, so it appeared to be larger than it actually was. We would shine our torches carefully, not wanting to disturb the bats, and look around. I'm not sure what we were looking for, but Dad always assured us that it was a magical cave. Why "Bumble-Bumble Elves cave"? Who knows, but part of the mystery was the name, and he told me that as a child, his own father had brought him here; so clearly it was ancient. Of course, to keep the magic going and to ensure that his well-laid plans were not exposed, he would tell us how the true powers of the cave and its inhabitant grew stronger toward dusk. And since this was a stop while going from Bangalore, there was never a chance we would be there after sunset. While always curious, we did not have the courage to ask him to stop by on the return leg. June would pinch my hand and point to the spot as we were coming back, and neither of us would have the nerve to ask him to stop. A thrill would run down our spines, but we would not speak a word. The duo in the front seats must have been stifling their laughter as we drove past.

Apart from Bannerghatta, our picnic jaunts included places like Thippagondanahalli, Hesaraghatta, and Magadi. We usually went with a couple of other families who had kids our age. These places had scrub jungles that held panther, bear, wild boar, jungle fowl, spurfowl, peafowl and partridge, and hence hunting was always on the cards. If we visited spots that had an opportunity for angling, the Seddons always came with us. "Tiny" Seddon was a great angler, and his family was great fun. These would be mostly day trips, while for full-fledged vacations we would go to places like Kodaikanal, Pondicherry, and the Nilgiris.

My dad had many friends at the railway colony behind the City Railway Station. We would go there often, and June and I would get to see the steam engines, while Dad talked to his friends. These were very exciting moments for us, as we would get into the engines and be given a tour by one of his friends. Though steam engines are associated with great amounts of soot and dirt, these engines would be spotless after every run, because the men who managed the trains were so dedicated to their jobs. The Anglo-Indians, who practically ran the Indian Railways, took pride in the way they ran the show, and I saw the same sort of dedication at the Telegraph Department, where my dad worked. Though the work at the department was not as hard, it ran like clockwork and was marvellously efficient, which suited my dad perfectly.

Before I got my first gun, as with most boys who had an interest in this sort of thing, the catapult was my weapon of choice. All it needed were parts from an old tyre, a forked twig and ammunition that ranged from pebbles to sun baked clay marbles and peas, of which there was never any shortage. If I was not in school, I would be at Cubbon Park with my friends, where I would climb trees, which I imagined to be giant ships, on which we were pirates, or we would play cowboys and Indians on the vast lawns that would become the American prairie. Unlike fake swords and daggers, the catapult was a real weapon and no play-acting was needed. We never shot at each other, but the feeling of a weapon, however small and insignificant, was very exciting.

My friend Sydney D'Silva and I used to go to Bannerghatta Road to raid fruit orchards, and hunt for Stanly bug-outs or bloodsuckers. Stanley bug-outs? That's what they were called, although I don't know how that name came about. They were not "bloodsuckers" either, but common skinks, harmless reptiles, and we caused considerable damage to their population by going on these adventures. We would ride out on our cycles with our packed lunches and catapults and spend the entire day in shady groves, climbing trees, swimming and fishing in tanks, and, of course, hunting these reptiles. The ones that died instantly were lucky while the less fortunate ones suffered in agony, for we just left them there. We did it with no remorse, and it was a terribly cruel sport we indulged in. We didn't have to wait for a weekend to indulge in this sort of fun. We often skipped school, and the closest haven for us to hang out then was the Mud Tank behind Baldwin Girls' school, where we would fish and collect specimens in bottles. Today, the tank is no longer there, and "Divyasree Chambers" stands in its place, though some of the trees I used to spend hours on are still around.

Another piece in our arsenal was butterfly nets, and we would spend hours catching beetles, butterflies and other insects. All of us had our own collection where the subjects were displayed in glass-covered boxes, mounted with special pins on plastic or cork or simply glued onto a small piece of plastic. These then served as prized possessions and were often involved during barters or bets at school. My trips to the jungles with my dad gave me a huge advantage over my city-constrained classmates, and I would often come back with some very exotic insects. One that stands out in my memory is an insect called the velvet *bootchie,* which we used to come across in the Segur area usually in the rainy season. It looked like a little velvet ball with legs. I used to find hundreds of them while walking up to Ooty, but they seem to have disappeared from those jungles now.

I always associate my trips with Sydney with toffee apples. American in origin, they were immensely popular among the Bangalore boys during the war, and we would eat these by the dozen. A bite from this whole apple impaled on a stick and covered with treacle would give you bits of the hard outer-coating and the crisp, yet softer fruit inside. Soda was available in a glass bottle that had a marble as a stopper for the gas inside, and we would often break bottles for the glass ball that would go into our collection. Meringues, and iced tea cakes were tea-time fare when I returned from school. I particularly remember eating blancmange, which came in five flavours. Then of course, there was the standard jelly and ice cream, which was mostly made at home in a hand-cranked ice cream machine. This was a family affair, and all of us helped to churn the ice cream over ice and rock salt to create the most delicious ice creams, which would, of course be consumed instantly! Most summer days ended with a couple of milkshakes at Lakeview, which cost about half anna each. There was no concept of an allowance in those days, and Dad's parsimony didn't make things any easier. However, Mum would give us pin money, usually a few annas every month.

After the Second World War, you could buy twenty-five loaves of bread for a rupee, and it is amusing that today, seventy years later, you get one loaf of bread for twenty-five rupees! For one rupee and eight annas, the four of us could eat a grand meal at good restaurant in town. For someone my age, money was never in rupees—only in pies, pice and annas. One rupee equalled sixteen annas, one anna equalled four pice, and one pice equalled three pies. Most of whatever we could scrimp or conveniently "borrow" was spent on food and trinkets at small shops, but the exciting places were Spencer & Co, and Nilgiris, the only two department stores at that time. However, we mostly depended on butchers, greengrocers, and fishmongers at Russell Market and as there were no plastic bags, we carried what we bought in cloth bags or wrapped our purchases in old newspaper. Bread, eggs, and milk were not bought from shops, but delivered home. Unlike today, the barber too came home, and June and I would have our hair cut in the garden, and we hated the clippers used to remove the hair from the back of our necks!

I was outdoors a great deal and often sustained cuts and bruises, but unless it was something serious, I never visited the doctor. Usually a spoonful of castor oil cured all maladies we suffered. Clothes were never bought but instead stitched by a tailor. We hardly ever bought new clothes and threw away old ones only after multiple rounds of stitching and darning on our Singer sewing machine, until they fell to bits. Clothes and footwear were bought one size bigger, as they would last longer! Shoes that were getting tight would have their toes cut out and used as sandals!

I hated lessons but loved sports so staying back at school was something I enjoyed. I excelled in most sports, including cricket where I represented the state school team as a wicket keeper. The fervour with which I hated academics often led me to find the most original of excuses not to go to school. Someone up there would have found it very amusing to see father and son providing similar excuses at the school and office, respectively, for not turning up on a Friday to get away on a long weekend. Dad and I usually started on Thursday evening and returned during the early hours of Monday. To then go to school for the full day, stay back for sports and then walk back home makes me wonder how I did not collapse on the way!

Like my father, I too had a fascination for all living creatures and had many pets while growing up. While they do not qualify as pets, one of my signature acts was carrying scorpions to school. I was quite a hero, even among the senior boys at school, when I would casually pull out a monster specimen from my bag, black and bristling. While I was always careful not get a vicious nip from its claws, the tail was always the danger end, and onlookers would watch in horror as I played a version of Russian roulette with the tail, as it aimed to sting me. There were a couple of things that were in my favour. The first was ignorance. The big black scorpions, while capable of leaving a painful welt, were practically non-lethal to humans. However, its sheer appearance made it seem twice as bad, or me, twice as brave. The other advantage I enjoyed involved a certain level of cheating. Thanks to some of the chokras at home, I had by then mastered the art of not only spewing the vilest of abuses, but also sandpapering a scorpion's stinger down to a nub, which made the creature practically harmless. Removing a scorpion's sting was equivalent to killing it, and carrying a dead scorpion, no matter how large, did not make for any worthy hero worship. So, through many trials and more painful errors, I picked up one of my many self-proclaimed PhDs—the type that loses its practical application after about a year or so!

When I was growing up, the closest we came to organised betting was with fighting quails, and this was something I excelled in. There was no concept of odds: it was a simple bet—the last quail standing versus the one that was incapacitated. Not a pretty sport by any stretch of imagination, but I became very good at it. Quails are notorious for their quarrelsomeness and are often kept separately, especially the males. I used to rear them at home, and my dad, unaware of my sinister plans, always wondered how a few would go missing. I took great pride in fixing their diet, which included guts from the meat we bought from Russell Market to feed the bigger pets. A pair cost about four annas, and I would spend much time choosing them from a shop at Russell Market. As part of the training routine, I would put the quail in front of a mirror, where it would tirelessly attack its reflection. I felt this prepared the quails for the ring and gave them good practice. Once they were ready, these feathered pugilists would indulge in a no-holds-barred match in a remote part of the school grounds, while a couple of boys were posted on the lookout for school staff, who absolutely forbade this sort of thing. Money exchange was minimal and we usually bet on trinkets like catapults, marbles, and comic books as prizes.

Quails were just one of the pets I had, and they were not pets in the true sense, as they were neither tame nor affectionate. I loved most mammals, and birds were tolerable, but I drew the line there. I hated snakes—unlike my dad. He had a morbid fascination for them and ever since I can remember, we always had snakes in our house—venomous ones like cobras and Russell's vipers as well as the non-venomous variety like pythons and *dhamans* (rat snakes). My dad would extract snake venom to be sold to local hospitals for a fair bit of money. My role in this entire exercise was to put the snakes back in the pits after their venom had been extracted. One might think that this job carried less of a risk, but these were snakes that had been woken up from their reverie, held tight and forced to bite on a membrane, and this left them extremely irritated. The job was a sweaty affair, which did my confidence no good. In later years, I had the added responsibility to take the venom to the middle-man who in turn sold it to hospitals and other organisations.

However, snakes were not the only non-human inhabitants of our house. Leave alone the numbers of animals, the sheer variety of species was astounding. Jackals, pangolins, mongooses, monkeys, squirrels including the Malabar Giant, rabbits, barking deer, a sambar doe called Dora, mouse deer, slender loris, huge tortoises and, of course, at any point in time a dozen dogs and cats. Domestic fowl, a pair of peacocks, geese, turkeys, parakeets, mynas, and a surly vulture represented the avian family. Looking back, keeping some of these birds in tiny cages would rank very high in my list of cruel acts; living in a one-foot by one-foot square jail for a life time must have been terrible for those birds, and I wish hadn't done that.

It is no exaggeration to say that most people viewed our home as a zoo, but the extent of this came to light one day, when my friend Merwan's scheme got exposed. As we let out part of the house to tenants, it was assumed that anyone seen within the walls was visiting a lodger. We would have many visitors, mostly children or young adults. No one was questioned nor given a second thought. However, one day, my mum heard voices raised in anger; someone was asking for a refund. Curious, she walked to the side of the house where the heated discussion was happening.

"Bloody hell, you said there were tigers, and that's why I paid so much. I did not come here to see some lousy jackals and snakes."

The cat was out of the bag and Merwan confessed that for a long time, he had been selling tickets to people for a guided tour of the menagerie at home!

Among our pets, Jackie the hyena was my dad's favourite and used to live on a large island surrounded by a dry moat, adjacent to Cubbon Park. One day, one of our tenants, Gilbert Briggs, a young boy, was playing with a hoola-hoop, the rage in those days. The hoop fell into the pit and he went to retrieve it. Jackie in the meantime had got hold of it and wanted to join in the fun, reluctant to let it go. In the tug-of-war that took place Gillie fell into the pit. While Jackie was usually very mild-mannered, he got scared when Gillie fell in, and attacked the boy and bit him. It became a contentious issue and questions were raised about whether such pets should be kept at homes. Though we managed to hush the matter, the municipality came to know about the incident and we had no choice but to move Jackie to Dad's house in Whitefield.

As I grew older, I brought home panther cubs from the forest on a couple of occasions. We refused to call all them anything other than Spotty. They would be playful when they were young, but as they grew older, they would be extremely difficult to control, often stalking guests and jumping on them with bloodthirsty cries. We never seemed to learn our lesson, and what seemed adorable pets at first would become dangerous animals, and we would have to give them away to the Mysore and Madras zoos.

Bruno complains of a toothache – with Kenneth Anderson

We had a few bears, but none of them were as affectionate as a sloth bear we called Bruno and none of them lived as long either. Bruno was like the third child of the family, extremely spoilt, and Mum's favourite. However, as years passed, he became infested with fleas and contracted some sort of disease, which caused him to lose hair, a heartbreaking sight. He got thinner and eventually passed away at a ripe old age. When he died, my mother showered her affection on a bonnet macaque named Jacko. Perhaps it was amusing back then, but in today's world, there would be such an uproar if a pet monkey was dressed up in pretty clothes, and adorned with lipstick, rouge, and *kajal*. I don't quite know why Jacko was dressed up like a girl, as he was a male. As is common with most monkeys, he had a habit of grooming others, and we would all take turns to have our heads massaged by him, often falling asleep during the process. However, as he reached maturity, he got extremely aggressive, often baring his teeth, especially if people got close to Mum, who he considered his two-legged concubine. He too had to be given away.

Although we had many dogs, they were all spoilt rotten and were terrible watch dogs. If there was one pet that guarded the house, it was a bar-headed goose called Ivan. We got him as a chick from one of our hunting trips and he grew up to be a temperamental and over-protective addition to the family. With two other regular geese, they were a vicious honking trio that attacked people without any sort of provocation. We had many exotic animals, and while they provided more excitement, they were wild animals, and we always had instances that put people's lives at risk. Looking back, apart from the threat to people, I can see how cruel it was to keep wild animals as pets.

Bishop Cotton was the one of the popular choices for schools for the English or Anglo-Indians. The others were Clarence and Josephs in the 1930s. It is funny that the Catholic versus Protestant argument spilled over to schools as well, for St. Josephs, our greatest rival, was Catholic, while my school, Bishop Cotton, was Protestant. My school was a prodigious institution started in 1865 by a bishop from Calcutta, who wanted to impart education in India. The students belonged to one of three houses—Pettigrew, Pope, and Pakenham Walsh, each house named after an influential individual at the school. During the years I was at the school, the principal was Canon Elphick, who is considered by many as the best the school ever had. The school had lots of blocks, each catering to either a batch of students or an activity, and a chapel and tuck room. Each class had two sections and had students from all over the country from varying backgrounds and religions, but the ones that stood out were Europeans and Anglo-Indians with a smattering of Parsis, Coorgis, and Malayalis.

We had just about three hundred students, so you can comprehend the student-teacher ratio. This translated into an uncomfortable situation with teachers' knowing each of us in far more detail than we appreciated. Examinations were conducted just thrice in one's schooling life—the Bangalore Middle School, the Junior Cambridge, and Senior Cambridge. The Middle School was an Indian exam that one had to write in seventh standard, while Junior Cambridge was an English examination, but conducted here in India. In the ninth standard, you had your Senior Cambridge which was common to both the Indian and English systems. I am therefore a Senior Cambridge fellow, or in today's equivalent, just about a ninth standard pass!

Most of our subjects were taught by cassock-sporting priests, who spent their entire life in service. They were committed to serving the school and the church for thirty or forty years, and, eventually, to be buried here as well. While choices were limited, and the concept of job hopping was unknown, these men dedicated their entire lives to the institution. Clearly, they were a different breed, perhaps the last of their kind. With practically no family and no prospect of going back to England, life must have been grim for those chaps. Despite their rather bleak prospects, most of them were fair-minded and their devotion to the education system was absolute. Detention was the most common of punishments, and they were administered by any of the staff for small offences. While it certainly was not a pleasant experience staying on in school and writing endless pages, it was not a big deal either.

Punishment for serious offences, on the other hand, lay in the hands (literally) of the school masters. Smoking and fighting were the most common serious offences, and if caught, promised a maximum of three strokes on one's bottom. Of course, the loophole in the system was that the actual punishment would be administered only after a certain interval, thus giving the guilty a chance to add a layer or two of inner clothing to reduce the sting. I had a friend called Chappell who actually would not wear "protection". While he cited that he was man enough to take it, I can't help wondering if his orientation was a bit different from the rest of us! I was not much of a smoker during my school days, but I did make up for lost opportunity once I finished schooling.

While most of our school masters were good chaps, every once in a while, we would have the privilege of having a sadistic one. An individual that particularly stands out was a chap named Moss. He had been a victim of polio and needed a cane to walk. His frustration and anger about his condition was vented on only targets who could not retaliate. His disability rendered him ineffective to carry out sneak attacks, so, every year, he would select about three or four boys and proceed to inflict misery on them for the entire academic year. He would goad them by mocking and ridiculing them, and the smartest thing a victim could do was to just take it; for the slightest whiff of impertinence meant detention or worse. He was so hated that at one point the head boy felt it was his right, as a representative, to do something for the masses. One night, he hid in a corner and then somehow managed to cover Moss with a cloth and hammer the daylights out of him. No one knows how Moss discovered the identity of the perpetrator, but the boy was expelled. Encouraged, Moss then broadened his target list and my friend Ronnie Philips came under his radar. Since Ronnie was a boarder, he was an easy pick for Moss, whereas I was spared, because I was a day scholar. Boarders could spend the last Saturday of every month with friends or family, and Ronnie used to come to our home. One Saturday, he showed up with a big bruise and when my mother inquired how he got it, he refused to divulge the identity of his tormentor. In those days, to snitch on somebody was against the unspoken code amongst boys who wished to be thought of as manly and honourable. But she persisted and since he was very close to her, he blurted out the truth. The dam burst that day and all of Moss's crimes echoed in our living room. My Mum seemed to take it surprisingly well, I thought. A short while later she drove off. I did not have the slightest inkling of what lay ahead, and the rest of the story became stuff of legend. She drove up to the staff quarters at school, asked for directions to Moss's room and marched on grim faced with a tow of boarders behind her on a sunny Saturday afternoon.

"Mr. Moss?"

It was a confirmation, not a question, but the occupant of the room did not quite realise it. The bolt was removed from inside, and my mother shoved her feet inside, pushed Moss aside and shut the door. I'm guessing it was her handbag, maybe it was something else, but the boys heard distinct yelps, as my mother proceeded to lavish Moss with some potent Anderson fire and brimstone, complemented with a heavy object. Although the room he was in was quite large, the speed of the attack combined with his disability meant that he had very little chance of defending himself. From the looks of my mother, who came out red-faced and sweating, the condition of the victim inside was left to one's imagination. Moss did not turn up to teach us for the next few days, and after that he stopped picking on the boys. I even heard that he gave up teaching and became a priest. If ever he was successful, Mrs. Blossom Anderson deserves special mention.

I would get caned quite often, mostly for fighting, and the comfort of letting my fists fly got me into serious trouble once, in my last year of school. I was passing by Seppings Road on my cycle, when I noticed a small crowd jostling someone. To my horror I saw that my friend Ronnie Butfoy was the target. He became a famous jockey and anyone who had visited the racecourse in the 1950s would have heard of him. Anyway, it did not once occur to me that this was outside the boundaries of school and here people did not fight fair. Adding to that was the immense self-belief that I was a boxer extraordinaire. I jostled my way through, and tried to reason with the crowd. I guess my Urdu was not up to the mark when it came to pacifying crowds, for the next moment someone had pushed me and I tripped and fell. The natural instinct, and this is something I had learnt at school, was to lash out. My fist met someone's face and from then on it was pandemonium. It was not much of a contest—a crowd against two school boys—but they were belligerent for some reason, and our weakness in numbers seemed immaterial to them. From an academic point of view, we were poorly matched; Butfoy was small built, and I was tall and lanky for my age and my frame made an easier target, and as punches and kicks were raining down, I took many … actually most of it, for the team. Just when I thought that I was losing control of the situation, someone walloped me with a starting handle. For those who are unfamiliar with this tool, the starting handle is what one used to wind and start cars of bygone days. I just blacked out and when I came to, someone was asking me if I could ride pillion. I nodded, and I remember a hazy ride to Victoria Hospital. I recollect a sad-looking old man, who, without too many questions, sat next to me and started shaving my head. I suppose he was one of those "all or nothing chaps", for he proceeded to shave off my entire crop of hair, not an easy job considering I was bleeding profusely. Without any form of anesthesia, I was given fifteen stitches— a handiwork so shoddy that even Boris Karloff would have felt sorry for me! It was a miracle because my skull had cracked, and the medics ignored that completely and focused on the ornamental patchwork to my scalp. Even today, I have a ridge running half way over my skull, from that incident.

While fighting and fisticuffs were frowned upon, the acceptable solution was to behave like a couple of proper English schoolboys and explain our predicament to the games master. He would then let us sort it out in the boxing ring. Till the bell rang, we would wildly lash out at each other, and eventually arms would tire, chins would droop and we would end up practically hugging each other in exhaustion. When the bell rang, our time was up and we had to shake hands and walk off. Although refereed by the games master, his role was simply to ensure that the fight was fought fair; he was not expected to announce a winner. However, the two pugilists and their supporters outside the ring knew in their hearts who had actually won. "Scrap On!" was the cry in school for such incidents, and the boxing ring would be surrounded by onlookers for these grudge matches. Although this was the accepted form of settling issues, boys would be boys and often, things would get settled outside the ring as well. Bullying, however, was not tolerated at all. It did not fit in with the English system of behaviour, and punishment was severe if cases were reported.

I took to boxing quite easily, and my build gave me a distinct advantage in the ring. Boxing as practised today, was fought by opponents of similar weight and not age or height, so I used to box with a lot of boys who were much older than me. My boxing master had the distinctly feminine name of Ian Maiden, but was a tough chap and taught me to use my height and reach to my advantage.

While I was fairly good at cricket, football, and hockey, boxing was something that stood out as the crowning sport during my school days. That Bangalore was regarded as one of the top pugilist cities is a fact unknown to many people. This was primarily because of the soldiers who were stationed here during the Second World War. Hundreds of people would flock to Opera Theatre and Hollywood City stadium to watch these matches. Adding to this was the fact that it was encouraged in school, and I soon realised that I had a knack for it. As with most schools, the entire year was based on collecting points for the house you belonged to. In boxing, entering the ring gave you a point, and if you won, you obviously got more. I was often bullied by my seniors to participate for the "honour of Pettigrew House".

Bishop Cotton Boys Cricket Team – 1950

We also had inter-school boxing matches and Bishop Cotton, Germain, and Baldwin were the three schools that had participated. It was hugely popular till a boy from one of the schools died and then it was banned. It is a very cruel sport and my parents never understood my fascination, but they had no real objection either. My dad was a firm believer in my "being a man" and "roughing it out", so he never interfered. One never wore any headgear then and the day you spent time in the ring, you ended up with a bloodied nose, bruised cheeks and cut lips, which would be looked upon with disapproval and mild concern by my mum, but she soon realised that this was who I was.

I used to train at the gym that was run by my neighbours, the Wollens. I practised alongside some of the best boxers in Bangalore every week. My hero was Gunboat Jack, an American, who was a welterweight boxer, settled in Bangalore. He was famous for getting into bar brawls, maybe because he was taunted for his colour. However, he was a true gentleman and I had the honour of spending time with him in the ring at the Wollen gym. Among the Anglo-Indians, the Suares brothers were famous during that time, and were heroes to boys of my age.

Food has played an important role in my life. While the fare at home was a mishmash of Indian, Tamilian, British, Goan, and French cuisine, the food at school was not as epicurean. During my early years, I would take snacks such as sandwiches with filling ranging from roast beef, eggs, marmalade and grape and guava jellies to school. Later, a chokra would bring a hot meal before the lunch bell rang and would take it back home after I was done. When I became a senior, I started to carry lunch in a tiffin carrier or eat at the canteen. Day scholars were not allowed to eat with the boarders, who would go back to their dining halls, while we would eat in our classrooms. The tuck shop was a common eating place and this was where, quite often, day scholars would give some of their home-made food to the boarders either out of generosity or compulsion, depending on their relationship. A system concept that I particularly enjoyed was option three—neither of the above. My friend, Merwan Chamarbagwala, was immensely rich, and apart from the food he would get from home, he also had an arrangement with "Tuckie", the guy who ran the tuck shop, to give Ronnie Philips and Don Anderson "whatever they needed", a privilege that got multiplied many fold during the years I was the school prefect. Merwan's father used to settle these accounts monthly, along with those of several other places in Bangalore where his son enjoyed limitless credit. The tuck shop was a huge draw for the boys in school. It was stocked with an assortment of delicious cakes and candies such as toffee apples, macaroons, flapjacks, lemon tarts, varieties of cakes and ice creams, and sweets such as bull's eyes, barley sugar, liquorice sticks, traffic lights, bon-bons and whoppers, which have disappeared from Bangalore today. Apart from sweets, snacks such as sausage rolls, potted meat/roast beef sandwiches, curry puffs, and chicken noodle soup were hot favourites.

Since Merwan came from an enormously rich family, he was the kind of friend most boarders desperately hoped to have! This was also because he was a day scholar and, every day, five-star quality food would be sent. His parents either believed that he had a colossal appetite or they did not pay attention to what and how much was sent for him and a lot of boys from our class benefited thus. Of course, the fact that I was the prefect implicitly meant that I enjoyed some privileges, and I am embarrassed to say that I could have my choice of chicken pieces and desserts over even Merwan himself! Although I was a day scholar too and in a far better position when it came to food compared with the boarders, my dad never believed much in eating out. Rather, he believed that money was not meant to be squandered away by paying a premium when one could have practically the same thing cooked at home for a fraction of the cost! I never had any reason to complain about the food at home, but the kind of stuff Merwan got was manna! The Koshy's restaurant on Brigade Road was a popular eating place in the later years and the Koshy boys, Mathew and Oommen, studied with me as well. The former was my classmate while the other was my senior.

Donald, Blossom and Mathew Koshy

I hated studying, and was never good at any of the subjects taught at school except Scripture! The languages taught at our school then were Urdu, Latin, and French. Hindi was not offered; Latin was considered a dead subject and French was for sissies. This did not leave me much of a choice and hence I became fluent in Urdu—well, as fluent as someone like me could ever become!

I always preferred the open skies, and at school, that meant sports. It was not just me, but all the boys played practically every sport in school and I was good at most. I played hockey and football for the school, and I represented Mysore State for the school cricket team. While test cricket was the only form of cricket then, we had our very own shortened version of the game—of course it was never called "one-day" cricket. My wicket-keeping skills and hard-hitting style kept me in the good books of my sports coaches, although I was constantly warned about how I needed to keep my aggression and "wild swinging" in check, for both hockey and cricket! Though hard to believe, in those days, there was even a competition for throwing the cricket ball the farthest! Cricket was my favourite sport, because it translated into a whole lot of time under the sun with friends, and I was legitimately bound to an activity that freed me from things like studying or homework. As is done now, we played cricket on mats that were pegged to the ground to give the ball a good bounce. I recall how once when I was playing on this surface, I had flicked the bowler to the leg-side and had run the first single. Trying desperately to complete the second run and beat the throw, I dug my bat into the ground. Unfortunately, it hit one of the pegs and the handle of the bat slammed into my groin. There were no abdomen guards at that time and I doubled up with pain and collapsed on the ground. I do not remember much after that, but when I came to, I was at the sick bay and under the watchful eyes of Hugwaffe, the school matron. A fitting name for a big-built German lady, who probably did bench presses in her free time.

"Take off your clothes, young man," was the order.

I meekly took them off.

"Take off your underwear," she thundered.

"Lie down."

She was trying to gauge the seriousness of the injury, but I was fourteen, and I could not help it … in a second I had a hard on!

"Get that away from here,' she roared, and I ran out of the room, with my clothes in my hands!

Regardless of the weather, participation in games was compulsory in our school. Even during the months from June to August when showers were common, during the games period, if the grounds were wet, all the boys had to run to Cubbon Park and back, which presented a unique and extraordinary sight. The distance was negligible, but it must have been a spectacle to see a hundred school boys running together in the pouring rain via Grant's road to Cubbon Park, in uniform. There was hardly any traffic to obstruct such an activity, and we would be completely drenched and bitterly cold by the time we got back. We, however, had to dry ourselves off and sit down for the next lesson!

Depending on the time of the year, there would be various seasons of games in school. This was not just restricted to sports such as cricket, football, and hockey but also non-official games. There were seasons for marbles, kite flying, top spinning and many more, and as a schoolboy all these were taken seriously as each victory gave you the rights to your opponent's stuff. I would look for excuses not to spend time on anything that was even remotely related to studying, and so I participated in these with as much enthusiasm as the other professional sports. It is such a shame that these have disappeared from today's schools altogether.

Although my dad was interested in wildlife, there was no scientific approach to the hobby. That, and my introduction to the avian world, was deeply influenced by O.C. Edwards, the famous bird photographer, who taught me Mathematics and English at school. He was a *pucca* (proper) gentleman and extremely considerate to the subjects he was photographing, a trait I did not pick up. The reason I was in his photography class was that if you were part of the group, you would be taken to places like Hesaragatta, Bannerghatta and Devrayandurga to spend some time in the forests, and photograph wildlife. He was not just an authority on photography, but he taught me about all living creatures, both plants and animals.

At home, the only day I was treated with any sort of special consideration was my birthday. There was no concept of a birthday party, it just meant a few friends coming home and having a good time. Birthday cakes were a must-have when I was in school, and as I grew older, home celebrations were considered a bit silly, till they were eventually phased out. Ribbon cake, which was made for many of my birthdays, was a speciality. It is a cake with about three or four layers, each of a different colour. How exotic it seemed back then! Maybe it was my imagination but each colour translated into a different flavour, and the confluence of these flavours as they melted in your mouth, encouraged by the exploding taste of icing, made my head swim! *Biriyani* was another must-have during birthdays, complete with nuts, raisins and fried onions. "Swami's", opposite the meat market in Russell Market, was a clear favourite among the Anglo-Indian families of the time to buy condiments, especially for birthdays, Christmas, Easter or any other excuse for celebration, which would have families land up there to place their orders. There was no music or dancing at these celebrations, and it was just my friends and, of course, my mum and dad who made their cameo appearance. I got a customary handshake from Dad, one of those rare signs of affection; hugging was considered unmanly back then, and both of us would have been mortified at the very thought of a kiss! I know I sound ungrateful, but even on birthdays, let alone Christmas and other days of celebration, I would have gladly given up all the attention and fun at home for a chance to visit the jungles—such was my craving for the outdoors.

I think that my fascination with guns was influenced by the kind of movies I watched growing up. Although I was only about six or seven years old, the Second World War had a profound influence on my life. It was all that people talked about, and I was at a very impressionable age. We would often go to the cinemas to watch war documentaries, which were usually about how British or American troops were advancing against a German or Japanese stronghold. While these were interesting, they were no match to the Hollywood fare that thrilled me. *Bataan* and *They Died with Their Boots On* were two of my favourites. I think General Custer was probably my biggest hero as I was growing up. Later, when I went to the jungles with my dad, I imagined I was Custer and Daniel Boone rolled into one! These movies were so influential that my friend Sydney and I would cycle all the way to Bellandur Lake during the last days of the war and watch seaplanes from a distance, enthralled at the spectacle and completely convinced that there were German spies around! Somehow Dad was not too fond of movies, unlike my grandmother, Mum, and June. They usually watched Shirley Temple movies, which I found to be a complete waste of time! Globe, Imperial, BRV Talkies, and Plaza were the theatres in those days, while Rex and Galaxy came up much later. Globe had the wonderfully quaint name—Crystal Picture Palace—and later it became known as Liberty Theatre. The most expensive tickets were half anna, and these were only when Mum came with us and we bought expensive seats, otherwise they were much cheaper.

Opposite the BRV theatre was the cricket ground, where I would go and play with my friends. This was also the location where the carnivals would be set up in Bangalore. It used to be a great source of entertainment for me and my friends. There would be boxing rings, dashing cars, giant wheels, a mini-zoo, and of course lots of food. We stayed on as late as we wanted, and no one got worried. Despite the excitement of the movies, or other forms of entertainment the city provided, my preference was always to be in the jungles.

Public dances at the BRV, Opera House and Bowring Club were very popular for the young and old alike, and for teenage boys with raging hormones, a source of both excitement and nervousness. We also had school socials we used to have once a year, and that was the only time that Bishop Cotton boys could formally meet the Bishop Cotton girls. It was a dance conducted with live music in a large hall, and many boys looked forward to the big event. Twerking was half a century away so foxtrot was the popular dance of the days. Apart from a few goody-goody boys, most boys, especially boarders, would jump the wall to meet girls from neighbouring schools. Suspension and caning were the usual punishments if we were caught for such escapades, and hence to have a conveniently arranged social event where boys and girls could get physically close to each other was rare and precious, not that the castigation or the promise of the social ever changed the way we cut class to meet girls during school hours. Two frequent offenders without any sense of remorse were my friends Sydney D'Silva and Ronnie Philips. Ronnie was particularly careless and enjoyed the privilege of holding a monthly pass to the principal's office for a caning. It was hard to say which he was more proud of, the welts on his hands or the hickeys on his neck! Going out with girls meant a pretty standard routine, and included watching a matinee show at the Plaza theatre, upstairs in the private box. These tickets were expensive, but that was the price one had to pay for a secluded spot and ample opportunity for hanky-panky.

As I was finishing school, socialising with girls became popular, and the girls were almost always from Cotton, Sacred Heart, or Baldwin. Even I did not realise the number of women I had dated till my sister June migrated to Australia and many women who met her would say, "Oh, you're June, Don Anderson's sister? I used to be his girlfriend!"

It may sound like I'm bragging, but I did not have to try very hard to get girls to go out with me. I had girls of all ages who asked me out; in fact if I ever walked up to a girl and asked her out, it was considered a feather in her cap. This was especially pronounced because it meant that I, Don Anderson, would pay for the date, and that was an unheard-of thing in those days! Dad was too stingy, so the money for these opportunities always came from Mum. As for expenses, it was just a movie and a meal. If it was ice cream, it was Lakeview; somehow Koshy's was not affordable on a date.

There was so much to do growing up in the 1940s and 1950s that I could not afford to waste it studying. I managed to scrape through every time there was a serious examination, and my parents were all right with that. Tuitions were unheard of, and there was no concept of replacing one's free time with more studying! There were students with all kinds of abilities—the brainy ones, the hard-working ones, and of course ones like me who were neither. Early on, my parents realised that I was not going to make it big in the traditional sense, so they had very low expectations of me. I do not know whether it was low expectations or whether they genuinely believed that I would someday find my calling, but I was given enough freedom to do whatever I wanted. By the time I finished what was back then Senior Cambridge, I had completed what was, back then, a fair milestone in terms of academics. Considering my remarkable academic prowess, I was allowed to stop studying further. The last school fees I paid in 1950 were two rupees and eight annas! It was not much and though we were fairly well to do, I hated the idea of my dad spending more money on trivial things such as academics. It was the principle of the thing—I encouraged him to spend it on things I wanted, and not on frivolous things like schooling. Like all idealists, I decided that I would earn my money doing something I enjoyed. Of course, my biggest dream was to be a white-ish hunter in India, having read Hemingway, but I had to remind myself of how futile that dream was. I was very choosy about the jobs I applied for, ensuring my enquiries only reached those places that promised a lot of free time. Naturally, there were not many instances where I applied and instead I spent months visiting the jungles and having fun with my friends.

Chapter Two

My Family

AFTER CENTURIES OF BEING ACCUSTOMED TO A certain lifestyle, August 1947 brought profound changes to the lives of the British in India. The biggest predicament they faced was the choice they had to make, between staying on in India, and emigrating to England or Australia, the popular destinations at the time. Until the Commonwealth Immigrants Act of 1962, all Commonwealth citizens could enter and stay in the UK without any restriction, a lucrative option for many families, who qualified to make the cut.

The term "Anglo-Indian" has been used loosely over the years and was initially a term to describe domiciled British citizens. At some point, it was used to describe those Europeans who had continued to stay back in India even though their bloodlines were strictly "pure". Lastly, it was used to refer to people of British and Indian parentage. Many people from these last two groups stayed on in India, marrying the local Indians and forming a distinct social stratum in some cities. Thus, there existed different types of Anglo-Indians, and the purebloods always distanced themselves from those of mixed ancestry while the latter found it hard to get acceptance from either the British or the local Indians. During the time leading up to the Second World War, the Posts and Telegraph Department, the Indian Railways, and the Police continued to be dominated by both domiciled Europeans and Anglo-Indians. They were given preferential employment in these areas by the British in the belief that they were capable of holding these positions because of their marginally "superior" bloodline or simply because of their education and command over the English language. The Anglo-Indians were God-fearing, simple, honest folk and their kind and trusting nature often led to their being swindled out of their houses and lands by many corrupt locals, especially in areas like Murphy Town, Richards Town, and other such places in the city that had large Anglo-Indian communities.

The decision by the Anglo-Indians to leave or to stay back was the litmus test to establish whether their choice was ruled by the heart or the head. For those who chose to stay on, their decision boiled down to one irrefutable fact—India was home. Staying in a city in independent India still promised a *dorai* a certain lifestyle, with ayahs, malis and chokras, and for a family in Bangalore, a respect that had not fully ceased when the British administration ended. White skin still managed to elicit a certain reverence, and it was hard to let that go and settle in another country where one would be as common as one's neighbour. Here in Bangalore, one could enjoy being practically the zenith of the social order with the parties and revelry, and if you were interested in shikar, as a certain section of the population was, jungles were less than four or five hours away in any direction you looked. So depending on what one's priorities were, choices were made.

It is funny that I was always thought of as Anglo-Indian, as I do not have a drop of Indian blood in me! My dad was Scottish, while my mum was of Burgher-Australian origin. As the term Anglo-Indian was loosely used to describe anyone with a bloodline not purely Indian, I became a member of this community. I'm guessing it was too complicated to create a new category with my kind of ancestry!

The union of Scotland and England in 1707 to form Great Britain opened the gates for Scottish immigration to India. Under the agreement, Scotland's wealthy families gained access to the East India Company and gradually dominated many positions in the organisation. The Scots turned their attention to new lands, either in adventurous aspiration to see the world, or from sheer compulsion to carve out their future with better opportunities. They came to India and other colonies scattered across the other side of the world, representing many professions and vocations. They came as traders, missionaries, planters, army men and, of course, they were all explorers in their own right. My family—the Andersons—was one such family that arrived here in India, searching for a new world, for fame, fortune and perhaps adventure. The surname

Anderson, incidentally is quite common in Scotland, being derived from St. Andrew, the patron saint of the country.

During my father's time, my family was believed to have been in India for at least four generations. The first members arrived from Glasgow as part of the East India Company. The earliest members identified are John Anderson Esq. and his wife, Mary Anderson Carnegy, whose remains lie in St. Mary's church at Fort St. George in Madras. They had a pair of twin boys, one of whom was Thomas Carnegy Anderson, who married Harriet Louisa Etheridge. They lived in Calcutta and later moved to Hyderabad state. They had seven children—Douglas, Mable, Forbes, John, Kenneth, Lillian, and Elspeth. Elspeth was married to Theophilus Neville Hearsey, grandson of the famous John Bennett Hearsey, who played a key role in the 1857 mutiny.

Douglas Stewart Anderson (1873–1938), my grandfather, was the eldest. He was born in Calcutta but grew up in Bolarum, in the erstwhile Hyderabad state. Although known as a railway colony, it was also a military base for the British forces at the time. Douglas served in the British Indian Army and was posted for a few years in Ismailia, Egypt, as part of the India Expeditionary Force E. He was part of the military accounts division, and during a posting in Bangalore, he met my grandmother, Lucy. After they were married, they went back to Bolarum where my dad was born. While in Bangalore, Douglas enjoyed duck-shooting jaunts to the lakes in the city. Ulsoor, Madiwala, and Hebbal tanks were his favourites, and weekend trips were not uncommon in the company of his friends from the army. Short and stocky, he would wear his deerstalker hat and big boots and go for a shoot, accompanied by his pet bulldog and bevy of hired help. Although I was not allowed to tag along, I remember him coming back with a game sling, which often held a brace of ducks. I would eagerly await his return to collect his brace of game, remove the birds, give it to the cook and clean his sling. I did not have much of a role, but those dinners were always special. He also had a special bench made of Scottish marble, and it was called "Douglas's chair", because no one else was allowed to sit on it! It lay under a rain tree in our garden, and he loved spending time there in the early mornings and evenings, having a cup of tea and reading the newspaper, while his pet bulldog, Bonnie, lay at his feet. After he died, the marble chair was used to make his tombstone, according to his dying wish, only for it to be stolen years later.

Douglas and Lucy Anderson - 1908

Douglas Anderson met Lucy Ann Taylor at a social gathering in Bangalore and they were married almost immediately after, at St. Mark's Church in Bangalore, in 1908. Lucy, my grandmother, was the daughter of George Abraham Bailey and Camilla Penelope Taylor. When she was just eighteen months old, her mother died during the cholera pandemic. Her father, who was part of the Irish regiment in Madras, left for Belfast shortly afterwards, leaving his daughter in the care of her two aunts, Mrs. Bower and Mrs. Bates, who had no children of their own and spoilt her completely. Subsequently, her father remarried and sent for his daughter, but she didn't want to go back and her doting aunts wouldn't allow it either. Thus, her father relinquished charge of his daughter and gave custody to her aunts who were extremely well-off and lavished every possible comfort on her, encouraging her to pursue activities like calligraphy, poetry, painting, singing, and playing the piano.

She attributes her late marriage (she was past thirty and an "old maid" when she got married to Douglas) to the freedom she was allowed by her adoring aunts. In a strange coincidence, when her aunts, Mrs. Bower and Mrs. Bates died, the causes of their deaths were the same. Both tripped over the same doorstep at Prospect House and broke their hips, within a year of each other. There was no hip replacement surgery in those days and both died of pneumonia after becoming bedridden. After they died, the house came into my grandmother's possession, and her husband furthered the existing structure. The credit for building Prospect House goes to Lucy's grandfather, John Taylor, who was the manager of the Mysore Commission for twenty-seven years. For his services, he was given the land adjacent to Cubbon Park by Sir Mark Cubbon, the British Commissioner of Mysore state, who was also responsible for moving the capital from Mysore to Bangalore. John Taylor's house on Sydney Road was a landmark for more than a hundred years, witnessing the births and deaths of many generations before it was demolished in the mid-1980s.

Although St. Andrew's Church was the default church for the Scots in Bangalore, my grandmother chose to be part of the St. Mark's church parish. She played the pipe organ for many years at this church, and that instrument became synonymous with her, for most Bangaloreans. She was a devout Christian and church-goer, and honoured her commitment of playing for the church service even up to a few months before she passed away. She was the head of the church choir and would organise picnics for the choir group every month, visiting places like Hesarghatta and Nandidroog. At times, she would take her grandchildren along and we would get into a rickety old bus, and a fun-filled day would ensue. She was headstrong, and once, even had a row with the head priest at St. Mark's, walking away in a huff to join the East Parade Church for a brief stint. Luckily there was a change of guard at St. Mark's and she was welcomed back with open arms. She was a very strict Englishwoman, but like all grandmothers, spoilt her grandchildren. June was her favourite and I a distant second. When it came to showering her time and affection, it was easier to devote it to June, as my interests in pets and shooting animals with my catapult were certainly not any source of amusement for her, let alone pride. She was not much of an outdoor person and spent most of her time devoted to encouraging her granddaughter's interest in the creative arts. She was a trained voice and wanted June to pick up those skills. Unfortunately, June was mostly interested in dancing, but like a good granddaughter gave in to the whims and fancies of her grandparent. Although she had a driver, my grandmother preferred to drive herself, in a 7 HP Baby Austin, mainly to Bowring Institute where June learnt ballet from Miss Shackle, a Russian teacher. The only time when I was allowed in the car was when we went to watch films together at the Liberty theatre.

To her credit, my grandmother was an ardent butterfly collector, the only hobby that I picked up from her. On rare occasions, I was allowed to accompany her and June when they went to Cubbon Park, with our dogs and butterfly nets, to enjoy an exotic picnic that would be laid out on the grass under the shade of large trees, while they would watch cricket matches in the distance. Unlike today, Cubbon Park back then was not a place for people to exercise, but for picnics and outdoor parties. On Sunday afternoons, there would be a lot of English families who would spend a few hours in Cubbon Park just enjoying the view, having fun and playing games. Unfortunately, it was also a place where people committed suicide, and despite being shielded by the grown-ups, June and I saw ghastly sights just across the boundary of our home. On special occasions my grandmother would drive us to Lalbagh, where there used to be a restaurant near the Glass House. Despite her English ancestry, she loved Indian food such as *dosa*s and *jalebi*s, and this was one place she believed served the best.

Quite a few of my family are buried at the Protestant cemetery on Hosur Road, including my grandparents and my parents. The old Protestant cemetery was very well maintained, but over the years, I have seen beautiful tombstones stolen, graves removed, and total apathy towards its upkeep. My father's grave had beautiful stones collected from the jungle streams he would visit, and one day I found that they had been pried out leaving ugly gaping holes. My grandmother's grave was much closer to the gate, and that too was robbed of an exotic piece of marble.

My mother, Blossom Hyacinth Minnette Fleming, was born in Ceylon (Sri Lanka). Her mother, Millicent Toussaint, was a Burgher from the well-known Toussaint family in Ceylon, while her father Clifford Fleming was a *pucca* Australian. He was born in a small town near Taree, New South Wales. Clifford's father served as an army doctor for Britain in a couple of countries and subsequently at the prison (Cellular Jail) in Port Blair, Andamans. The family would spend holidays in Ceylon owing to its proximity, and that is where Clifford met Millicent and married her.

Clifford and Millicent moved to India when Blossom was about ten years old. They had eight children: Rita, Gemmy, Jill, Zinny, Curly, Blossom, Tommy, and Sonny Boy who drowned at Ulsoor Lake while swimming, when he was a teenager. Blossom was literally the black sheep of the family, as all her siblings were fair with blond hair and blue eyes while she was swarthy. My mum was tough as nails and had a bad temper too. Not many people know this, but she was also a crack shot, with a few panther and wild boar trophies to her credit. The Anderson women, June and Mum, were an integral part of our jungle trips when we were young, and June learnt how to rough it out although her asthma restricted her travel. As we started to grow older, Mum's absence was conspicuous, and eventually it was just Dad and myself.

My parents got married when they both were just nineteen years old, in 1929. It was quite a scandal for the Anderson family because they eloped and spent their honeymoon in Pondicherry where Mum had family. The only time in his life that my dad was not a miser was when he was courting my mum, and during this odd but brief phase, a funny incident took place. He was driving from Richards Town back to Prospect House with my mum's words still ringing in his ears on how she found cycle rides romantic, when Dad, who was so smitten at that point in time, actually made a deal with someone on the road and exchanged one of his father's Ford cars for a bicycle!

Blossom Anderson with a jackal pup and a panther cub

In 1942, my Dad's salary was Rs. 100 a month, a fair amount, but the war was taking its toll on the cost of goods, and he had no choice but to look at other sources of income. He heard that the American army was looking for a place in the cantonment area, so we leased our home out to them, and they used the property to make parachutes for the war. We received a princely rent of Rs. 250, and we moved to a place that was two miles beyond where St. John's Medical College stands today. Back then, it was just farmland. It was a five-acre piece of land, with a fresh-water well and was owned by Rev. King, a Protestant priest. The rent was only Rs. 30 and my Dad, the miser that he was, felt that a profit of a Rs. 220 a month was worth putting everyone, including himself, through minor discomfort! In terms of size, though much smaller than Prospect House, it was still fairly large, had an outhouse for the servants and, of course, space for some of the animals we brought from Prospect House. My grandfather had passed away by then, and my grandmother lived with June in a small cottage on Palmgrove Road. Those were tough times, and most well-to-do families found it hard to cut back on their lifestyles, while the poorer ones found it tougher, even to survive.

Those who could afford, used cycles, while the next strata used a "Victoria" or *gharry* (horse-drawn carriage) to move around, and only the affluent families had cars. Petrol was rationed and most families like ours reduced consumption. My dad started to ride a motorcycle to work, and as his timings at the telegraph office did not coincide with my school time, I had no choice but to walk twelve miles every single day. I started doing that at the age of eight. School would get over by 3:30 p.m. and I would then wait till 5:00 p.m. for games, which was compulsory in those days. The sport depended on the season and this would go on till 6:30 p.m. I would have to walk home after that, lugging my bag and sports equipment, through Austin town, Vivek Nagar and all the way back, on streets that had no proper lighting to speak of. It would take me about two hours, including the many stops I would have on the way! I am sure that not a single eight-year-old could do that today, even if they were allowed to, for they would just collapse with exhaustion. It goes without saying that this did not leave me any time for my homework, and I often used that excuse when I got into trouble at school for faring poorly. Looking back, I am proud of the way I stuck it out, walking those distances, never complaining, but then I did not know better. However, my mind would be filled with memories of Prospect House, which seemed like a distant dream. For a short while, we hired the service of Anjenappa, a bullock-cart driver, to drop me up to a point on my school route. Unfortunately, that did not last very long, and he found employment elsewhere. Luck smiled on him when he started his venture into the meat business. He soon had his own shop at Johnson Market and eventually moved on to open what would become the famous Ham Shop on M.G. Road. He stopped coming to the shop on M.G. Road as I grew older, but while he was there, and if I happened to drop by, he would proudly announce to all the customers in the shop, "I used to be bullock-cart driver for that *dorai!*"

The war ended in 1945, but getting Prospect House back proved to be difficult, as the process was buried under military red tape. We therefore stayed at a rented place on Cornwell Road in Langford Town before finally regaining possession in 1949. I lived in Prospect House for almost forty years, and it broke my heart when we had to sell it in 1985.

June got married in 1951 and moved to England, and since it was just Mum, Dad, and I living in that huge house, Dad decided that he would lease parts of it to small families. At any point in time, we had about six to eight tenants. Some of the ones I remember were the Pococks, the Peters, the Briggs, Colin Bone and his wife, Sonny Leonard and his mother, the Ellis family and the jockey Butfoy among others. Although the period these families lived there often overlapped, each of these families played a part in my life. The Briggs family was perhaps the one I was closest to. They were Anglo-Indians of Scottish ancestry and hence were given preferential treatment by my dad. Old man Briggs and Dad got along like a house on fire. He had seven children, three boys— Donald, Gilbert, and Chippy—and four girls— Margaret, Shirley, Carol, and Alicia. I taught Gilibert (Gillie) hunting and Chippy angling, and they hero worshipped me no end. In fact, people would refer to them as my left and right hand, for they were always ready for adventure and to rough it out. Chippy, the daredevil, was so at home at Sangam, where I used to take him angling, that he would swim fearlessly in the gorge at Mekedatu.

We leased part of the property in the early 1960s to a gentleman who started a petrol pump, which still stands today. Most of the tenants were wonderful people, but from the early 1970s, things changed and every other day saw fights about rent, upkeep and other fun issues. The law at that time was heavily in favour of the occupant of a rented property, and we were made to jump the hoops by some of them. The worst of the lot was a Malayali family, to whom, in the end, I ended up paying a huge amount of money to vacate the property. The whole episode with my tenants and how they made me and my family suffer left a bitter, lasting memory, which would, in turn, impact many people in the future. After Mum died in Whitefield in 1987, I was too tired to keep fighting with the tenants, and in my frustration and anger listened to the wrong set of people who managed to buy it off me for seven lakhs. Only when I tried to sell it did I realise how complicated it was. As the land was a gift from one Englishman to another, I was not allowed to keep the proceeds from the sale, or so I was told, and I didn't have any papers to prove otherwise. So, I was only allowed to keep what I got from the sale of the two buildings, a fraction of the value of the property.

While my Dad was always buying land that bordered his favourite jungles, he rarely invested in Bangalore city itself. However, over 1961 and 1962, he bought two houses with the royalties he received from the publishers George Allen & Unwin, as his books had become international bestsellers. "Bijou Cottage" at Whitefield was the first, and he later bought a property of five and a half acres in Bannerghatta. He lived in Whitefield, but would go over to the Bannerghatta property during weekends in his Morris Minor, a car designated for Bannerghatta trips for some reason.

During this time, he and Mum developed irreconcilable differences, and he moved out of Prospect House to Whitefield, where he lived with an Anglo-Indian lady by the name of Margaret. It is hard to pin down what these differences were, but they had grown apart and his fascination for animals and the occult had become borderline obsessive. My Mum was the tougher of the two, and she had grown up with many siblings in a big family where sensitivity and patience were not virtues to be proud of. Middle children like my Mum were fighters and adapters, and having never enjoyed any sort of individual attention while growing up, combined with her tough-as-nails Australian blood, made her a force to reckon with. My dad, on the other hand, had a Victorian upbringing and being an only child, was totally spoilt, and lavished with attention his entire life. As most married couples, they had their fair share of disagreements, and we would often witness precursors to the third world war, though better sense would eventually prevail and normalcy would return. However, as they grew older, they grew tired of fighting, and came to the conclusion that perhaps it was in everyone's best interest if they lived separately.

He moved to "Bijou Cottag" in 1962, and it was an embarrassment compared with the home he grew up in, as the total area was just short of an acre. However, there was a natural wilderness to the place, and that suited him very well. Whitefield was the back of beyond in the early 1960s and was almost like another city, cut off from the rest of busy and commercial Bangalore. It was full of Anglo-Indians, who had decided to move away from the madness that Bangalore was becoming. It was hard to say whether it was sheer laziness or something that my Dad planned, but the land was overrun with weeds and bushes that just seemed to welcome all kinds of snakes. In fact, that small plot of land was so famous that snake charmers would come there when they ran out of stock! He had nearly bought the house in 1957, but for some reason decided against it. In 1961, it was still unsold and he ended up buying it for Rs. 5,000 from a gentleman by the name of William Saldhana, who owned the adjoining piece of land as well. Saldhana wanted to rent the place, but Dad convinced him to sell it, although he did not buy the adjacent mango *thoppu* (grove) that was on sale as well. It was here that he lived during the last years of his life; a recluse because of his illness. There was a large verandah in front, and behind that were two large bedrooms. The verandah and the rooms were filled with his trophies and mine, and also notable were posters of the film *Harry Black and the Tiger*. There was an outhouse, and of course lots of cages that were filled with his pets including pythons, a slender loris, hyenas, jackals, geese, an iguana, and even a small *mugger* (crocodile). He had become famous the world over and every other day, there would be someone who landed up to talk to him, hear his stories and get their books signed. However, after he was diagnosed with cancer, he became very selective about the people he met. He only wanted to meet *swamis* (religious people) and those he perceived would help him with his illness, and shunned common folk.

The property in Bannerghatta did not have a name, but was right along the periphery of the forest and extremely beautiful. Dad's neighbour was Sundar Raj, who had a house there even before we bought our property. Sundar Raj was a Tamilian from Mysore state and an old family friend who owned a shop called Gun Craft on M.G. Road, next to the Deccan Herald office—a shop every hunter, practising or aspiring, in places like Bangalore and Coimbatore, knew about.

**With friends outside Guncraft. Owen on the left and
Sundar Raj on the right**

Gun-making is a fine art. One needs to be an expert to understand the nuances a few millimetres can make and Sundar Raj was a master at his craft. He worked on and repaired all the guns that my Dad and I owned, right from fixing scopes to getting ammunition and everything else in-between. His hunting skills on the other hand were lukewarm, but he was keen on coming along with me to shoot wild boar in the scrub jungles close by. He enjoyed angling as well and had a fair bit of luck, even landing a 45-pound mahseer at Sangam once. He was a few years older than me and his sons Suresh, Udhank, and Ravi looked up to me as their hero and I used to take them for short treks through the jungle. There was no Bannerghatta National Park back then, and while I never let them handle the gun, they were excited just to come with me and carry the fowl I shot, feeling extremely proud. Although I don't particularly remember the incident, Udhank often replays a particular story, apparently one that is so etched in his memory that he just has to relive it every time he has an audience. Apparently, I was walking with the boys behind me when suddenly three partridges flew out of a bush in front in three different directions. I shot two with my 12 bore shotgun, one with each barrel, reloaded and shot the third bird, all in a space of less than ten seconds, and that became a part of folklore! When I stayed there, there was never a question of buying meat from the market; wild fowl was the substitute for chicken while wild boar replaced beef and mutton.

I do not remember how it became popular, but from the early 1950s, Sundar Raj would lease parts of his property at Bannergatta to families to come and have camps. He grew *sapota* (sapodilla), mango, coconut, guavas, and other fruits on his four-acre plot of land, which was built on an incline. It was a wonderful place. It had even a stream and we would go there very often with some of our tenants, especially the Briggs family. He had employed some people from Guntakal to look after his land, and over time, they fell out of favour and eventually ended up buying one property by the side and one above his property on the incline, something that he did not appreciate. He attempted to buy those lands from them, but they held on and wouldn't alter their stance. What made matters worse was that my dad, who was so enamoured with these properties, paid the Carols, one of the families, a very generous amount of money and bought the land that was adjacent. Sundar Raj became very bitter towards my dad, accusing him of going behind his back and abusing his hospitality. From then on it was open season with both Sundar Raj and my dad embroiled in petty disputes over several issues. The reason for most quarrels was the stream that flowed on both properties. Sundar Raj would be upset that it would sometimes flood his property, while my Dad would refuse to entertain his complaints by stating that nature took its own course. Of course, Sundar Raj would then demonstrate how that could be changed by diverting the water further up, and my dad would send legal notices to him. My dad was, in fact, famous for doing things the "official way", often sending court summons and official notices, and was involved in dozens of cases, which took up much of his time and energy. After a point Sundar Raj got fed up with the barrage of documents arriving on his doorstep, and one day, with no provocation or warning, fired his gun at my Dad who was on his property, but at some distance away from him. He certainly had no intention of hitting him, and my Dad knew that as well, but the embarrassment and shock of the incident forced him to resort to write another formal complaint! According to Sundar Raj, and I'm paraphrasing here, this is what Dad's letter said.

"On the 5th Day of December 1960 at 11:00 a.m. in the morning, Mr. Sundar Raj of Bannerghatta raised his .22 rifle to his right shoulder and fired a single bullet at me, standing forty feet away. The westerly wind that was blowing at approximately

10 km caused it to hit a papaya tree I was standing next to. If the wind direction had changed the bullet would have changed course and hit my chest, and considering this as attempted murder, I would like to report this heinous crime and implore strict action be taken against Mr. Sundar Raj."

On receiving a notice from the lawyer, Sundar Raj came over to our house and spoke to my Dad.

"Mr. Anderson, and I call you Mr. Anderson for you are older than me; to others- you are just a bastard. I've just finished reading your long and interesting novel about how the direction of the wind saved your life. Let me tell you something. I have been working with guns all my life, I understand bullet trajectories better than you know the back of your hand. If I wanted to hit your left ball, I would do it, mind you, your left ball specifically, so please stop writing letters about the westerly winds and papaya trees, you are wasting your time."

He certainly won the battle on that day.

Although he was at loggerheads with my dad, he was very fond of me and was great pals with my mum. He was an avid agriculturist and would spend hours perfecting his method of planting seeds and saplings. Once he and I decided to start a joint project of planting mango trees and bought saplings together, from Lalbagh. He had an advantage over me as he lived in Bannerghatta and had all the time in the world to execute the perfect plan. He even came over and explained it to me:

"You need to dig a pit two feet square and two feet deep and aerate for twenty-four hours. After that you need to mix red mud, and manure in a certain proportion etc."

I did not have time for all this, I only spent weekends there, and he would mock me saying that I was scratching the earth like a chicken before planting the seedlings and that I would never get my trees to grow. As luck would have it, most of my trees grew while his did not, and that certainly did not amuse him. Some of the mango trees that both of us planted remain and can be seen from his property, which belongs to his son Suresh, today.

Our house used to be exactly where the Bannerghatta butterfly park now stands. On our land, we had a big rock on an elevated spot, and if you stood on this rock, you had the entire jungle in front of you as a panorama. This used to be my Dad's favourite spot on the property. Every evening he would sit on this rock and say his prayers. Mind you, he was not a particularly religious person in his youth, but as he grew older, his beliefs got stronger. I am not sure if they were Christian prayers, but more of alone time with God.

His frame of mind is quite evident in this poem we wrote, entitled **"The Church of Stone"**.

Do you believe in a God above?
Then come to my Church of stone
For there I learn that He is love
And I speak to Him alone.

My church of stone is a wondrous spot
It's foundation is the ground
For its roof, the dome of heaven I've got
And its walls, the hills around.

Come at any time you may,
Solace you'll surely find;
The door's always open, night and day
And you'll get peace of mind.

The rising Sun just tips the glades
As it peeps o'er the hills to the East
In pink and blue and purple shades
That fade in the mists of the West.

It falls on my little church of stone
And turns it all to gold
A purer, richer, lovelier throne
Than any king of old.

All day you may sit and cast your gaze
Down a valley between the hills
For mile and miles, lost in a maze
Of rocks and trees and rills.

And you should watch the setting orb
Sink behind the hill to the west
In one crimson, vermilion, orange daub
No painter's brush could best.

Nearer at hand the jungle lies
Mysterious, and silent and still
But you think no more of time that flies

As your spirit drinks your fill.

Of solitude and blissful rest
Of heart and mind and soul
You learn the value of what is best
That's where you reach your goal.

All this you can see and know and take
In this little church of mine
Nor wealth nor architect could make
A place for me, more fine.

Its seat is just a chunk of rock
But it bars no colour caste or creed
The organ is the chirping of forest birds
To welcome all in need.

For here at any time you want
A blessing you'll surely find
Perhaps the healing a body that's sick
Or rest or peace of mind.

At sunset hour you'll find me there
Seated in my church of stone
And I need no priest to tell me where
To look for God's high throne.

For this where He speaks aloud
And tells me of his love
I can read that message in the clouds
And the moon and stars above.

He asks me what I've done for him
But I hang my head in shame
For I've never bothered to think of Him
Self and sin have dogged my name!

Although I've often let Him down
And hurt Him all I could
He's never failed me once
And I know He never would.

These are the thoughts of Him above
That come when I sit upon this stone

Lost in the wonder of his love
Meditating my insignificance alone.

That's why I cherish my church of stone
Poor and humble though it be
For it's here I meet God face to face
And get the comfort He has for me.

After he died, I made a bird bath next to his favourite spot, and I would find some solace in seeing the birds that frequented it. It continued to be there for years after I sold the property, but when the government took it over and built the butterfly park, it was destroyed. The land was on a gradient and not very rich, but it was at the edge of the forest that extended right up to Madras state. It was extremely beautiful and crowded with animals that seemed to wander into our property. Dad was never one to kill for sport, and by the mid-1960s had stopped carrying a gun. A short walk from the house would get you to a jungle that was overrun with partridge, spur fowl, monkeys, wild boar, deer, the occasional panther or bear and, of course, a never-ending barrage of elephants. When I was working at the Binny factory, I would leave from home at five in the morning and my co-workers could not believe me when I used to say things like,

"This morning, on the way to work, I passed a herd of twenty elephants."

It was not something any of them could ever echo! That was Bannerghatta in the 1960s—wild and not a place many people thought they would like to live in, unlike Whitefield. In fact, elephants are regular visitors to Sundar Raj's property to feed off the fruit trees that stand, even today.

The house was never in good shape nor was it very comfortable, but it was practical and I was not the type who looked for drapes and matching cushions. It had a tiled roof, mud and brick walls and a red oxide floor. It was modest compared to Prospect House, with just two 10 x 12 foot bedrooms, a 12 x 15 foot living/dining room and a bathroom. My Dad was such a miser that we had practically no wooden furniture, but frugality took on a new meaning when my dad decided to have sofas made from left-over cement after some construction work! We just put bolsters on these cement sofas and things were as comfortable as they could get, or so he said Once, Sundar Raj had waited for me at home for a length of time, (in one of those rare times when I had kept anyone waiting) but I had just got home from work, and it was a spur of the moment trip. When we entered our house on our return, there was a strong smell of decay. We traced the odour and discovered that Sundar Raj had accidently sat on and squashed a rat snake that had crawled between the cushion and the cement chair! The added charm if you were a serpent in the neighborhood was that the Anderson home had a huge aviary full of pigeons, so snakes were a common sight at our home. Despite the absence of any valuables in the house, it was protected with padlocks and deadbolts, and even the skylight was reinforced with barbed wire, a source of amusement for those who knew dad!

After my Dad passed away, I continued to visit the place on weekends, from 1975 to 1986, and during that time, I hired an Anglo-Indian chap by the name of Eric Coleman and our chokra, Thangavelu Jr, to look after the place. When they were sober, they were hard workers, and the three of us put up a fence around the entire property, and made a *kutcha* (crude) road from our property to the main road; the road still stands today, although it has been considerably improved upon. However, most of the time, the two caretakers were intoxicated and did as they pleased—drinking themselves silly was their favourite pastime. Most days they would go to Bannerghatta village in the morning, drink all day, lie in the shade somewhere and repeat the process all over again. On rare occasions, when they felt the necessity to come back home, they would attempt to stagger back, often hearing the news of elephants on the path. Then would begin this rigmarole where they would get on the hillock behind my house and shout for me to come and get them, and considering their state of inebriety, it was a commendable feat that they could manage to make so much noise and catch my attention. I would then ride up on my motorcycle, light some firecrackers and scare the elephants away. Then came the part where the three of us would try to get back home on my motorcycle on an untarred road with no street lights, while the two rascals would be swearing on their mothers' graves that they had not touched a drop of alcohol that day! It was by sheer luck that we were never attacked by elephants during these joyrides, because Bannerghatta was famous for such incidents. In fact, immediately after I had sold the farm, someone was killed right on my property by an elephant. I sold it for Rs. 10,000 to a Parsi chap who started a flourishing business growing mushrooms. He then sold it to the government, who was purchasing land from various owners there to set up the Bannerghatta National Park in the early 1980s. It was I who got the acquisition notice from the government. I have always had a morbid fear of dealing with officials, especially since I am a British citizen and I had this irrational apprehension that one day I would get deported to England. What would I do if that happened? I knew no one there and I was sure that I would not survive more than a few days in England. Thus, I kept this big secret close to my heart and only a couple of my closest friends ever knew. I was very careful and would get my Indian visa renewed every five years and my British passport every ten years. This meant dealing with the Home Ministry at the Vidhan Soudha, and I was always jittery during those times.

I moved from the house in Whitefield to Eejipura in 1987. Whitefield had changed considerably from the 1960s when my dad had moved in, although it was still considered the back of beyond. The Anglo-Indian community had thinned down, and often you would find a lot of anti-social elements after dusk. Although all these things never bothered me, I moved out of Whitefield and found a small property in Eejipura, just off the main road, which had a small house and an outhouse. Whitefield House, the place where my Dad lived, had been sold off and a new building had come in its place. At a rent of Rs. 1,000, it was a good deal for a house, a fairly large garden and an outhouse for the hired help. Thangavelu Jr, who grew up in Prospect House, was someone who served me at Bijou Cottage and then back again at the house here. By now, he had a big family—Tresa, his wife, and their children—and all of them lived in the outhouse. As was his dad, Thangavelu Jr was absolutely loyal, but he had started to drink heavily, and could not be relied on to do his job. His sons Sambo, Bimbo, Duddu, and Kumar were grown up now but in the manner of their father, they too were heavily into drinking from a young age. As the boys got older, they started making a lot of trouble, often creating a ruckus and asking for money. Their ingratitude and insolence were shocking, and after their mother died, I paid a large amount of money and severed ties with them permanently.

———

June

My sister June was born in June 1930 and was christened Margaret June Blossom Lucy Anderson, a trim name indeed! She attended Bishop Cotton Girls' School and graduated in 1947 after completing the Indian

High School and Matriculation Exam and the Senior Cambridge Overseas Exam, receiving a first class for both. She was the brainy one, something she inherited from our dad, while all I inherited was my mum's rebellious streak! June's brilliance was not restricted to academics alone—she played all sports, was part of the Mysore state hockey team and was also a state-level shot putter. She was a very pretty child, always considerate and helpful and it was only natural that she was everyone's favourite. Her biggest fan was our grandmother, and they shared a very special bond. I only wanted to play rough sports while June was interested in books and painting, something that her grandmother encouraged. The two of them would sit on the verandah while my grandmother would attempt to pass on the creative skills she had learned as a young girl, in the same house, decades earlier. But June's first love was dancing, and somehow that went beyond the purview of my grandmother's proficiency. Whenever I saw an opportunity, I would creep up behind either of them and then jump onto June like a tiger, spoiling whatever peace and quiet existed. I would either whack her or take away one of her dolls, and these are the moments I suspected my grandmother was not as old as she made herself out to be, for in a trice she would jump up to stand between June and me.

"Go away you horrid boy, leave my child alone" would be ringing in my ears as I escaped, only to hatch my next despicable plan. After June got married, she went away to Wellington, in Coonoor to stay with her mother-in-law, Laura, and when she came back, she saw that I had appropriated her bicycle.

"You forfeited it," I stated.

One thing led to the next and in no time, much to our grandmother's horror, we started a brawl of sorts that spilled onto the road in front of our house. My poor grandmother was frantically shouting, "For heavens, sake, you can't hit my child! She's married!"

When June was about ten, she was supposed to have had her tonsils out at Victoria hospital. She was terrified and started screaming. Her grandmother, as always, came to her rescue saying, "Don't upset her, she'll get an asthma attack."

So, everyone calmed down, and then my mum said, "Look at Don, he's always sucking his thumb, so let's take his tonsils out" and before you knew it, I had my tonsils removed instead! I came back home feeling very ill, while June laughed her head off. Of course, the thought of revenge made me recover much faster than most people would have imagined and then I gave her a good bashing, but she always tells me that I should be thankful to her, for I would never have a sore throat ever again in my life.

Happy days – Donald and June

As children, our favourite haunt was a milk bar called Lakeview on South Parade, where milkshakes cost two annas. One day, coming back from Lakeview, we came upon a Brahminy kite sitting on a tree. It was just after my sixth birthday, and I was extremely trigger happy. Without a second thought, I shot it with my Daisy air rifle and it fell to the ground, wounded but not dead, for it was fluttering about. To save an additional pellet, I took a stone and repeatedly hit it on its head till it moved no more. On the way, June kept crying inconsolably and much to my chagrin, told Dad. He was most upset about the cruelty dealt out to the bird and was determined to teach me a lesson. He was on friendly terms with the sub-inspector of police, Merwyn D'Souza, whose office was in the building adjoining our home. I was produced before D'Souza and Dad announced,

"My son has committed a terrible crime, and he needs to be punished."

The sub-inspector played his part, and personally escorted me to a dingy cell and locked me up. Much to their dismay, I was the least bit bothered and instead used the opportunity to sleep on the dirty and very smelly moth-eaten blankets that were kept in the cell. I was very comfortable with the phrase "To hell with you all", as they found out that day! After a couple of hours, I was taken out and firmly forbidden to do such a thing again. Like any typical six-year-old, there was no promise from me regarding this matter and I disappeared as soon as we reached home, but I caught June in the gardens and threatened her. "You're nothing but a sneak, I'm going to teach you a lesson."

My grandmother had a small greenhouse on the property, which was her pride and joy. In fact, this love for gardening was passed on to my parents, who maintained the greenhouse for years later. Knowing June's fondness for spending time there, I hid in the greenhouse with my air rifle in hand. When June came in, I gently raised the gun to my shoulder. "Aim for the heart", I told myself and gently squeezed the trigger. Luckily, the marksmanship that would made me famous in later years was still in its nascent stages and the pellet missed its mark. June dropped down like a sack of potatoes though, but then got up and ran, to eventually collapse on the portico. On examination, it was found that she had been hit on her shoulder. The scar has remained since then, and she is proud to show it off even today. As for the wrongdoer, back to the jail I went, and to make matters worse, my air gun was taken away till I learnt to be responsible. Unfortunately, there are not many places in a house you can hide things from an inquisitive six-year-old, not even in a mansion like Prospect House. I soon figured out that the air gun was kept behind a particular wooden almirah, and I proceeded to use it as I pleased, always taking care to put it back. Of course, my dad never knew I was doing this and constant practice made me a crack shot.

I do not blame her for hating me those days, as I was always fighting with her, and the poor thing was almost never at fault. I hated school and anything to do with studying, and I would ask, cajole, and then bully her into doing my homework, often pulling her hair, twisting her arm, and even sitting on top of her. Growing up with a mean and bullying brother taught her to be tough, and in later years she joined me on trips to places like Javalagiri and Devarabetta. It was no small feat to cycle there, especially in the summer. She was about fifteen and I was about eleven, and we would ride the thirty-five miles to Devarabetta, taking almost five hours to do that. We would leave the cycles at the forest guest house and walk to each of the three waterholes in the evening, observing wildlife. Food was usually brought from home, as the village was some distance from the guest house, and we did not want to lose time. We would get *vindaloo* and eat it with bread, and dessert was usually condensed milk. Although we were warned by Dad that condensed milk would dehydrate us, we did not give it much thought and would finish a couple of tins each in a day! After our long walk, we would come back to our abode, sleep the night and then ride back home the next morning.

While condensed milk was a treat on our trips, ice cream was something we indulged in when we were in the city. There were two options, Lakeview on M.G. Road, or the ice cream man who would ride all over the cantonment area, with a small cart that had a distinct bell. Can you believe that the sound of the ice cream bell could be heard inside our massive house? That will give you an idea of how silent Bangalore was in those days! Anyway, as soon as we would hear the bell, we would rush to our cupboards to get our money. Once when I was about eleven or twelve, the familiar bell rang and both of us rushed to open our piggy banks. June realised that she did not have any money, and she very politely asked me if I could lend her some. I was excessively rude and replied in the negative. She pulled my hair and we gave Prospect House yet another wrestling match. Of course, our grandmother came in to separate us and after patiently listening to both our versions, she felt that June was certainly justified in her actions and not only gave her money for the ice cream but also some more, for the grief I had caused her! Such was the blatant favouritism that my sister enjoyed!

Some people instinctively defend underdogs, and my Catherine ayah was one such person. While everyone believed that June could do no wrong, my ayah believed that I was a saint and would vehemently defend my actions. She accused June of playing to the gallery and would tell Mum that I would grow up hating people if everyone accused me of wrongdoings all the time! However, since the opposing counsel was my grandmother, who was also judge and executioner, Catherine ayah's passionate appeals never managed to reduce the punishment doled out to me. One of the few times that got June into trouble was quite by accident. Under her explicit reassurance that she would not push too hard, I agreed to get on to our garden swing. I was not used to it, and immediately asked her to stop. Noting the fear in my voice, June started pushing me higher and higher, and I think for the first time in her life, she had the pleasure of having me at her mercy and watching me squeal like a little girl. But then I jumped off, and while it was not from a great height, I tumbled down. June was so terrified at what she had done that she started to cry, while I yelled blue murder, accusing her of trying to kill me. The poorly executed assassination attempt got June three smacks (only) from Mum, and that threw my grandmother into a fit of lament while I was compensated with all kinds of rewards. As with most siblings, a lot of unintentional accidents happen that infuse our childhood with interesting stories. Once we were playing leapfrog and just as June was about to jump over me while I was half bent, I flattened myself and she lost her balance and fell on her face. She cut her lip badly and had a huge bruise on her face. Another time when I was chasing her, she ran indoors and slammed the door behind her. I crashed into it and nearly broke my nose. While I was physically stronger than her, she could be extremely unkind. There was a time when we both walked to school before we got our ponies. She was older and I would piteously cry out, asking her to slow down so that I could walk with her. But she would say, "No, you're too ugly", and march on. I would follow her, whimpering, sucking my thumb and sniffling all the way.

I was always getting into trouble, and I instinctively knew the right buttons to push to get someone worked up. My mum had a younger brother called Sonny Boy, who had drowned when he was very young. Since then, she had a morbid fear of water bodies. One day, after I had got a pasting from her, I announced that I was going to drown himself next to the bamboo island in Cubbon Park. My initial claims were not heard by anyone, but I then proceeded to run around the house declaring that no one loved me and that I was going to make it easier for everyone by ending my life. Naturally that got everyone worried, especially Mum, but by then I had cleverly disappeared and could not be found. It was late in the evening and people started looking for me, with torches in their hands, but it was of no use, and they just could not find me. My dad went next door to the police station and requested one of the constables to help. At about nine o'clock, June was walking past the garage, when I noticed her and could not control my laughter any longer. She looked inside and saw me sitting ever so smug hidden behind some boxes. She was so angry at my having upset so many people that she grabbed the first thing she could lay her hands on, an empty paint tin, and swung wildly at me. It struck my head, which started to bleed, and I began screaming loudly. Naturally she got the blame, and everyone forgot how much trouble I had put them through. What discomfited everyone was Catherine ayah's incessant "I told you so! One of these days, something is going to happen to this boy, because he doesn't get any love and affection in this house!"

June, too, loved the outdoors and would come along with us whenever she could. This was not often, because she suffered frequent bouts of asthma, aggravated by the pollen in the Bangalore air. She started school at the age of four but had a severe attack and was bedridden for many months. However, she was so bright that she came back to school and took up her lessons as if she had not missed a single day and our grandmother deserves a lot of credit for that. She studied and excelled in French, English, and Maths. She wanted to be a nurse and had applied to the Lady Curzon hospital when she was just sixteen. Although she had excellent grades, they felt that she was too young, and asked her to come back the following year. My Dad was not very keen for her to be a nurse because he was worried about her asthma attacks. She met Jack at a dance a few weeks after her exams while he was an officer cadet training as part of the British Indian army. While the writing was on the wall, no one could have predicted the events that would unfold and change their lives forever.

Jack Vivian Jones, her husband, was born on 16 November 1927 to Laura Caroline Gertrude Netto and Harry Jones in Golden Rock, Trichinopoly. Jack completed his Senior Cambridge at a school in Mount Abu and later attended the military university at Lahore, where Harry was posted at that time. With both his parents connected to the army, it was hardly a surprise when Jack decided to enlist in the British Indian Army. He got posted to Bangalore, where he met June. They were engaged in April 1947, and by July, Jack had got commissioned and was posted to Lahore and was in that city the day India got Independence. His regiment was called back to India, but the situation was so dangerous that they had to wait until nightfall to start. Under cover of darkness, the trucks drove out of Lahore, and the three hundred miles from Lahore to Delhi seemed like three thousand, and he knew that death was always around the corner.

June got married when she was only seventeen years old. She was supposed to get married in 1948, but there was so much turmoil that the army cancelled everyone's sabbaticals for the foreseeable future. That, and the fact that she was so much in love, were reasons compelling enough and they got married on 27 December 1947 at St. Patrick's

Roman Catholic Church in Bangalore, which was incidentally the same church where Jack's parents were married. They went to Wellington, in the Nilgiris for a while, protected from the bloodshed up north. Then Jack was posted at Fatehgarh, eight miles from the Taj Mahal, a place June describes as "Hell on Earth".

Jack Jones and June Anderson - 1947

Fatehgarh was a very important place during the great Indian Uprising and the British had a big fort there. In 1857, the Indian soldiers mutinied against the occupants of the stronghold and even though the British took refuge in the fort and in the church, they were dragged out, slaughtered in cold blood and their bodies thrown into the well at the church. June, who had been brought up on a staple diet of ghosts and spirits, was constantly perturbed when they stayed there.

She had never lived with people from the north before and found them to be extremely aggressive and rude. The men often gave her dirty looks or spoke in a most disrespectful manner to women. Bangalore was such a sheltered city in comparison, and testament to the cloistered life she had led was the fact that she had never seen a Sikh before. Although she stayed within the cantonment area, with Jack away, she was alone and inconsolable most of the time. Eventually they got quarters, a house with just a room and a bathroom. The thatched roof of the house was full of scorpions and there were snakes in the garden. There were no fans or refrigerators and unlike Bangalore, it was unbearably hot. They lived on a road that led to the river, and every day, she would see dead bodies being taken for cremation. She would tell me years later, that looking back it seemed silly, but she used to be terrified of the processions that went by. They would be chanting loudly, while June, cowering behind the curtains, would sneak a look at the corpses, and that would frighten her even more. She would often wake in the middle of the night, screaming, for in her dreams, the corpses would come alive, and they would be chanting! Although she was married, she was just eighteen and still a child.

When June was pregnant with her first son Donald, she was very lucky to get the attention of a hospital. The state government had officially given orders to shut down the missionary hospitals there, on the suspicion that hospitals were responsible for the conversion of the local population to Christianity. Most people knew that she and Jack were British and assumed that they stood for everything that had oppressed the locals. The local government would rather let people die than allow missionary doctors to treat them, lest they convert their patients to Christianity. Luckily, June managed to reach there as one of their last patients, and being a Christian already, she was probably seen as a zero-risk patient. The doctors were allowed to tend to her and she delivered her son, Donald, named after me. The army was very strict about sanctioning leave, and Jack was allowed just a single day's leave when his first son was born. When Don was about eight months old, they were posted to Ambala in the Punjab. She was expecting Chris, her second son, by then, and the quarters they were given were out in the wilderness. They had a Muslim cook who wanted to go with them, but the other officers said the Sikhs in Ambala would slaughter him, and hence they had to take a Hindu cook, Babu Lal. Ambala was a Sikh stronghold, where you would find Sikhs carrying their *kirpans* (knives) or their swords strapped to their chest and June was terrified of them. Don got very sick with dysentery and nearly died when Jack was at the front fighting Pakistanis.

She was on her own with a very sick child, when she had her second son, Christopher, at a local hospital there.

Close to twelve million people were displaced and another million lost their lives during the Partition in 1947. Most of the atrocities were committed in Punjab and Bengal, and Jack, who was posted in Punjab, got ring side seats to some of the most horrific acts committed by human beings. People were burnt alive, looting and arson of homes were common, women and children would be dragged out of their homes to be raped and tortured. Instances of mass suicide by women were not uncommon, usually by self-immolation or by jumping into wells. Those who survived were often mutilated with signs of the religion that motivated the violence. It was a war against the defenceless, with each side trying to outdo the other. Jack could not take it anymore. He had seen trains full of dead people stacked like cattle, he had seen babies lynched and lying unclaimed on roads, bodies butchered and dumped in wells, and this was more than any sane man could endure. He decided that he did not want his family growing up in a land where violence of this scale occurred, and deep down had made up his mind to get away from there as soon as an opportunity presented itself.

Sometime during 1950, while in Fatehgarh, Jack received a letter from the British High Commissioner offering British citizenship, as he was registered as a son of a British serviceman serving overseas. A large number of the British in India wanted to go back after Independence, and those who served the Queen in the manner of the armed forces had a slightly better chance. It did not take much deliberation, especially for Jack who had seen the most horrific scenes during the Partition, and they replied in the affirmative. In fact, after four or five months at his next posting at Ambala, his Commanding Officer handed Jack his papers, honourably discharging him from the army. He was informed that he would be paid gratuity for the time he served, plus three months' pay. But this was untrue, as they were to find out when they reached Bangalore, and he did not get a single rupee as compensation. They were in real financial trouble and having two small boys did not make it any easier. Chris contracted malaria on the journey back to Bangalore from Ambala and Don had still not fully recovered from his bout of dysentery. The future looked so bleak that they were now reconsidering moving to England. At least in India they had family who would take care of them. They borrowed some money and Jack went to Madras to see the British High Commissioner. He was a kind-hearted gentleman who patiently heard why Jack wanted to get away from it all, and also booked their passages to England and lent them money. While that was a huge blessing, they still had to borrow much more from many people including Dad. This was used to buy the bare necessities for their journey to England and have some in their pocket when they landed there. The ship they were booked on had some engine trouble, and they were put onto a much smaller one—one that had been used to carry troops in the war against Japan and that was certainly on its way to the scrap yard after this voyage. Neither of them had ever been on a ship before and were violently ill. They hit two gigantic storms, and both times, they came very close to capsizing. Most people on the ship fell ill, but not due to sea-sickness alone. The ship echoed the sounds of the people it was ferrying, creaking and groaning all the time. The only two people on the ship who seemed unaffected by all this were June's boys, who were full of beans and found this to be a great adventure.

After three awful weeks, they landed in England. What a shock it was after India! England was grey and dull, and the people were extremely unfriendly. No one cared about each other. There were bomb craters, they did not have decent accommodation, and everything was rationed: it was a nightmare. Every day they wondered if they had made the right choice, coming to England. However, it was an irreversible decision and gradually they convinced themselves that things would improve. Deep in their hearts they knew that even if they endured a lifetime of hardship, they would ensure that their children led comfortable lives and that was the singular thought that kept them going. Fortunately, Jack's parents, who had moved to England by then, took them in and gave them a room in the basement of an old Victorian home at Earls Court, and this one room, bath and kitchen was their home for a year. June thus moved from a palatial mansion in Bangalore to a tiny one-bedroom house you could cover in less than fifteen steps. She stayed there and looked after her children, while Jack found employment at a local factory. Life was incredibly hard and she would often wonder what she had done to deserve this sort of thing. Slowly the government realised that the influx of immigrants from India needed housing and started to build satellite towns for the same. One of them was Basildon New Town and they moved to 6 Beeleigh West, a tiny three-bedroom terrace house. It did not have any floor covering, and they had practically no furniture to speak of, but it was heaven after the mouse hole in London and by then June had had her third child, a daughter, Jackie. They soon realised that the locality they were staying in was becoming a rough neighbourhood, and they decided to move again.

About this time, Dad had finished his first book *Nine Man Eaters and One Rogue*, and he had sent June the manuscript to take to the publishers, George Allen & Unwin. They were delighted with the content, and it went on to become one of their biggest grossing titles ever. Dad gave her a massive chunk of the first royalty he received and they put that down as a deposit and bought a three-bedroom bungalow in Essex. She lived there for three years, and by then, both Jack and she were tired of the English weather and the people. Australia was the "Promised Land" for a lot of people and everyone talked about going there. Jack and she applied to emigrate halfway across the world although they were not really serious about it. Moreover, Australia had a "White Australia" policy at that time, and they were very strict about who they were allowing in. It was a series of policies favouring immigration from only European countries. The policy came to fruition in 1901 and it took nearly seventy-five years to abolish it. It was primarily against non-white populations, an extremely racist policy. When June and Jack had their interview in England, they were looked upon with suspicion as their accents sounded odd. When they mentioned that they were from India, they were informed that their lack of money would almost certainly not qualify them to move. June was sinking into despair, realising that they had reached a dead end when suddenly they were informed that their request had been approved. They got a notice that stated that they had three weeks to leave England. It was very short notice, giving them hardly any time, and they ended up giving away all their material possession to blood-sucking agents who took advantage of their situation. The tickets were £20 each, and £100 back then was a fair bit of money. However, they got my mum's sister, Curly, who had moved to Australia in 1922, to sponsor the children and they finally said goodbye to England!

They boarded the SS Oriana, perhaps the last of the Orient Steam Navigation Company's ocean liners on 9 February 1964 and landed in Perth on 28 February. Those days Perth was such a backward place—the only thing one could get there was fish and chips! It took decades for White Australia policy to be lifted and only then with the influx of provisions, were they able to feel that life was normal again. Australia was a tough country and it was bloody hard work for the two of them. For three years they struggled to make ends meet, with three growing children. Those were very tough years for them, and both June and her husband held more than one job at the same time, for the extra income. June still missed India a lot, the warmth and the confusion and the noise, but she certainly did not miss England. June would long for our parents and of course India and all its wonderful people, and would send such letters every month that it depressed Dad a lot. They moved many times, eventually settling down at Canning Vale in 2005.

June left India in 1951, four years after she got married, and despite her poor financial condition made it a point to visit us every four or five years. She would always be horrified at how Bangalore and the people had changed and by the mid-1980s she had stopped coming altogether. I think her greatest disappointment was the fact that no one seemed to cherish or even revere the past, and the sale of our ancestral home was the last straw. She realised that she had nothing to look forward to after our parents passed away. Her children had no recollection of India, and they had been brought up in England and Australia and had no connection with the country she grew up in.

She still loved the jungles, though not as much as me, and she would always ask me to include her for a few days on trips just to see me happy and in my element. Naturally, Jack had to come along too, and one of the trips made me realise how ill-suited he was for this kind of thing. Sometime in the late 1970s, they were visiting and had brought a movie camera, which had me excited. We were driving in the Nilgiris and had reached a spot when a herd of elephants started to chase us. There was never any real danger and I was laughing, but suddenly the car stalled and things started getting a little scary for the visitors. The matriarch of the herd used this opportunity to trumpet and charge at our vehicle. I no longer carried a gun, and although deep down I knew that the elephant would not carry out the charge, I was a bit concerned. As for my companions—they were shrieking in terror, even June. As expected, the pachyderm veered off at the last minute and I took the camera and moved into the jungles to get better shots of the herd. I was away for a good ten minutes and when I returned, I saw June with a jerry can, caught in the act of washing Jack's backside. Although I did capture it on film, I did not say much. There was an uncomfortable silence in the car for the next few minutes, and then our driver spoke to Jack reassuringly in broken English, "Don't worry Sir! It's quite natural, and a lot of people have this sort of reaction on seeing elephants up close."

"Oh really," said Jack, feeling marginally better, "You've had 'this' happen to passengers who have had this sort of experience before?"

"Oh no, Sir, I'm not talking about other passengers. I was talking about myself!"

Despite how much I bullied and hurt her, June loves me and continues to support me through the years. She has been an incredibly caring sister, and I have never done anything good to deserve that kind of affection. Not just during our early childhood when I suppose all siblings hurt each other, but even when I was old enough to understand things, I chose to be extremely selfish and only did things that suited me. Despite all this, she convinced me to move to Australia and promised to pay for my fare, help me get started and look after me, but by then I was too set in my ways and could not think of leaving behind the lifestyle that I had grown accustomed to.

Chapter Three

Friends

AIR MARSHAL MALCOLM "MALLY" WOLLEN, MOST noted for his role in the 1971 war to liberate Bangladesh, was six years older than me. He was my senior at school and I always looked up to him with a certain awe and respect, whereas his younger brother William or "Willie" was closer to my age, more fun-loving and easy-going. Mally was the Services boxing champion and chairman of H.A.L among other important various posts he held. However, the fact that he was a highly-decorated fighter pilot was what impressed us the most. He was awarded the Sword of Honour, the Flying Trophy, and the President's Plaque in addition to the Vir Chakra and the Param Vishisht Seva Medal. He was never the type to boast but we would bother him no end to tell us tales from the wars he fought against Pakistan. The Wollens also happened to be our neighbours at a certain time of our lives when we lived on Cornwall Road and during this time, he and I got close, for they would conduct boxing camps at their house. They had a huge garage that was converted into a sort of a boxing hall, complete with a ring. Although I was younger, I ended up sparring with a lot of Mally's friends. As I had volunteered for this, no punches were spared when I stepped into the ring. I didn't really mind at all, because it helped me get tough and learn to defend myself, not to mention channel my energy into some sort of physical activity when I couldn't visit the jungles.

Willie was older than me but we got along well and had some great adventures in the jungles. His wife, Winsome, did not like the fact that he chose to spend weekends going on hunting trips with me, rather than spending that time with her. Adding fuel to the fire was the fact that we were hunting animals, and that was unacceptable to her. Willie was the kind of guy you could always count on if you got into trouble. I remember an incident when we had gone hunting near Ramanagaram, and it got dark quite early that day. I had already fired thrice with my rifle, missed on all occasions, and I knew this was going to be one of those days. Soon, dark clouds filled the sky, and we were hurrying to get back, as we didn't want to get caught in the rain. Suddenly, without warning, there was a thunderclap and almost immediately I noticed a sloth bear running in our direction. It couldn't have seen us in the fading light, but it was trying to make a getaway and was headed straight to us. I fired but missed the bear completely. The law of averages was catching up and I knew that my luck was about to desert me. My second shot hit the bear, but instead of stopping it, seemed to give it more impetus. It was bellowing in rage, confused and looking for the creature responsible. It was too late, but I realised that I didn't have any more cartridges; the chamber was empty and I didn't have any in my pocket either! I could have had six in total, but I had always believed that carrying five brought me luck, and it looked like my theory was about to get tested! All this happened in a matter of seconds and the bear was practically just a few yards away, standing on its hind legs and roaring with pain and anger. I had forgotten all about Willie, till I heard a voice. As cool as a cucumber, Willie, who didn't have anything to protect himself, handed me a cartridge from my gun bag, saying, "Here you go."

It was almost point blank when I fired my last shot, but the bear dropped down on all fours at the same time, and toppled over, practically inches from where I stood.

I was amazed at Willie's bravery and composure. Anyone else would have fled the scene, but he had stood right by my side and saved me from certain mauling or worse!

With Willie Wollen

Willie was never keen on hunting anything, perfectly happy to stand behind the scenes and watch me in action, but one day, at Hugh Hailstone's place in Mudiyanoor, he declared that he wanted to go shooting. I wasn't keen, but he was adamant and so we all got into our car and started driving. The sun was beginning to set and we switched on the car headlights. We had hardly gone a mile, when the lights picked up a pair of eyes on the road. I applied the brakes and waited. A hare hopped on to the road. Willie was in an unusually belligerent mood and demanded that I hand over my shotgun. I thought that he might have had a bit too much to drink but I handed it over, reluctantly. The hare was a sitting target, frozen like stone. Willie got out of the car and fired, completely missing the animal and almost falling back with the recoil. He staggered to his feet and found that the hare had disappeared. He was cursing under his breath, when the little rodent reappeared on the road, seemingly unaffected by what had just happened, or perhaps it was another hare. Anyway, Willie felt that it was mocking him with this act, but he had had enough of the gun, so cursing the little hare, he picked up a fair-sized stone and threw it wildly. Incredibly, his aim was spot on and knocked the creature senseless! It was so bizarre but it happened in front of our eyes. Thereafter we always ribbed him, that even if his "gun" didn't work, he had other methods to get the job done! Believe it or not, there was another incident with Willie and a hare! Once Willie, Merwan and I were driving in the Nilgiris on the ghat section and had stopped for a break. As I started the car and switched on the headlights, I spotted a hare that was right in the middle of the road. It was facing away and hadn't sensed our presence. Suddenly, out of the blue, a horned owl swooped down and knocked it senseless. I thought it was a lucky break, it meant meat for our next meal without spending a cartridge! So, Willie got out of the car, clapped his hands, and the bird silently glided away into the darkness. He picked up the lifeless body of the creature and put it into the boot of the car. He was extremely excited at what had happened and had described more than one recipe he had in mind when we reached our destination. He felt he deserved credit, as he was the one who scared the owl away. When we reached our destination, he opened the boot, and to his astonishment, out jumped the hare, very much alive, and scampered away into the darkness!

Once, we were going to Hogenikal with Willie, Merwan, and my dad, in Merwan's car, when the radiator developed a leak. We were miles away from any garage and were in a fix. Then dad had this brainwave that we could fix it using eggs! I had never heard of this before, but considering that we didn't have a better idea, we were ready to try that. The theory is that if you drop a raw egg (only the white), it would cook inside the radiator and plug the leak. To our surprise, it actually worked, and we did manage to go some distance, but then the problem surfaced again. We had no option but to use our drinking water and hope that we could somehow reach Hogenikal where we could get the radiator fixed. Then water ran out and we were stranded…we just had to get more water. Again, dad came up with an idea. He suggested that the closest source of water was in our bodies, and therefore it made sense that we use that. His suggestion, that we pee into the radiator, was met with much amusement by everyone, but we realised that it was a logical one, considering the circumstances. So, Dad, Merwan, and I peed, but when it came to Willie, he refused.

"You buggers, there's no way in hell you're getting me to do that," he yelled and walked off.

We laughed at his discomfort, and shouted after him, "If you don't pee, it's your responsibility to get someone else to contribute your share."

Willie replied that he would choose the latter. Soon enough, we had a bullock cart pass us by, and the occupants got the most bizarre request they would ever hear in their lives. "Sirs, would you mind peeing!" …in Willie Wollen vernacular. This was years before Morarji Desai popularised a certain concept and so poor Willie was treated to some very colourful language while we sat there and laughed our guts out.

Although we knew each other from earlier days as neighbours, he and I were also colleagues at Binny's. He was far cleverer than me but was stuck in a clerical job that did not do any justice to his intellectual capabilities. He got promoted as a manager, much later than he deserved, at the garment factory at Hebbal. His wife, Winsome, became the head of the Richmond Road Post Office, that is operational even today. After he migrated, he would come to Bangalore every two years and we would go to the jungles, and he would be extremely depressed when it was time to go back. Willie was one of those people who reluctantly migrated to Australia, because his heart belonged here.

Sonny Leonard was a trouble maker and yet a great friend of mine and Dad has written about him in his books. He was such a klutz, but a very lovable one at that, so despite all the trouble that he always managed to drag in with him, he was often forgiven because it was never intentional. His mother and he were our tenants at Prospect House and though he was younger than me, he was always around and so I would take him along on many of my trips, although armed with considerable caution! He was not well educated and earned his livelihood as a lorry driver. They were not particularly well off, so Sonny would drive for days at end, scoffing at our concern when he would drive during the nights on the Bangalore-Bombay route. Unfortunately, he was a heavy drinker, not a particularly enviable trait for someone in his profession. As predicted by most of us, he died in an accident, although it was never ascertained whether he was intoxicated at that time. He did not call his mother the day he was supposed to reach his destination and a couple of days later, the news came about his demise. Either the accident had been horrific or the post-mortem was botched up, but add two more days to that, and the result was one of the most unforgettable sights I have seen in my life. I have seen people mauled by panthers or bears, seen automobile accidents, but the sight of Sonny Leonard's body swathed in bloodied bandages and coated with eucalyptus oil left an indelible mark in my mind. We brought the body home despite my Mom's protests, as a token of our concern for Mrs. Leonard, but the whole house was reeking for days after. Weeks passed but the memory of that gruesome spectacle was still fresh in people's minds. I convinced Thangavelu to seed the idea among the occupants of the house that Sonny met his end far earlier than he deserved and would seek retribution against all those who did not treat him kindly. Knowing that almost everyone in that house would have hurled abuses at him at one point or the other, I'm sure the thought crept into people's minds that perhaps they should have treated Sonny better. The other partner in crime was my Dad who, without direct reference to Sonny, suddenly and quite vocally, spiked his interest in the afterlife, and damned souls seeking retribution. About two weeks had passed when I put my master plan to work. It was a Sunday evening, and a half moon bathed our compound. I got myself covered in bandages, and literally doused myself in eucalyptus oil, and started moaning from the depths of a corner in the garden. I quickly realised that humans are not the most discerning when it comes to hearing spooky moans far away. I realised that I had a more powerful weapon than my voice. I did a quick circle around the house, spending time under the windows, and ran back to my original point. Sure enough, I could hear the questions, "Do you smell eucalyptus?" When three or four questions of the same nature were voiced, my Dad asked the very question that was on everyone's minds. "Hey, the last time this house smelt like eucalyptus was when..." If there was ever an award for acting at Prospect House, my Dad deserved it for his performance that day. I'm told that he stopped mid-sentence and pointed out and gasped, "By God, its young Sonny." On cue, I could see heads peeping out from the windows and I delivered the coup de grace with my loudest groan. It was met with the desired result, for pandemonium broke loose and for a moment even Thangavelu seemed to have got forgotten the act, for I could hear him above everyone else, begging for mercy!

I remember a trip I did with my Dad and Sonny to Gulhatti in our brand new second-hand Studebaker. Dad was driving while I sat on the top, where we had fixed a carrier, with a flashlight. Sonny and I were taking turns sitting on the roof of the car, trying to outdo each other in spotting game. While he was on top, I held my rifle, but when we switched places, he was given strict instructions not to touch it, because

I knew that he was a fiddler and trouble always followed him around. Suddenly the car went over a small pothole and the next moment there was an explosion. Dad hit the brakes and I nearly fell off the car. I steadied myself, shocked and angry. Sonny jumped out of the car with that familiar guilty look. I knew that he had definitely done some *golmaal* (mischief). That's when I noticed a big bloody hole in the roof, inches away from my butt! Like a cowboy he not only loaded the rifle, but faced it to the roof of the car, and had his finger on the trigger when the car went over the pothole. Perhaps the other instances were not as life threatening as this one, but one could never be too careful with Sonny around. The Leonards were not very well to do, so I often took Sonny along on my trips much against my better judgement and regretted my decision each time.

An oddity in our gang was Father Freeman, the erstwhile principal of Philomena's college in Mysore. A Catholic priest, on the education board, he had his hunting days behind him when we became friends. While a firm believer in the Christian way of things, hunting had always been a weakness and we teased him mercilessly about how certain bits of his pedagogy had been conveniently altered to suit his hobby! He was a youthful eighty-one when he became part of our entourage and did his bit during our trips, never asking for any special consideration on account of his age. He used to live at the retirement quarters at St. Martha's hospital and I met him through my friend, Gene Edwards. He was determined to enjoy every moment with us youngsters, geriatric hindrances be damned! He was known to be an excellent shikari, having shot sixteen tigers, and although those days were things of the past, his love for the jungles was as strong as ever and in our motley crew he found kindred souls, whose idea of having a good time lay far away from the city. He was soft spoken, and more enthusiastic than us who were a good thirty years younger than him. He would always ask that he carried one of the guns when we went out hunting and although he didn't do much shooting after he joined our gang, he personified toughness till he passed away at the age of eighty-six. He brought a different perspective to our group with opinions on life slightly different from ours and we always appreciated that.

Then there was "Tiny" Seddon, who at 6ft 7 inches was anything but that. But somehow the name stuck and although he was only a bit younger than my Dad, he preferred to come along with my gang as he got older. He was a fantastic angler, a champion mahseer fisherman, and a small-time hunter. I never accompanied him on his hunting trips, as he only shot animals from his car. He had a beautiful silver A1 Ford, and whoever went along with him had the responsibility of shining the spotlight while he shot small game. I've held the spotlight for him, and even at a young age, he earned nothing but my contempt for the manner in which he shot his game. In all other aspects, he was a great person. He never drank, nor smoked, but was full of merriment and always a good sport, especially considering the many jokes we made about his size. Tiny's work often took him to Shimoga and Bhadravati and those naturally became the places where we had our picnics. Two of our standard stops were the rest houses at Tarikere and Arsikere. We all loved food, and the cook at the Tarikere rest house was exceptionally good. He was a Muslim who knew recipes quite different from the usually fare we were used to at Bangalore and so these trips were extra special for gluttons like me. The roads were full of game in those days, and every morning and evening we would go out in the car and get jungle fowl or spur fowl for the meal. Of course, if we ever got something like a sambar, we took our bit and the rest was given to the cook, who then sold it to the people at the closest village.

A good friend of Tiny's was "Baba" Cariappa, who was in the army. He was under the impression that his profession automatically qualified him to be an outdoor person, a hunter and angler, but that couldn't be farther from the truth. He would come along for wild boar hunts and duck shoots, but was never successful. He would accompany us to Sangam for angling, but always left empty handed. His lack of contribution to the pot hardly put a dent into his enthusiasm when it came to sharing the spoils. In most situations, it wouldn't make a difference, especially at duck shoots, where the rule was to divide the spoils equally among all the participants, irrespective of how many birds were shot by an individual. If you shot the most, what you took home additionally was just pride. In Baba's case, at times it was a little hard to watch him get an equal share when he had contributed nothing! However, he loved good food and the way he lovingly described how the boar or fowl was going to be prepared would make us forget our mild annoyance.

**Spoils after a duck hunt – Baba Cariappa, Clive Greenwood,
Tiny Seddon and Donald**

Gene Edwards was another excellent friend I had. I met him when he
was about thirty, and I, a few years younger. A champion boxer in his
younger days, among all my friends, he was the one who was always in
the mood to have fun. Forever playing the fool, he loved to entertain and
was extremely popular with both sexes. Originally from Hyderabad, he
was posted in Bangalore as the manager of Castrol for the state and that
meant a lot of travelling. Although he was never interested in hunting,
his enthusiasm spiked after I started to sidetrack him during the times
I accompanied him on his tours to Mysore, Bhadravathi, and Shimoga
where he promoted his brand. One had to pass through many forest areas
and inevitably we would have a small deviation and hunt, and although
he never became a shikari like me, he started to love the jungles. He
loved angling as well, and with a few friends, we would visit fishing spots
in Sangam, just camp by the river under open skies. I remember the first
and perhaps the defining trip that got him interested in coming along
with me. I had mentioned to my friends that I was visiting Ramnagaram
to shoot a panther, and somehow everyone was held up with some
chore or the other. Gene, who had never been to one of these before,
volunteered to come to see what the fuss was all about. We were delayed

74

leaving Bangalore and arrived at our spot much later than I would have liked. As we approached the bottom of the hillock, we noticed that the panther was out already, enjoying the gentle warmth of the setting sun. I asked Gene to move to a rocky outcrop that gave him a good view of the panther, while I attempted the bizarre pursuit of stalking a panther, going uphill! Every now and then I had to stop and look at Gene for directions, and true to his word, he never took his eyes off the animal, always letting me know in which direction I had to move next. At one point I realised that I was perhaps close enough, and so, crawling on my knees, came to a small clearing, waited to catch my breath, aimed and then shot the panther, who didn't have the slightest idea it been stalked just as it did its prey. It dropped dead in the same spot. I felt extremely pleased with myself, for I had never tried something of this nature before, but Gene, who had a ringside view to all this, was thrilled. As he kept repeating over and over again to all our friends, "It was like watching a film!"

He died of lung cancer and his death left me inconsolable. He started radio therapy and before his second sitting he told me, "Don, I have a bad feeling about this," and he never came back.

My friends and I would hang out at Crown Café opposite Wood Street, where we would spend many hours. Over the years, my circle of friends would change and there would always be those who would go away and come back, but the evenings at Crown Café with the guys exemplified the carefree life I lived at that time. We would have kababs and biriyani and drink beer either in our cars or at the restaurant itself. Whiskey was the "guys' drink" back then but we had to depend on someone bringing it from abroad as it was not made in India. I didn't drink much, but I was a heavy smoker, and Charminar was my preferred brand. Those cigarettes didn't have any filters and it's a miracle that none of us developed serious ailments. Sometimes we would walk from Crown Café to the Bandstand where we would listen to music. Anglo-Indians dominated the music scene in Bangalore and live music was common at places like the 3 Aces. Although I didn't enjoy this as much as my hunting forays, I used to enjoy hanging out with my friends, both men and women. We would get boisterous occasionally, but no one bothered us, because Bangalore was a place where everyone was so easy-going, and knew that we never meant any harm. Although I never played billiards, I would often visit

Tom's billiard's parlour on MG Road. A lot of chaps from colleges and even schools would come there, and I slowly realised that I was getting too old to be visiting that place! The other place that my friends visited was Metro, which stood where Cauvery Emporium stands today at the Brigade Road – MG Road junction. It was supposed to be a restaurant and bar, but in reality, it was a knocking shop that a lot of men from the cantonment area visited.

It's hard to comprehend that a dangerous situation in the jungle would ever be associated with laughter, but let me narrate one such incident. I was about fourteen and had gone on a trip with my brother-in-law Jack and my friend Sydney D'Silva. Jack wasn't interested in shooting but was a good sport and came along to enjoy a guys' day out. This time we went to Javalagiri and left Jack at camp, while Sydney and I decided that we would go for a walk. We had walked for a couple of hours without seeing anything and were returning to the forest rest house taking the long route. The sun was setting when we heard loud bellows from up ahead. There was absolute panic—cattle were running helter-skelter and people were chasing them. There was so much dust in the fading light that it was really hard to make out what was happening. By the time things settled down, we could fathom that a tiger had killed a cow a few moments earlier, but was not able to carry the kill away because the other cows chased it away. We were excited. A tiger no less! Could there be a bigger prize? This was 1948 and tigers were not uncommon in these parts. There was no time to tie a machan, and the cowherd and his companions were not inclined to set one up. It was dark, who knew when the tiger would return? None of them wanted to go to the village and come back with one of their local muzzle loaders. We promised to avenge their loss by sitting up and bagging the tiger when it came back. With just our knives, we proceeded to hack some branches and made a terribly unimaginative hide. Our pulses were racing as we settled in for the night. We didn't have food, water, or blankets, as we hadn't planned to stay up. We hadn't informed Jack that we would stay up. None of these concerns crossed our fourteen-year-old minds, as we realised the possibility of shooting our first tiger! I can never stay awake the entire night, and that day was no exception. I had a little shut-eye, dreaming of skinning the tiger, and winning the admiration of the villagers. I woke up with a start. I could feel that something was not right, and I could feel the hair on the back of my neck stand up. I couldn't put my finger on what it was. Sydney, too, was intently peering out through the hide. I heard a soft growl some distance away and, immediately, I stiffened. Clearly the tiger had seen us and was making obvious his displeasure on finding company next to his meal. Although there was some moonlight, I couldn't see where the sound was coming from. I motioned to Sydney to stay silent. We didn't know better so both of us were sitting facing the dead cow, and we now realised our folly. What if the tiger came from behind? It was too late to change positions and the growl meant that in all probability we were being observed. I desperately tried to scan the bushes but it was of no use. Then I heard another growl, and poor Sydney started to shake. He was so scared that it looked like he was having convulsions. I put my arm around his shoulder, gave it a tight squeeze as if to say, "pull yourself together, old chap", but it was of no use, it started to get worse, and to my horror, I could sense that he was about to scream. I put my hand over his mouth to stifle the sound, and held my rife in the other, just in case. That's when it happened, Sydney couldn't bear it anymore, and, pushing my hand away, switched on the torch and collapsed on top of me, laughing! With tears streaming down his face, and in between gasps, he somehow managed to tell me that the growls I heard were from his stomach, as he hadn't eaten for a long time and his seizure was nothing but suppressed laughter! I felt very sheepish after that, and the tiger, who must have been most surprised to see two giggly teenagers tumble out of a bush, must have left in disgust, for he never came back that night.

Sydney D'Silva was in a way my definitive "best friend" for most of my school life. He was a happy-go-lucky chap and a good sport. He had neither hobbies nor vices, but was always happy to tag along with me for a lot of my adventures. He lived in a small house opposite an office called Mesquite & Company on St. Marks Road, very close to where Koshy's restaurant stands today. As he lived close by, we spent time at either of our houses every day. I remember that it was very normal when we were ten or eleven to walk to each other's house and this had to happen before nine o'clock. Bangalore was the first city in India to receive electricity and during the war, lights would be turned off at exactly 9:00 p.m., and this routine was so punctual that you could set your watch or clock by it. Our parents trusted us and, more importantly, trusted people in that area.

The wonderful sights I would see on my way back home are so deeply etched in my memory that I smile every time I think about them. I would pass dimly lit but wonderfully cheery houses alive with the sounds of the families gathered around their radio, listening to the BBC on their Ekco radio or records on a gramophone. The houses would be surrounded by large gardens casting spectral shadows, and the quiet roads would echo our footsteps as we walked in a hurry…one could never be sure what ghosts one would see under the trees, waiting for young boys!

Next to Sydney's house was the home of a girl who caught Sydney's attention and to be truthful I was enamoured of her too. She was an English girl, extremely curvy, and her short frocks and long legs gave us much to imagine. She lived with her grandmother whose sense of sight and hearing were suspect. So, she would carefully sneak her boyfriend in, and we were always curious what happened after he got in the room. Our knowledge of sex and the female body was limited to a few magazines that were falling to pieces, or older boys who proved their superiority having seen it in the flesh. Most houses in those days had tall rooms and skylights that could be opened. It didn't take much imagination or even ideation to realise that it was the one place we could use to be initiated into the adult world. It was not easy. We had to execute our plan when she invited the chap over, and when both Sydney and I were at his house. It meant that we had to jump the wall, climb up the huge tree next to the house, drop off from one of the branches on to a landing and observe the forbidden, all the while ensuring that we did not get caught, not just by the occupants of the house but also by people in other neighbouring houses. Unlike today, in those days, most of the women were home-makers, and there was a good chance that someone would see us. And if one noticed two fourteen-year-old boys on the top of a house they did not belong to, it usually meant that they were up to no good.

So, after many "so near, yet so far" opportunities the winds changed in our favour. Sydney's mum was away visiting relatives, so we waited patiently, hoping that the couple would get together. The gods smiled on us in the late afternoon, making the entire morning's wait worthwhile. It was a well-executed plan, as it had been thought through down to the smallest detail. Sydney was on guard and gave me the signal of two short whistles. Like trained soldiers, we did our respective bits, and in no time we were next to the skylight. Sure enough, we were well rewarded with what we had hoped to see, and with an aerial ringside view too! While the sights we were seeing were not entirely unfamiliar, the feeling that a voyeur gets the first time he sees something like that is so strong, it can cause very different reactions in different people. I held on to the skylight as hard as I could, breathing heavily. I could hear blood whirling in my head. We had to look around furtively to ensure that our actions were not spotted, but again the gods were kind to us. All we could hear were the sounds of trilling birds. There were no shouts from down below, no one had caught us yet, and it seemed like a perfect, sunny day. Then something changed. The visual cues were so strong that poor Sydney couldn't control himself, and with a low moan, he shuddered and fell. As he fell, he knocked hard on the glass of the skylight, and it didn't take much detective work for the couple below to see the source of the sound. The chap was first shocked, as was the girl, and then rage took over. To his credit, he still had the presence of mind not to shout and reveal his presence in the house but to shake his fist at us and jump off the bed. That day, we understood first hand that fear produces more adrenalin than anger, as we both ran to save our skins. We did get a head start, for we were clothed when the race began, and we did not have to look out for a grandmother on our escape route. We didn't get caught that day, and it was a happy ending in more ways than one, for us. I don't know if he saw our faces, but we never saw him again. The number of times we repeated this story at school got tiresome after a while, but we became heroes for having seen such an incident live!

It's funny that my friendship with Sydney started with a fight. We got into an argument in school over something, and while I cannot for the life of me remember over what, at age eight or nine, it was worth having a physical fight, it finally came to that. Unfortunately, it was a Friday and the typical way of resolving fights at school, through a boxing match, couldn't be administered, so as gentlemen we mutually agreed that he would come to my house and sort it out there. We decided that we would deploy the same rules as the gym, only the venue would change. This was met with much cheer from the onlookers, who loved incidents of this type. He was much shorter than me, and in the heat of the moment, that had not mattered to him. However, half an hour before the fight, he came home, apologised and requested if we could call off the fight. I don't think he was in the wrong, but he was smart enough to know that a private apology was better than a public humiliation. I, too, was not too keen on hammering someone much smaller than myself as it would do no good to my reputation if word got around. Anyway, that fight turned into friendship and we have been firm friends since that day.

We've sometimes had disputes that threatened our friendship, but somehow we always found ways to put aside those differences. Financially, he wasn't well off, while I was. To add to that, he always attracted "nice girls" while I always got girls who wanted to have a bit of fun. As we grew up, we kept score of the number of women we slept with, and often challenged each other to get certain girls in bed. While I may have won the battle, he certainly won the war and made better life choices, and today he is considerably well off and has a family while I have nothing. Such is life!

A friend of Dad's who used to accompany us during our hunting trips was Wiele of "Wiele and Klein", the famous photography studio in Madras and Mysore. He was a German and the rigour with which he was taught the language in Ooty as a youngster was very impressive, for when he spoke English or any of the Indian languages, he spoke with a strong guttural accent. And it was not just his accent that was off.

Once he got me into a hell of a bloody mess, after which I stopped taking him along on trips. The two of us had gone for a trip to Shikaripur and, leaving my friend at the village, had gone out to scout for animal tracks. I was making my way back to the village when I noticed that a war dance was going on. Apparently, Herr Wiele had believed that women were easy in the village and, approaching a certain gentleman, had asked in earnest in his faultlessly rasping Hindustani, *"Ladki milta?"* (Can I get a girl?) It was a bad day for Wiele; the man he approached was like the village headman and his perfectly innocuous question was perceived to be aimed at the headman's daughter who was standing close by. The village was ready to lynch him, but as in most situations in these villages, there are tried and tested ways to appease a crowd. A pooja of a certain value did the trick, as also a promise that I would never bring such people to their village again!

I learnt to drive my first motorcycle, thanks to my friend Ronnie Philips, at the age of fifteen or so. He was the son of a planter who lived in Shimoga. Neither Ronnie nor his family were ever interested in hunting, believing it was both cruel and dangerous.

**Wiele with Rex Wilson on the left and Blossom Anderson
on the right**

Ronnie was a boarder in Bishop Cotton's school, and his family would come down very often to meet him. Ronnie was, in many aspects, the definitive good boy and always asked his parents for permission to do things. After a long phase of negotiations, he finally got consent to come with me on a trip to Javalagiri. I did not volunteer to inform him that a panther hunt was on the cards, as knowing him, he would have specifically asked for permission to shoot a panther and that would have been the end of that story. So, with half-hearted but officially documented blessings, Ronnie and I set off on a borrowed motorcycle, promising to be back at a certain time at my house. We reached the forest rest house by noon and waited for it to cool before we set up our task. By now Ronnie had been informed of my plan, and he was very excited, the thrill of doing something without informing his parents giving him an adrenalin rush. I don't remember how, but we managed to find a friendly village cur who didn't particularly mind having us tie a rope around his neck, and it followed us quite contentedly. The poor thing had no idea of our malicious plans and once we tied him up as bait, proceeded to wriggle and yelp, but it was of no use and I managed to pacify it with some leftovers from our lunch. We decided to sit on the ground, with absolutely no cover, just a blanket wrapped around the two of us. We were very confident that a panther would come, especially hearing the odd bark from the mutt. We were incredibly lucky as, within an hour, we saw a small panther launch itself out of nowhere and kill the dog right before our eyes. Much to our dismay, it managed to break the rope and carry the victim away into a nearby bush, where we could hear but not see it. The sun had set, but it was a brilliant moonlit night, so I felt that this was a perfect opportunity for me. I handed my blanket to Ronnie, took my Dad's shotgun, and walked cautiously towards the general direction where the panther had disappeared with its meal. A while later, I heard the faintest of sighs, and my hair stood on end. I flashed the torch around and there, about fifteen yards away, was the panther, just staring at me. It was some distance away from the dog and it didn't seem very afraid, so I cautiously walked closer. Small steps, ever so slowly, with the gun cradled in my arms, up to a spot I believed was a decent distance for a shotgun. Then I let fly. I had aimed for the neck, but it did not have the desired result, for all it did was to get it to charge. Luckily, the panther did not run straight towards me, but to my side, so as it ran past, I swivelled and let fly a snapshot with the other barrel. I was sure I had hit it this time but the panther disappeared into the bushes and was lost from view. We had promised our parents that we would leave at daybreak, but the code of a shikari—not to leave a wounded animal to suffer—was ingrained in my very impressionable mind even at that age, and so we decided to stay the night and finish the job. We waited till the sun was high the next morning, and it was past nine when we started out. We had no guides because I was supremely confident in my tracking skills. It was a humbling experience; despite shooting the panther at least once, we could not pick up the trail. When we couldn't do it as a team, we decided to split up. An incredibly stupid move, considering that Ronnie was unarmed, but by noon, we had to face the fact that we were terrible trackers, and we started to walk home, dejected. As we were heading back, we noticed that a crowd had gathered around the guest house, and in a few seconds, pandemonium broke loose. The crowd rushed towards us, led by Ronnie's parents, who had come there believing the worst had happened. Ronnie got an earful, but the relief that he was safe softened the blow, and so I bore the brunt of their anger. They refused to listen to my point of view—such as the ethics of a shikari and other lofty statements—and I don't blame them, for what I had done was borderline insane and they behaved as any parents would. They got into their taxi and stormed out of the village. Ronnie was very upset with his parents for a while. As for me, I never did find that panther.

While I knew how to ride a bike, it always meant borrowing one from my older friends, who in turn had to ask permission from their older siblings, so the probability of getting one when I actually needed it was non-existent. My dad had a great fascination for automobiles, and by the time I was fourteen, Dad had about fifteen motorcycles in his garage, and that was temptation enough for me to ask for one. By then I had been riding on the roads in Bangalore and felt that my demand was fully justified. Surprisingly, he replied in the affirmative, but weeks went by and his enthusiasm seemed to diminish considerably. Then one day, he and I went to Hoskote and the belt of the bike broke. Apparently, it had been my responsibility to check that before we left. He was so furious that he made me push the bike back to the city, which was a distance of almost sixteen miles. That was the last nail in the coffin. I was convinced that the only way to drive home the point of how badly I needed the bike was to run away from home. Sure enough, with a well-placed note on my parents' nightstand, I proceeded on my maiden urban solo adventure. After the first few steps outside my house, I realised that I hadn't thought this through very well. The romanticised notion of a starving homeless son being pacified by his parents with a motorcycle seemed a distant reality; so, I took the next best course of action and went to stay with my friend, Merwan. His mother didn't think twice about my arrival but she spoke to my Mum, and soon I was picked up by my Dad and taken home. He didn't say a word, but next day we went out to get a bike. My Dad being... well, my Dad, he convinced me that only a second-hand bike made sense and so I got a distinctly second-hand looking 1942 single cylinder 5 HP Army Norton for 300 rupees in 1948. After the war, a lot of the bikes were sold off at very cheap prices, and the best brands one could choose from were BSA, Triumph, and Norton.

Although the first option for anyone buying a motorcycle in those days was Simpson and Co. on South Parade, the bikes I bought were never new. My next motorcycle was also second-hand, a scarred remnant of the war, a 1942 500 cc BSA with a sidecar. Does its registration number MYB 3047 seem familiar? It would if you have seen the iconic film *Sholay*. While the sidecar kind of cramped my style, it was something different and at that moment in time, it was cheap and translated into luggage space. It was in terrible shape when I picked it up, and I had to spend a lot of money to do up that bike. If I were to describe the sidecar,

I would say it looked like a coffin on wheels. I'm guessing it wasn't the brightest engineer who drew up the plan, because once you got in, you had this helpless trapped feeling. The funniest incident with that bike happened when we went duck hunting once, on Kanakpura Road. After multiple rounds of coin tossing, Ronnie Philips found himself to be the designated driver while the losers, Sydney and I, had to resign ourselves to the sidecar. I pulled "bulk rank" on Sydney and forced him into the back of the sidecar, while I sat in front. Ronnie was very careful that day, avoiding all the bumps and potholes. It would be accurate to say that the part of the motorcycle that he was sitting on avoided the ruts and dips, but not the part we were squeezed into. Our exclamations and expletives were directly proportional to his speed, and the mathematical equation touched infinity at a bend near Somanahalli. We were on a narrow road that bisected a large tank, when Ronnie felt that this was the one spot where the biker and his machine became a single entity. It was certainly an inspiring thought, as most bikers feel this during their time on the road. However, it certainly was not the speed, the section of the road, or the time, to forget that we were attached to his bike. We got on to the tank road at tear away speed, and then I remember a sudden silence and the feeling that the road wasn't so bad anymore. A peaceful feeling enveloped us for just a moment. The sidecar had detached itself from the motorcycle, and gone over the escarpment at a ridiculous angle, sailing over the wetland below. Sydney was yelling blue murder and as we stuck our heads out, we saw a man planting something, directly in our path. Hardly a laughing matter, but it was quite comical to see his expression, for out of the blue was this coffin-like contrivance flying out of the sky, and in it were two heads screaming in terror. He dropped everything and ran like hell. Of course, we landed in soft mud, which cushioned our fall, but we had a few broken bones and cuts and bruises after that incident. To even out the damage, Ronnie had fallen into the small pond on the other side, and had bruises all over. Despite incidents like this, I was always able to get the bike fixed; there was no concept of throwing anything away those days till it fell to bits. Years passed and I wanted a newer motorcycle, so I sold this one to a guy who eventually loaned it to be used in *Sholay* by Amitabh Bachchan and Dharmendra in a famous song. I didn't even know about all this till my friends told me. Of course, I became a bit of a celebrity and I even convinced myself to watch the film just to see my old motorcycle on the big screen.

My next motorcycle is the one most people remember me with, in the sixties. No surprise, it was second-hand as well, a twin engine 5 HP 1956 model Norton Dominator, an absolute dream machine, with a top speed of 100 mph. Its first owner had been killed in a road accident, and a few years later, the original owner's brother and his pillion rider were killed near Mysore when they hit a water pipe on the road. The father of the deceased driver didn't want anything to do with the bike, clearly believing that the bike was cursed. So, before he lost any more members of his family, he sold it for a paltry sum of Rs. 800, a steal in those days! It became a part of a lot of my adventures over the next nine years. In fact, this was my show-off bike. After many a panther hunt in Ramanagaram, I would drive into town, ensuring that my route included South Parade. I'd turn the handlebars by 180 degrees and have my panther slung across them. How silly it seems now, but boy, did that make people take notice! I eventually sold the bike, and within a month, believe it or not, the driver and his pillion got killed on the Ooty ghats!

A common sight in Bangalore in the 1950s

While I had many bikes, the flashiest one was a 1000 cc Red Indian "Chief", yes, again a second-hand bike, extremely heavy, and not the easiest to handle, but it certainly would make heads turn. It had a beautiful sound, and I would drive on MG Road, with either a girl behind me or a dead panther in front on the tank, and that made quite an impression.

I've been very comfortable with automobiles, owning many over the years. The love for them was passed on to me by my father. Before the war, his prized possession was a T Model Ford he named "Sudden Death". It literally had no body, it was just a square box roped to the chassis. There were no mud guards, which effectively meant that apart from appreciating the visual aspect of the road, one could taste it as well. However, those were seen as funny incidents and for the bunch of ragamuffins that we were, this was the least of our problems. The horn was placed next to the driver's seat—well, it not really a seat but an old petrol tank with one of my Mum's cushions on top. Similar discarded cushions were placed in other parts of the car, and they served as seats for the other passengers. The car cost about forty-five rupees, and I think the year was 1941 or 42, if I notice how old I looked in the photograph. It ran on kerosene which cost two annas a gallon. So, Dad being the miser he was, would fill two annas worth of petrol, just to get started, and then would switch over to kerosene after a while. Thus, one could go to Madras and come back for fifteen-twenty rupees including refreshments on the way! One of the other T Model Fords had regular seats in the front and the back was a wooden box that doubled up as a machan that Dad used to tie up on the trees when he sat over a bait or kill. The wheels were twenty-one inches across and very narrow, so this could go across practically any terrain—the equivalent places in today's world are those that need a 4-wheel drive. The best part of this wonderfully weird machine was that it was so light that there was no chance of it getting bogged down anywhere, so the absence of tarred roads was not a problem. If one got into slush, a single person could help push it across and we would be on our way. Dad had twenty-three spare engines for the T model Ford, and dozens of spare wheels. Although he was no mechanic, he knew just about enough to ensure that the cars could run. Cars in those days had no gears, your clutch doubled up as gears, as you released it you went forward. The simplicity of those cars was something else! If you looked under it, all you saw was an engine, some plugs and a dynamo!

"Sudden Death"

After this came the A model Ford, again many of which were hoarded in my house, spread across many shelves and crevices in our garage. While an excellent car with nineteen-inch wheels and a better engine and actual doors, it somehow never matched the simplicity of its predecessor. We had many other cars including four or five Studebakers, but the prettiest of them was a 1920 Bugatti racing car we bought from an Irish gentleman who was moving to Australia. Dad would take me around for short drives, and race on the wide roads of South Parade early in the morning on Saturdays. That was the only time we could drive so fast. It would be freezing and both he and I would cover ourselves up and put the engine to test. It was a special feeling, but shortly it developed problems and we had to sell it at the Gujj (Gujjulee, a place opposite Russel Market where one buys and sells old things) for 225 rupees.

Like all shikaris, I too am extremely superstitious. While the biggest ace up my sleeve was a mantram I used to chant to bring me good luck, the next best talisman was my friend, Reggie Freeman. He was an Anglo-Indian, who worked in the Merchant Navy, and that meant that when was in Bangalore, he was here for a good four to five months. During these months he didn't have an everyday job, so he ended up coming with me to the jungles, practically at my beck and call. I don't remember how it started, but there were times when I would literally beg him to come with me on trips. For every story where I shot them, there are nine others where I would come back empty handed or not even see one altogether. You can call it what you want, but with Reggie by my side, my luck was just incredible! My outings with Reggie were after I had joined Binnys, so I had to make the best of my carefully planned trips, and I did not want to leave anything to chance. Poor Reggie, there are times when I selfishly would ask him to leave his girlfriend behind to come hunting with me to Ramnagaram. No wonder he longed to get back to his ship! My Norton bike, my .423 rifle, Reggie Freeman, and I were an inseparable quartet and we had many adventures together!

This collection of friends would be incomplete if I didn't mention my Dad's very good friend, and my hero, Eric Wilkinson. He was a very handsome chap, well-off, and almost always in a silk shirt, a fashion statement those days. He hunted with a shotgun, mostly shot fowl, and he was a marksman extraordinaire. He taught me to imitate the cries of the birds, to identify them, and understand their behaviour. If people think that shooting jungle fowl and partridge is easy, they couldn't be further from the truth. These are extremely clever birds; they know when to stay motionless and when to fly away. While on foot, you are likely to see practically all animals, but you will be lucky to see jungle fowl, champions of deception. You will hear them and see scratch marks on the soft earth, but one has to be really skilled to track down and shoot them on foot, and Eric had no equal. Anyway, Eric was in the Merchant Navy, working on the training ship "Dufferin" and knew every possible cuss word that ever existed. We Anglo-Indians do not shy away from swearing, but Eric could embarrass even us. He bought me my first drink, and as for my first cigarette, I stole it from him! Thanks to him, I added a lot of colourful verbs and adjectives to my vocabulary. Once Eric took me to see the circus which was at the Parade Grounds next to MG Road. Back in those days there was no concept of rules, they could best be described as guidelines, and so, despite warnings, Eric and I slipped past a few people and went right up to the cages that held the big cats. He was irritating a particular panther by scaring it and generally playing the fool. Soon the panther got tired and lay down, and Eric decided that he would put his hand inside and stroke it! The outcome was inevitable, and he was mauled so severely that he had to be taken to a hospital and have multiple stitches.

While most of the people I have described were friends, I also had a business partner at one point of time. Paddy Keeler had served as captain in the British Indian army for a short period and he and I decided to form a professional hunting company. He would liaise with various clients from abroad and oversee business acquisition while I was the expert who would take them on their shikar. India in those days held such a deal of mysticism and romance that foreigners thought of this land as one overrun with tigers, elephants, poisonous snakes, and other deadly animals. If they didn't get you, the millions of germs that were floating all around certainly would. While this kept away a lot of people, the primitive urge of man to hunt animals, especially exotic ones in the country, brought a small but steady stream of visitors. Most of the organised shikar firms were in North and Central India, the most well-known being Allwyn Cooper in Nagpur, an outfit started by V.C. Shukla, who went on to become a famous politician. They organised big-game safari and photo expeditions of wildlife in Central Indian forests, including shoots for Robert Ruark and Khan Saheb Jamshed Butt among other famous hunters of that time. In fact, it was my dream to work for Allwyn Cooper and I applied for the role of a shikari. They were keen to have me on board, on the condition that they would not pay me a monthly allowance but only a commission on the shoots that I undertook. In the meantime, I was supposed to move to Nagpur and wait for clients to turn up and pay for all my expenses. I was not comfortable with that arrangement and I declined Mr. Shukla's offer. At that time, South India did not have such a company and both Keeler and I felt that this was an area with practically no competition, and so it made sense to start this venture. He had prior experience in this sort of thing, having been associated with organised shikar somewhere in the North, and therefore he set about getting a company registered, ensuring the documentation was in place, spreading the word around in both the United States and England, and we did have a short-lived but profitable business called International Hunters. Perhaps I was naïve or maybe I was just so happy to earn money that I never really looked into the financial aspects. He was older than me, considerably wiser, and an Irishman to boot! My dad, who was never happy about this partnership from the start, would often warn me, "Never trust the Irish", and I would laugh at him, for he genuinely had no rhyme or reason for his chant; it was something he had heard growing up, and I refused to let his myopia affect what I was enjoying. But I began to grow suspicious of Keeler and we had a couple of showdowns on the issue of payments. What made it worse was that he demanded kickbacks from every individual connected to our business. We were really not a professional outfit; all our hunts were in BR Hills, and Hugh Hailstone's property served as our base. I got to know of his ludicrous behaviour when he demanded bribes even from the shikari guides! He would collect tips from the clients on the pretext of paying those poor guys and instead of giving that to them, would demand that they pay him from their wages, threatening them that if they didn't, he would get more qualified people from Mudiyanoor on his rolls. Our best customers were from America; very wealthy, easy-going, and most appreciative. The most famous of them were the father and son duo of Barnery Berlinger, Sr and Junior. They had hunted in Africa and visited us in 1956. We had a grand time, and although we didn't get a tiger, they got a huge panther. All this and more is documented in the book *Danger Down the Sights* written by Barney Berlinger Sr. They visited India again ten years later, but by then our outfit had been long disbanded.

Merwan Chamarbagwala is probably the one friend that most people would recognise as he is mentioned in my Dad's books. We studied together at school for many years. Both he and I were day scholars, although from different spectrums of society. He belonged to one of the wealthiest Parsi families in Bangalore and loved to flaunt his wealth. He took a great liking to me, as this afforded him an opportunity to give a tough-guy impression to the world. He liked to create a perception that he liked roughing it out and shooting dangerous animals. In reality, he was a nervous chap, and the only creatures he shot were spotted deer. However, he loved the outdoors and having an adventure. It suited me fine because he would finance the entire trip, and wouldn't interfere in my shooting, as he always stayed at camp, and to be honest he was a fun-loving chap.

My trips to the jungles were mostly in his cars, and we would all take turns driving. As none of us were keen on that bit, often we would draw lots. The food would also be supplied by Merwan, and it was usually a protein rich diet. There was no question of buying food, everything was prepared at home, Merwan's home to be specific! Like any self-respecting Parsi, he loved food, and the Chamarbagwala family had kitchens well-stocked with not just food, but fantastic cooks as well! We would have dishes such as smoked beef, pork *vindaloo*, fried chicken, accompanied by chappattis or ghee rice. Biriyani was another favourite and no meal was complete without liquor. I was never a big boozer, and the prospect of getting high or tipsy in the jungle never held much appeal for me. I had to be on top of my game, be in the best physical shape and mentally alert, as expected from a hunter, and I always managed to do that. Merwan owned many cars that served as our trip vehicles, the two most memorable ones being an open Cadillac and a Jaguar. He used to stay at No. 2, Residency Road, and after school would go to his father's printing press to collect the newspaper *The Sporting Star*. This newspaper ran a contest, something similar to the lottery, and was extremely popular in Bangalore in the mid-fifties, although they did get into some legal problems that indicated that this constituted gambling.

In the late sixties, Merwan, Willie Wollen, my Dad, and I would do many drives to the jungles, usually over the weekend. Despite my Dad's love for the wilderness, there are times when I genuinely didn't know whether it was that or the food that Merwan would bring on the trips that enticed him to come along. As he grew older, his fondness for sweets and puddings just kept increasing and Merwan, the sly fox that he was, would announce the menu well in advance. The rule of the trip was that everyone had to do their share of all the work including driving, and poor Dad, he would actually work out deals with Merwan where he would take up Merwan's share of the driving and get an extra share of the confectionaries! We were all working by then, so it meant leaving after work on Friday, driving most of that night, doing some hunting and then driving back on Sunday night, reaching home and then going back to work. Merwan later went to England, got some sort of degree and came back. He chose to settle down in Bombay and became a millionaire.

The jockey, Ronnie Butfoy, was another friend of mine and also a tenant at Prospect House. Despite his short stature, he was full of energy and it was hard to say what he loved the most—road rage, hunting wild boar, angling, getting into fights, women, or getting into fights about women. Whatever mess he got into, he gave it a hundred and ten percent. Before he was my tenant, he would come from Calcutta during the racing season and his gutsy attitude was not restricted to just the racing track. He was a very good dancer and a regular at the dances at Bowring Institute. Once I received a call from him at around 2:00 a.m. He sounded frantic and begged me to come rushing to Bowring as he was in a spot of trouble. From the tone of his voice, I knew that it was not some trivial matter, and as his reputation of getting into ugly situations preceded him, I didn't think twice. I was barely clothed, but I ran, gunned my motorcycle and reached Bowring Club in a couple of minutes. I rushed inside and there he was, coolly dancing with a girl! He waltzed up to me with the girl in his arms and said,

"Don, those guys want to have some fun, do you mind?"

I looked around at half a dozen guys, all wearing expensive suits and murderous looks, waiting for Ronnie to stop dancing. He then had the audacity to turn to them and say, "This is my friend Don Anderson, and he'll be on my side."

Still dancing, he came over to me and said, "I appreciate the intervention, and your quick response, but if we are going to have a pow-wow, I suggest you do it without your hard-on."

He was a legend in Bangalore, even winning the Invitation Cup in 1973. I would never go to the races, for I was not the betting kind, but everyone in the city would talk about his exploits during those years. He got married when he was very young and migrated to England.

Ever since I was in school, I've always had women of all ages attracted to me. I don't think that I was ever a smooth talker or a convincing flirt. I have been told that I was good-looking, and I think the women I dated were as shallow as me. I never had to woo or court anyone, especially in my younger days, and one could say that I was spoilt for choice. My first experience with a woman was when I was fifteen and still in school and she was in her mid-twenties. That opened a floodgate of casual encounters for decades to come. It was incredible, the sheer number of women who were open to the idea of casual sex and they fed my voracious appetite and bloated my ego no end. Drive-in theatres would find me there every Friday night if I wasn't out in the jungles. The number of women were excessive by any stretch of imagination and while most of them are no more, the ones who are alive today live across the far reaches of this planet, in Australia, the UK, America, and of course there are those much closer to home, in Bangalore. As years passed I was convinced that I could never settle down with one girl, as there was not just the constant temptation to stray, but also opportunity to fulfil that temptation. At some point, I even regretted that I was not given the opportunity to attempt the Indian system of an arranged marriage; I might have got married then. To their credit, many of the women I had affairs with had great marriage potential, but I could never even comprehend the notion of being with one woman for the rest of my life. At any point in time, I would be dating two or three women during my twenties and anyone who wanted more than their share of my attention and time would be slowly eased out of my plan. I never thought of having children, for I know I could never give them the attention they needed. I knew that it would often come down to choosing between my wife and children, and the jungles, and it would be a painful but easy decision for me every time. I am not proud of what I did, but then I'm not ashamed either. That was the life I chose to lead, and I think that the suffering I am going through in my last years has some connection to the pain I caused in my youth.

Chapter Four

Shikar Days

THE JOY OF SITTING IN AN INDIAN JUNGLE IS AN *indescribable feeling and if you truly love the wilderness and all its creatures, an evening can provide you more entertainment than any cinema, and the best part is it will be like no other evening you've seen before, even if you've done it a thousand times already. Like my dad, I too started to enjoy the thrill of doing this over time, and towards my last days of hunting, I never felt disappointed if I did not shoot anything.*

The feathered species are the first ones to announce the lengthening of shadows. The red jungle fowl and the peafowl give their distinct cries as they settle in for the night. Most birds are diurnal and their gossip and song at the end of the day are replaced by the more somber notes of the owl and nightjar family. The owls give a low eerie lament while the soft "chuck-chuck" of the night jar increases its tempo till it sounds like a small machine and then gradually ceases. The mammals have their own signature sounds—the bell of the sambar as he warns his herbivorous brethren that their nemesis is about, echoed by the sharp cries of the spotted deer. The sound of breaking branches are often the only giveaway as otherwise elephants are silent feeders. Unless mating, tigers and panthers are extremely silent, and the sounds that bears, hyenas and jackals make are not that loud to be heard over great distances. When camping out in the jungle, one must know how to recognise these calls of the animals that will tell him if a carnivore is on the prowl. The belling of the sambar, the shrill call of the spotted deer or the hoarse bark of the muntjac—all point to a predator. These herbivores also call at panthers but only an experienced hunter can

94

easily tell by the extent of excitement and uneasiness conveyed in their cries, especially that of the sambar, as to whether a tiger or panther has been the reason for their cries. Jackals too give a high pitched unearthly "wheaanwhhhhh" as they spot danger. A better sighted ally is the langur sentry, who will never fail to show his excitement with his hoarse bark. Birds such as peafowl and jungle fowl are less reliable as they will sound an alarm for even a mongoose, but every sound is invaluable feedback. While these sounds can certainly get you excited, it is no match for the feeling that will overwhelm you when see an animal, any animal, come close to where you are sitting. Of course, if it's a tiger, panther or elephant, your adrenalin will shoot through the roof, but even a wild boar, snorting and complaining, looking for food, if right under your tree, makes for a most exciting time. There is magic in the air, and to those who have never experienced it, I would say that it's a loss that cannot be made up for. It would be unfair to even hint that animals are the only source of interest in the jungles. Far from it. Trees that are hundreds of years old, some still standing, while others have crashed to the forest floor. Vines and parasitic creepers that lie entwined, wild flowers that grow on shrubs and bushes, fruit trees like figs that provide sustenance for the herbivores. Dry river beds and sandy nullahs, rock precipices and deep caves, desolate waterholes and green jungle pools. These are all part of the mystery and excitement you come across while on foot, and no two days can be alike, not even the experience with the same animal.

Many people who have had the good fortune of hunting in India will unanimously agree with me that this sport is one of the most exciting, thrilling, and enjoyable things in the world. However, contrary to what most people think, my jaunts in the jungles were not always about *shikar*. Even as a young boy, who was confident about handling a powerful gun, I still enjoyed the trips where I just appreciated the wildlife I got to observe. I did not need anyone preaching to me nor talking to me about conservation. There were times when I would ride up to Devarabetta on my bicycle, leave it at the rest house and sit at one of the three waterholes all night long just to enjoy the solitude and enjoy nature at its best. The rest house was a fair distance from the village and so I had no choice but to take packed food with me—usually vindaloo with chapattis—which lasted two days, and that is all I would have! Butter in those days was available in tins, but once opened would spoil quickly in the hot weather, so I would finish a whole tin in a single day!

Hunting in Bannerghatta

I have lived a decadent, selfish life, taking and doing what I wanted. It may sound as if I am gloating, but I am merely putting on record the way I lived my life—the rules I made for myself, the absolute lack of respect or concern I had for any other living creature other than myself. When I was out in the jungle with my rifle, I attained a state of nirvana, for I felt like God. I was so confident about my skill as a hunter that I knew no creature could ever hurt me, and I took some really extravagant risks during those times. I have no explanation as to why I do not have even a scratch to show from those days. My parents, too, seemed to believe that I was invincible, and they never said stuff like "be careful". I will not call it luck or karma, or attribute it to my shikari guides or even my own skills either as a tracker or as a hunter handling a firearm, for there is no logical explanation. Going by the law of averages, I should have had at least a dozen serious injuries, but I never had even one. I had my rules as a hunter: I never shot females or young animals or stole eggs from nests. This does not absolve me from what I did, because I realise that the only difference between hunting with a license and without one, is a piece of paper and the number of lives taken.

Although I have never been seriously injured, the same cannot be said for my companions. Let me tell you of one such unfortunate incident that happened in Bandipur during the late 70s. A friend of mine from school had come back from Australia and I was keen to take him to the jungles, as he wanted to shoot some pictures. He was not keen on travelling by motorcycle, so we decided to hire a taxi. It was supposed to be the three of us, but when the driver finally arrived to pick us up, we saw that there was an additional person. The driver begged us to let his friend come along, for his courage had failed him when he heard that we would be driving through the forest. I was not keen but somehow let the uninvited guest come as well. That evening, after we finished driving around and getting the photographs, we came to the area where we had booked our accommodation and decided to get a bite to eat. The driver and his friend wanted to smoke a beedi (Indian cigarette) and so we stopped at the small tea shop by the main Ooty-Mysore Road. It was getting late, and we were perhaps the last customers at the tiny tea stall, which was lit by a single petromax lantern. The last beedi was stubbed out and we had finished our tea and were walking back to the car, when out of the blue there was an angry trumpet and we could see a tusker running straight for us, almost from behind the tea stall. My friend and I were already some distance away and we had a head start. We ran in different directions and headed for the buildings we could see some distance away. The driver ran past our ambassador car, and away from the buildings, perhaps thinking that in complete darkness the elephant would not be able to see him. Unfortunately, his companion thought that the safest place to be was inside the car, and on reaching it, tried to open the doors. As luck would it, it was the only time during the entire trip that we had locked the car, and the five or ten seconds it took him to try to open the door made the difference. We did not see or hear anything, but when we regrouped, we found that the poor chap had been killed. Perhaps the elephant had just whacked him with its trunk for his lifeless body lay a few feet away from the car. We took him to a hospital at Gundulpet where he was pronounced dead. This incident and some that I will mention later are testimony to the fact that the risks one would take while in the jungle in those days could be life threatening.

When you are in the jungle, it is a good idea to be always prepared. Although nothing can teach you better than experience, you gain an advantage if you pay heed to the words of those who have been there before. Typically, when you are sitting up over a kill, in near complete darkness, you will not hear the tiger or panther arrive. Despite their size, they are soft-footed and extremely wary about approaching their kills, especially man-eaters and ones that have been shot at before. Only once the feline starts feeding will the crunching of bones advertise their presence. It is pitch dark and you will have no idea which side it is facing until you switch on your torch. You only shoot at specific points on its body, so the direction it is facing—away from you or towards you— makes a big difference. You need to have nerves of steel and be ready because you get just one shot, and that means you have to see its position, raise your gun, locate the spot you want to hit, exhale, and fire. If you shoot and do not bring it down with your first shot, and if it has not seen you, the animal will run in the direction it was facing when the shot was fired. So, if you are on level ground, and by some circumstance the cat has been facing you, you can kiss your life goodbye, for in a flash it will be upon you.

I will not defend my hunting some of the larger animals as some sort of service I did to protect people, but the truth of the matter is that tigers, panthers, and wild dogs were treated as vermin in those days, and hunters were rewarded for killing them. Bears and wild boar were not considered "gameworthy" and shooting them did not particularly interest anyone. Elephants inexplicably, have been protected since 1873, and unless declared rogue, one would get into serious trouble if one shot them. Again, I will not pass judgement on policy, but the fact remains that hunters like me, indulged in hunting based on the strict rules laid down by the forest department, although one could always question our conscience for the acts we committed.

Today, everything is done from the safety of cars and jeeps and I am not talking just about tourists who visit the jungles, but even those who work for the forest department. I remember a time when the officers who worked for the department either rode on horseback or walked the area they were responsible for. It is hard to explain but like the old-timers, I can vouch that one will feel a deeper connection to the jungle and its dwellers only on foot. Imagine a walk on a moonlit night—your senses are so heightened that every cricket chirp or a twig break will tell you something. None of your senses are superior to those of the animals, but carrying a small two-cell torch, wearing light rubber boots, and paying attention to the signals can ensure that you have a thrilling experience.

When we visited the jungles, our first preference was to stay in forest rest houses. They were built in very picturesque locations by the British in all the south Indian states, and although there was considerable red tape to get permission to stay in one, it was always worth the effort. Many of them still stand today, such as Annaikatti in the Nilgiris, but others have been reduced to rubble—the one at Gulhatty, for instance. The ones that survive today are a considerable improvement on their erstwhile state, as back in the day, they were fairly basic. The thatched roofs would be covered with dry straw and came alive at dusk with rats and other creatures that would spend all night rummaging, squealing, and making such a ruckus that if one was not accustomed to this, one would find it very difficult to get some shut-eye. The presence of rodents would invite snakes that would follow them onto the roof, and that is another story altogether. The only recourse we had was to have a wick burning all night and stuff our ears with cotton to ensure nothing went in.

Hogenikal Forest Bungalow - 1939

I had been going to the jungles from a very tender age with my Dad, and I have some vivid memories of those trips. It was in 1947, the year India won her independence, that I shot my first panther. I had started visiting Javalagiri with June when I was about ten years old, and by the time I was thirteen, I started going alone. Looking back, it's remarkable how much freedom my parents gave me, but then again, the world was a much safer place back then.

I had practised enough with my shotgun and felt that the time had come when I would be able to shoot a panther. Javalagiri was familiar territory and I cycled there with the firm intention of bagging "Spots"

Although my family knew that I carried my shotgun, in their minds it was for protecting myself in case I was in a tight spot. I cycled for a couple of hours with a friend, Colin Bone, who was older than me, feeling deliriously happy, as I had just been given permission by my dad to go on a hunt. Colin was not interested in hunting, but my gun gave him the confidence and so he said that he would tag along for the adventure.

Panthers were so common in those days that it was not long before I heard one sawing, from the rest house. It was late in the afternoon and the sound was incessant. I asked the guard at the rest house and he explained that someone had shot its mate and it could be seen on the periphery of the village on most days. Considering the fact that it was advertising itself, I thought it would be easy to find, and I felt as though I already had my first panther in the bag. As we got closer to the source of the sound, Colin's bravado vanished, and he stated that his girlfriend would be furious if something happened to him. Making a mental note never to have a girlfriend of that kind, I waved goodbye, walked a while and started to stalk the panther. I had never done this before, and the going was difficult. I wanted to be absolutely quiet, did not want to get my shotgun to touch the ground, and most of all I wanted to reach the panther before it stopped sawing and I lost it forever. I was doing an awkward crawl, with the shotgun in the air, stopping when the sawing stopped, and it seemed like ages. My knees and elbows were sore, and at a slight corner, I sort of got up into a half crouch to take a breather. Ten feet away was the panther, sitting on its haunches and staring at me most inquisitively. I do not know who was more shocked, but I shot off both barrels in an instant. The recoil was so powerful and since I was not fully balanced, I fell over backwards. I had missed my opportunity, for when I got up there was no sign of the panther. I was disgusted with myself and trudged back to the rest house where Colin was waiting anxiously after he heard my gun go off. The next day, we waited for the sun to get high in the sky and managed to get a few villagers to help us track the panther. To my utter delight, we found the panther a few yards away from where I had shot it. I explained to the villagers of how this was my first trophy and they helped me skin it. However, it was a shoddy job and I never managed to preserve the skin as proof of my initiation into hunting.

Let me follow that up with the story of the first man-eating tiger I shot near the village of Gajnore, many years later. Even in those days, the land between Ubrani and Gajnore never held any thick forest, but was a desolate country filled with stunted bamboo, date palms, and thorn trees. The villages were few and were found mostly along the banks of a river that meandered through this area. The Mysore government had issued a notification and reward for hunters with licenses to kill the man-eater that had become a menace. It was supposed to be particularly cunning and had avoided the hunters at the expense of two of its brethren who had been mistakenly shot. Its modus operandi was to carry off travellers on the highway between Chitraldoorg and Shimoga town. The tiger never had the courage to charge a cart but would always sneak on these groups of people when they stopped for a break. Of course, stories are grossly exaggerated and it was not long before the rumour that it would jump on to bullock carts and carry away victims became extremely popular and practically brought all traffic to a standstill between dusk and dawn. On every occasion that it made a kill, it would leave the bullocks and only carry off humans, a frightening prospect, for, at minimal risk, it could have killed the tied bullock which would have given him a larger meal. Instead, it chose humans, making it a connoisseur of human flesh, and I wondered how I would ever get it, considering I had never done this sort of thing before. A long period of immunity had encouraged such confidence in the tiger that it even made occasional raids into the town, sometimes not even waiting for nightfall. Apparently, there was a reason for the tiger's impunity. The villagers believed that its behaviour was punishment being meted out by the gods who wanted to teach the villagers a lesson for abandoning ancient values and giving in to temptation from the bigger towns.

I landed up at the travellers' bungalow about ten miles from Gajnore. The country was open for several miles on all sides of the bungalow, the forest beginning some four miles west where the road descended a kind of ghat into the valley leading to the Bhadra river. It was this spot that the man-eater was said chiefly to frequent. For once I could not afford to tie baits hoping for it to turn up—I knew that it would not take baits and I did not want to kill another innocent tiger. However, on two nights, I sat up on machans at likely places, yet no tiger came. When I was at Gajnore, I would hear of its exploits at Ubrani, and when I would go there, obviously a couple of days later, it would have moved on. It was frustrating. I had taken a week off, and my time there was drawing to a close. On Friday morning, the luck that had so far eluded me, changed. Unfortunately, it ended the life of a young man, who was taken from the field where he was working. If I could have convinced the distraught relatives to leave the body where it lay, I might have got a shot when the man-eater returned to complete his meal. However, I did not know anyone from this village, and I did not have such single-mindedness as to ask them to leave the body as bait. However, I vowed to avenge the death of the man and was racking my brains to find a way to do this. Clearly, the man-eater would come back, but how soon would he discover that the body had been removed? Would it come close enough to give me a shot? After much deliberation, the only solution I could think of was to get the meat of a goat (the cheapest option) and wrap it in clothes in the hope that this would at least convince the tiger to approach the kill. Knowing its penchant for human flesh, the first mouthful would perhaps give the game away, but then, I hoped I would have had enough time to get it within my sights and give a satisfactory response. My idea was met with such scepticism that some of the elders even laughed. "*Yejmanre*, this is not an ordinary tiger, but the devil himself. Taking away the body would be acceptable but attempting to fool it…will bring immeasurable misfortune upon us."

I gritted my teeth and explained that things could not get any worse than having a man-eater around. Luckily, money is an expedient in most situations like this, and I managed to get help to set up a machan as well. It was an uneventful night, although several times I got up with a feeling that I was being watched. It was just paranoia, but it was a horrid feeling, and despite the rifle by my side, I felt very vulnerable. Early next morning, feeling dejected, I got off from the machan and started trudging back, when all of a sudden in the distance I saw a dark shape. It was looking straight at me, and I froze. I do not know why, but I started to shiver, and it was not because of the cold. Then, with a small shake of the head, it trotted off. It was a jackal! I nearly sat down in relief. Clearly my nerves were on edge!

By mid-day I knew why I had not seen the tiger that night. A mile away from the bungalow, it had killed a small girl who had gone to edge of the field to answer the call of nature. I was informed that the girl had been eaten completely so there was no point waiting for it there. Then, for the next two days, there were no kills, and I had to get back to Bangalore. The man-eater then disappeared for a bit, and it was believed that it had wandered off or died, and people were relieved. Their joy was temporary, for within a month it struck again, repeating its tactics of sneaking up behind a bullock cart that had halted for a break, carrying off the lone cart man, who apparently believed that the man-eater was no more. As the incident had happened close to the village, the tiger did not get the opportunity to finish its meal. The place where the body was found was just beyond a culvert that went over a small stream. Perhaps it was fate, but I had decided to visit the place on the same weekend, and I had no sooner got off my bike than I was informed about the incident that had occurred that morning. Needless to say, the body had been taken away for the last rites, but I was sure that the tiger would return. Although the man had been killed on the main road, his body had been dragged for some distance into the undergrowth. It suited me fine, for I was able to find a ficus tree close to the spot and, with help from the locals, to put up a machan. There was no cadaver, and I had no choice but to get a buffalo to satiate the man-eater's hunger, and again hoped that it would not get too perturbed about the switch. The machan was a small *charpoy* (a traditional bed slung with rope) fastened securely to the branches of a tree, and surrounded by a screen of boughs, while below me was the unfortunate bovine at a spot where two jungle paths intersected. Soon, the last rays of the day disappeared and the moon began to cast spectral shadows as it rose from the earth, bringing out the sandy road in pallid clearness amongst the shadows. It started to grow cold and quiet at the same time, the birds of the forest having gone to rest till the morning. Far away, I could hear the faint bark of the village dogs, and the only other sound was that made by the tree crickets. Soon it became so dark that I was resigned to spending the rest of the night dependent on my hearing, not my sight. I have neither acquired the patience my dad had nor his ability to stay awake through the night, and, embarrassing as it may sound, after a while, I fell asleep. I got up with a start—a distant roar from the east had woken me up. I gripped my rifle, but there was silence, and then I heard it again, this time from a different and somewhat nearer point, and then again, betraying the tiger's zigzag course. I was hoping that it would come on to either of the paths and see my buffalo, or at least hear something worth investigating. Judging from the last sound, it was still a furlong away, so I took a chance and shone my torch at the buffalo, and realised that it was fast asleep! It had not heard the roars, so it was either a heavy sleeper or tone deaf, and neither suited me. I wanted it to give itself away, so I used a rather unsporting method of throwing a couple of my cartridges at it, hoping to wake it up. I do not understand buffalo too well, but its low grunt in response seemed to say, "Just go back to sleep, you two-legged moron."

Famous last words, for that perhaps betrayed its presence and in less than a minute came the sound of the tiger's rush and then, in almost complete silence, it killed the buffalo. All I could hear were the sounds of its legs kicking out, furiously at first, and then feebler and feebler till it completely stopped. The day had not dawned, and my watch showed the time as 5:10. For a few minutes the situation remained as I have described, and then I heard the unmistakable sound of a heavy body being dragged along the forest floor. Under the trees, it would have remained veiled from my sight, and had it dragged the body in another direction it might have retreated into the jungle, but on the light-coloured mud road, there were no shadows, and the pre-dawn light gave me that one small window of opportunity to silhouette the tiger, and I did not miss. My perfect shot killed it on the spot, and soon, the glorious morning sun bathed my first man-eating tiger and me in soft light and created an unforgettable memory.

Unlike my dad, I do not believe in ghosts or the supernatural. However, there have been a few occasions in the jungles when my iron-clad theory has been questioned. I was frequenting a small village called Thali (called Little England by the British) to get rid of a panther that had started attacking the villagers. It had started out killing goats, but it had gradually lost its fear of humans, and from baring its fangs to actually jumping on herdsmen, the progress was rather rapid. I knew that it was a matter of time before the inevitable happened and I wanted to prevent it from happening. I went there every weekend for more than a month to get rid of it, but I never seemed to have any luck. What worked in my favour was that Thali is very close to Bangalore and I could afford to go there as often as I liked. Soon it was the peak of summer and the Thali lakebed lay bare in most parts. I knew that this was one place where the panther would come to quench its thirst after sunset. Since I was not sitting over a bait, there was no reason for the panther to walk into my sight, and so I had to think of something else. I had to be at a spot where I could watch the waterhole from all sides, and the only way, however stupid it may have been, was to sit right next to the waterhole itself. This was a massive risk knowing that this panther did not fear humans, but I was young, and perhaps foolish, so I asked a couple of the villagers to dig a hole in the sand, deep enough for me to sit in, but one where my gun could be pushed out without having to get up. I got into the depression and asked them to cover it with some branches and grass. Considering that I had to sit in it all night and also have room to manoeuver in case the panther came from a different direction, I got them to make some adjustments till I was finally ready. The duo left, muttering to themselves within earshot that they would never see *dorai* ever again, which certainly did not do my confidence any good. The setting of the sun turned the sky to various hues of pink and purple, and soon the birds of the night came alive. I realised that it was going to be a tough night, for the heat from the sand was making my vigil extremely uncomfortable and unlike a machan on a tree, I did not get any respite from an occasional breeze. If it can be believed, despite all this discomfort, I fell asleep. Then the oddest thing happened. I felt that someone I knew was warning me of danger. It was not as in a dream, but as if it was happening in real life. "Look up! Look up!" came the repeated cry. I woke up with a start but was careful not to make a sound. I sat there, feeling sweaty and drained. I will never forget that moment as my eyes got accustomed to the surroundings and saw the crouched panther staring at my hide not more than fifteen yards away. I bagged the panther with a simple shot, but I have no explanation as to who or what warned me and allowed me to wake up, else I would not have lived to tell my tale.

While I always follow up a wounded animal and put it out of its misery, I must tell you of one that I did not. I had received word from the Madras government that a rogue elephant had caused considerable damage near Kodekarai. I knew the superintendent at Hosur who had sent me a telegram to get rid of the beast. I only had the weekend free, since, on Monday morning, I was expecting some foreigners from Binny's, who were coming for an inspection. I was sure that I could bag it over the weekend, as elephants are not as hard to find as tigers or panthers. I left for Gerhetti on Friday evening and reached the bungalow. I was impatient to get started, which kept me tossing and turning all through a night that seemed to have no end. At last the day broke, and I was up and ready for a quick meal of leftover sandwiches and freshly brewed coffee. My tracker was on the verandah, waiting for me, and after a quick discussion, we started off. The sun was gently kissing the horizon, and our path lay shrouded in a gradually rising mist that was playing hide and seek with the lofty crags that lay in the distance. Soon, the pink eastern sky turned grey and then the sun became a dazzling white ball of fire rising above us and making the going tough. After about five miles, we reached a small patch of cultivation where the bull's artistry was evident. The crops were completely damaged and were interspersed with its fresh spoor in the soft mud. It did not seem to be in any particular hurry or have an agenda for the tracks kept criss-crossing each other. It was unbearably hot now, and I had to stop at intervals to parch my thirst, but my tracker seemed oblivious to the conditions. I realised that we were moving at the same pace as the elephant, as the tracks and dung were as fresh as when we started off. We stopped and ate our lunch under the shade of a bamboo clump at about three o'clock, ensuring that we had no company. We knew that the heat would slow it down, and although the pachyderm had no idea that it was being followed, we had to be careful. Suddenly my tracker gesticulated with his arm and squatted, and I froze. Gradually, I edged closer towards him and was rewarded with a magnificent spectacle. Standing under the shade of a large tree, nearly motionless, except for the occasional flap of an enormous ear, was the rogue. Its tusks were not long, but quite thick, and I gauged that it was a young bull. I was exhausted but the built-up adrenalin got me shaking. So, I sat still for a good five minutes, realising that the wind was not blowing to its advantage. The bull was a long way off, but some thirty yards from it was a small bush and that was what I set my sights on. If I reached that spot undetected, I had a good chance of bringing it down. I crawled out on my stomach, one inch at a time. It was extremely hot and the burning sand made it extremely uncomfortable. I reached the bush, where, knowing I was fully concealed, I got on to my haunches and then slowly to my knees. I tried to synchronise my movements as it threw dust on his back—it gave me a small window of opportunity to mask any noise I might make. As I cocked my rifle, I felt the wind change, and I trembled, waiting for the inevitable. I could see the tips of its trunk curl in my direction, and in an instant it was on guard, ears flattened against the sides of its colossal head. It moved in exaggerated slow motion to face me, almost as if it did not want me to know that it had discovered me. I did not allow that to happen, for head on, I had no chance of bringing it down. My rifle spoke, but clearly I had missed my mark, for it did not crumple down into a heap as I had expected. Instead, a scream of rage and pain was all I could register and it was off. Apart from being too tired, all the frustration of the morning bore down on me as I did the stupidest things possible. I fired into his disappearing haunches, as any inexperienced amateur would do. I certainly did not miss, for an ear-splitting response ensued, and the jungle then receded into a hush. I tried to avoid the disapproving look of the tracker and instead peered in the direction where the pachyderm had vanished. More for my benefit than his, I exclaimed, "He cannot have gone far. The two bullets would have certainly caused grievous injury," No words were needed but my tracker's scornful eyes said just one thing, "I wonder which of the two creatures had something up its rear end!"

We reached the spot where the first bullet had hit it, and I saw a large blood spatter on the ground. I was keen to follow up, but my tracker objected saying that though he could cover any distance, the sun would be setting in about a few hours' time, and we were a considerable distance away from civilisation. He felt that as it got dark, we were certain to meet tigers, bears, ghosts, and other creatures that seemed to spawn from his fertile imagination. However, his jibber-jabber was in vain, and I pulled *dorai* rank and vehemently decided that we were going to get the elephant, no matter what. I reloaded my rifle and two people with diametrically opposite expectations set off, following the blood spoor. The jungle showed unmistakable signs of the tusker's passage through it. The bent and broken sprigs and bamboos crushed and trodden down, liberally besprinkled with blood, indicated that it was hit hard and must have been in considerable pain. Soon the topography changed and we came into an open area where the elephant's rage was all the more evident. Small trees lay uprooted and broken, rocks were strewn around—I had never seen anything like this before. Clearly my tracker had not either, for he realised what it meant if we came across this creature, or rather if it came across us. The *dorai* with his ridiculous shooting skills would ensure that both of them would never see their families again. Although he begged and implored me to abandon the quest, I paid little attention to his entreaties. Despite my high strung state, an idea suddenly occurred in my clouded brain. I now had a chance of making up for the previous two gargantuan mistakes. Being under the impression that the elephant had gone in a westerly direction I thought that it would have to break cover from the dense foliage and charge up an incline to reach me. So I asked my companion to shout, clap and draw attention, while I sat ready with my rifle. His expression said it all. If all white men were as mad as this *dorai*, the world had no hope. I felt sorry for him, for he tried to be a good sport about it, but all that came out was a hoarse gurgling sound. So, I yelled at the top of my voice, though it did not quite echo the way I wanted it to, and the sounds of crickets were the only sounds I could hear. Leaving my tracker who refused to move an inch further, I started to follow the path that the elephant had taken. I then realised that I had got it wrong. There was no blood trail or broken saplings. It had gone in an entirely different direction, and a sickening feeling took over. I had assumed that the elephant had gone in a direction where the forest cover was the farthest from where we stood and that had given me the confidence to put on a show. The truth was that he gone in another direction, perhaps even backtracked, and none of the other possibilities would have given me the advantage I assumed I had. The setting sun gave us our last admonition, and I realised that I had been beaten. I had to reluctantly admit defeat and started my long and incredibly nerve-wracking trudge back home. I was lucky that I had my tracker, for he managed to get us home in almost complete darkness. He did not show up the next day, and I knew that even if I got a new tracker, I would never be able to find the elephant. I was extremely upset with myself for the two shots and, more importantly, for letting the animal live in pain for whatever time it had left.

...And that's how I would shoot an elephant

During a jungle trip, there are many precarious situations one lands up in, but I had so much confidence in my rifle and in myself that I never felt I was ever in a situation beyond my control. Yet, sometimes there are problems that cannot be solved with a gun. Ticks are a prime example and are usually transferred from animals like cattle and dogs, found in villages, to humans. In the forest, ticks are found on almost all animals, and one has to be careful not to get bitten, for not only can they transmit viral and bacterial infections, but they also can cause acute itching that will not go away for months on end! In the summer, it is a good idea to stay away from sleeping in places like cattle sheds, for you are sure to have the most uncomfortable night of your life!

As you would have ticks in the hot season, in the dry season, if you visit certain jungles, you are bound to be covered with leeches. Here again there are two types. The first one is thin, almost like a caterpillar, while the other is thicker, almost as fat as one's thumb, and grows to the size of a zero-watt bulb. Both are potentially harmless—all they do is fasten themselves to some part of your body, drink your blood till they are about to burst, and then fall off. No pain, no side effects, but the sight of these creatures especially in large numbers on one's body is a revolting sight, and it takes considerable will power (and experience) not to yank them off.

Once I had gone duck hunting with my friend Clive Greenwood to a tank in Byramangala. We had shot a few rounds, and it had not been a particularly successful morning. The couple of teals we had shot had fallen in the middle of the tank, so Clive and I waded in gingerly. There were a lot of weeds at the edge and a constant buzzing of small insects. As we felt our way along the bottom of the slime-covered water tank, I found one bird. Clive had no success, and thus, after a while we decided to get back. It was December and the water was quite cold. Luckily, the sun had come out by then, so we wanted to get out of our soggy clothes and get warm. As we were clearing the last of the weeds, I noticed that Clive, who was walking in front, had something on his neck. It was a slimy leech, the fat kind, and the sight of it on his neck was nauseating to say the least. I mentioned it to Clive who got out the tobacco juice from his bag. By then some of the locals had arrived at the tank and were in the process of collecting water and doing other morning chores. They were mildly amused by the sight of two white men whose idea of fun was swimming in a muddy tank on a cold winter morning, fully clothed.

Clive exclaimed, "Bugger all, I'm sure there must be others we can't see!"

I was confused and unconvinced, because I thought he meant that other villagers would be hiding and watching this spectacle, till I realised that he was talking about the leeches on his body. He proceeded to peel off his clothes in a hurry, muttering obscenities. I tried to stop him, considering that there were women around, but he was a man on a mission and could not be stopped.

"I'll be damned if I have one of those things on my dick," he cried as took off the last piece of clothing. He then demanded that I do an unhurried inspection of his behind, the frontal self-check having been completed. The villagers must have seen some strange sights in their life, but watching a man undress and get himself inspected by his friend must have ranked high on their amusement scale. Luckily, I was saved from the ignominious task of applying tobacco juice on different parts of his body in front of a sell-out crowd, as it was just the one critter on his neck. A few dabs and in a couple of seconds it fell off, where Clive's foot crushed it, bringing out the blood it had guzzled from his body.

"Your turn," said Clive, but I refused, considering the amused Byramangala entourage. I ran my hands all over but did not feel anything. Of course, the wet clothes were stuck to my body and it was done in a hurry. I reached home and when I took off my clothes, to my absolute horror, I discovered a big fat leech stuck onto my private parts. I let out a mild scream, not too loud, but the chokra, Thangavelu, who happened to be in the next room, came running in.

"*Ennachu dorai* (What's happened, Sir)?"

No words were required for the sight was fairly self-explanatory. He disappeared even before I could say anything, while I was figuring out the best way to reach a room where I could get salt or tobacco juice. He re-appeared with my hockey stick and advanced upon me, reassuring me that if I stayed still, he was confident of getting it off.

"Don't be a bloody fool, Thangavelu. What if you miss?"

"Don't worry, *saar* (Sir), I have killed many snakes in my lifetime and I am sure that with one mighty swing, I can kill this as well."

"Fool, does this look like a snake to you? This is something else…and one can't hit it or pry it off."

His snort of derision clearly indicated that he knew better than me in this situation. He disappeared again, and I marvelled at his quick thinking—perhaps the good chap had gone to get me something to get it off. But, far from it; he brought something even more potent—my mother. Needless to say, after getting my mother out of the room and with some help from Thangavelu, I managed to get it off.

There were so many tanks in Bangalore that were frequented by migratory birds, but slowly, with rampant unchecked hunting, the birds disappeared. We found it more productive to visit areas away from the city. Kanwa reservoir was one such spot, but I preferred another tank at Maddur, off the main road. This place, apart from the seasons of shooting, also had another memory—something unique. The company I kept had a few regulars, but there were always friends of friends who became part of our gang on and off. One such chap was Squadron Leader Milikens, who was a test pilot for Hindustan Aeronatics Limited. He was one of those guys who always came up with bizarre but brilliant ideas, and I had taken him on many trips to the jungles. We had gone to Maddur for hunting wild boar and for some angling when we came upon this lake where we could see hundreds of wild geese flocking on the water. They were far away, on the other end of the lake, so it was impossible to get them with our guns. We asked around and understood that the gaggle would never come to the near end, having learnt the hard way that they would be shot at by the locals with their muzzle loaders. The far end of the lake was covered with impenetrable jungle, and I believe that practically no civilisation lay in that direction, so the birds had got their facts right. But how were we to get to them? Then Milikens had a brainwave. It seemed so odd and bizarre that I thought he was joking, but the earnest look on his face convinced me that he was serious. We would put his wonderfully harebrained idea into action in two weeks' time, and I convinced my friends Tiny Seddon and Baba Cariappa, who were keen on duck shooting, to come along as well. We reached the lake before dawn on the arranged date and waded as silently as possible into the shallow parts of the near end, holding our guns. Then came the big surprise. It was like a scene from a movie. As dawn was breaking, a small plane was first heard and then could be seen approaching the other side of the lake. It was Milikens! That was the plan! I am not sure what story he gave his superiors, but he had actually managed to get a plane out from H.A.L to Maddur. His plan was to fly over the lake on the other side and frighten the birds and force them to fly towards us! Like a kamikaze pilot, he flew low and right into the nesting colony, scattering the birds. That was when we realised how the best-laid plans sometimes do not work out the way you want them to. For there were no geese, only domestic *kokkus* or storks, thin ungainly birds not worth firing at! We waved our hands and tried to indicate to him that these birds were not worth it, but I guess the difference between goose and stork in sign language was non-existent. Poor Milikens! He must have been confused by the absence of gunfire at our end of the lake, and repeated his manoeuver, going even lower, but was met with the same non-violent response. Disgusted, he flew back to his base, surely cursing us. The next day he was really pissed off with us, with me in particular, and accused us of treating him like a joke, while he was risking his neck. I think what really irked him the most was that his brilliant idea did not provide results as expected.

Tank hopping was a common pastime of ours, and we mostly did it in Mandya district, which had dozens of small lakes and tanks. In the mid- and late-1950s, the assortment of birds in these places was hard to believe. Spotbills, mallards, pin tails, wigeons, whistling teals, bar-headed geese, and brahminy ducks were some of the birds that fell to our guns. These have all but disappeared just like the lakes. We would line up at various positions, and someone would have the first shot, and then others would follow. There was no blind firing; each shot was carefully done, but done fast, because in a matter of seconds the lake would be empty. We would collect our trophies and then head to the next tank. On a good day we could get thirty or more for the bag. Irrespective of how many one shot, at the end of it, the spoils were divided equally. You could shoot perhaps fifteen ducks and you would end up with five, which was not fair, but that was the unwritten code.

Outside a Poojaree cave

When the season for wading birds ended, it would be the time for quails. Quail shooting is best done during December and March, and the cultivated fields are often a great place for this. My particular favourite was a place near Begur on the Mysore highway in the patches with tall grass. Nowadays, it is next to impossible to see quails while you are out in the jungles, but in the 1950s, Bangaloreans who ate mutton and beef all year round used to look forward to wild quail, till, of course, quaileries sprang up to cater to the local demand. I continued to explore a lot of places where I could spend time hunting birds. Places like Thippogondanahalli, Savandurga, and Manchinbele were frequent haunts of mine for partridge, and Huliyodurga was the de facto choice when it came to jungle fowl.

Like most hunters, I would be superstitious about the clothes I would wear, and even had lucky pants and shirts. Unlike what is shown in the movies, I never wore light khaki clothes and pith helmets. I would wear greys, greens, or dark blues, and very old ones at that, ones that had seen plenty of wear and tear but which covered my arms and legs and protected me against insect bites and thorns. "Wait-a-bit" thorns are particularly tricky, and greenhorns who try to force their way through will be left lacerated, for these thorns are about one-fifth of an inch but extremely tough and will not break. The only way is to move backwards ever so slowly and try to disengage oneself. Another superstition I followed was to never take a camera along, for the few instances that I did so, I saw absolutely no game. Early on, I would either leave the camera at camp or have my friends carry theirs, but I never took one along into the jungle.

The Indian jungle is not really as dangerous a place as most people from the cities believe it to be. I would say that most perceptions are based on the imagination of armchair tourists, and the rest is a result of exaggerated stories often falsely embellished each time to make the storyteller appear a hero.

Guns

I must have been three or four years old when I received a pea-shooter blowgun from my grandfather, and I was so fond of it that I would sleep with it under my pillow. A considerable upgrade was a silver electroplated Daisy air rifle that I got on my sixth birthday. I was thrilled to bits because until then all my hunting was limited to the catapult, something I had become an expert at. The air gun is what I practised with and it made me a good marksman, for I would spend hours in our backyard shooting small targets.

However, in my opinion, the first real gun that brought about the genesis of my hunting days was a 12 bore double-barreled shotgun my dad gave me for my ninth birthday. This was a hammer shotgun, which meant that one had to cock the hammer before firing. Forays into the jungle, armed with my shotgun gave me a whole new thrill. Here was a gun that I thought would protect me against any creature that walked the earth. I did not have the strength to cock the hammer, and each time I had to ask Dad to do that for me. I would walk in front with the cocked gun, while he followed some distance behind. I had to be very careful not to trip and fall, for if I did, the gun was sure to go off. I started to go for walks on my own and it was the ultimate thrill for me to walk alone in a scary forest with a powerful gun, though I was reassured by the fact that my father and camp were not too far away. More often than not, I would not come across anything, as I had not mastered the art of tracking or moving without making a sound, so I would come back to camp and have Dad un-cock the gun. Looking back, I am grateful to him for entrusting me with a weapon so early in life, but it eventually led to a frenzied passion, something I could never grow out of for most of my adult life.

I owned a few shotguns after that, including a. 404 double-barrelled Jeffrey, but the best one I had was a Greener 12 bore shotgun that I fitted with a bulb, and it served me well for close-quarter shooting. When it came to shooting elephant or bison, I used the. 470 Nitro Express, but it was such a heavy rifle that despite my strength I would often have a bloody nose after firing it. I had to make do with this weapon because I could not get my hands on the. 416 Rigby, which was then supposed to be the best rifle in the world, popularised by Harry Selby while hunting big game in Africa. This was brought to India by the British, and to counter it the Germans flooded the Indian market with their. 423 Mauser. I was lucky enough to be presented with one by Hugh Hailstone, one of Dad's friends. Until then, the popular rifle in the Indian market was the IOF .315 sporting rifle, which was the civilian version of the British military Lee–Enfield rifle made at Tiruchirappalli. It had a heavy bullet, and I would use it to hunt boars on the outskirts of Bangalore. I also had a. 30-06 Springfield and a Military model M1 Garand but I was not very fond of using either.

My dad, of course, had his. 405 Winchester, one he bought for 50 rupees, and he was very proud of both the gun and the amount he paid for it. It was a cheap big game gun with an underlever, but the problem with all Winchester rifles was that if you did not handle it the right way, you could jam it up. Despite that risk, he never parted with it, and to its credit, it never let him down. At that time, there were three gentlemen who were as famous as my dad for hunting game. They were his friends Pat Watson, Dick Bird, and Russell Green from Madras. Of the lot, I would rate Dick Bird as the best. He was the postmaster in Santaveri, in the Baba Budan hills, and I remember our many visits there over the years. He was not just a top shot, but also an excellent tracker, extremely fearless and did most of his shooting on foot. He shot many tigers and at one point would take clients from Bangalore and Shimoga for shikar. There is an interesting story about Dick—he had made friends with a few Americans clients who worked at H.A.L., Bangalore, and as a gesture of gratitude for their hunting trips with him, they promised him that they would drop off money the next time they passed by. The Americans had a sense of humour, for the next time they did pass by, they were in an airplane, and true to their promise, they dropped a parachute with a huge amount of money that helped Dick buy a coffee estate which he managed till he passed away.

Pat Watson, on the other hand, was not as daring or even as skilled as Dick. He had lost a leg at Birur, and perhaps it was this handicap that made him resort to his style of shooting, which was on a bullock cart at night. His shooting was done mostly at Kadur, and often Dad and I would visit him. Kadur is 130 miles from Bangalore. Our train would leave at nine at night, and we would be there at four in the morning, and then we would walk the ten miles to Watson's camp. In my opinion, shining a torch and shooting an animal from the safety of a bullock cart is quite unsporting, so Dad and I would spend the night at a waterhole while Watson indulged in a bit of shooting.

My dad also had a .500 Black Powder Express Hammer, and although it was a lovely weapon, he hardly ever used it, always relying on his Winchester. During the years he went hunting, neither he nor any of his contemporaries considered shooting with a scope, and this continued till the mid-1950s. My friend, Clive Greenwood, is responsible for bringing scoped shooting to Bangalore, although it had gained popularity in the

Central Provinces by then. I considered myself a good hunter with open sights, but with a scope, I became deadly. The fitting of the scopes was done at Guncraft by Sundar Raj, who was a master of the craft. I remember one particular time when I wanted both sights and scope fitted for my. 315, for short and long-distance shooting and Sundar Raj was ready for the challenge. He added an extra mount and the stock had to go up half an inch on the butt. He did that and realised that we had a situation where I couldn't put the cleaning rod right through, so he improvised and extended the hollow right through the stock.

Ammunition was getting expensive, and while I only squeezed the trigger when I was absolutely sure I had to, the same could not be said of my friends. I was teased mercilessly for my parsimonious attitude—they tell me now that my favourite sentence in those days was "Guys, what you hold in your hands are not anti-aircraft guns."

What that meant, of course, was not to fire till one was absolutely sure of the shot. Luckily, the fact that I sold cartridges back to Guncraft for reloading, remained a secret between Sundar Raj and me, or else my gang would have got another reason to mock me! Stories of my miserly nature and many others would be discussed at Crown Café on Monday evenings, when we would all meet up after work to exchange notes about the hunts during the weekend, over beer and kababs.

All this came to an end in 1972 when the Wildlife Act was passed. It saved the future of Indian wildlife, but gradually it took away the freedom that people such as I had all those years. Not the freedom to hunt, but the freedom of movement. Even without the Act, my hunting days were on the wane, so I was not particularly upset, although there was a tinge of sadness about giving it up altogether. The Act was not passed overnight; there had been a lot of rumours, and many amateur shikaris went overboard with their last hunt. Suddenly the forest department folk started to look at me with suspicion, and it was ironic that licensed gun holders like me, who always followed the rules, bore the brunt of this treatment, while poachers and others who were hand-in-glove with the department got away with so much more than just moving around in the jungles. For a long time after the Act was passed, the forest department did not cancel any licenses, but stopped issuing new ones. What that meant was that some government officials continued to hunt animals and justified it by stating that they still held valid licenses. In fact, a few months after the Act was passed, a senior official, who was connected with the passing of the Act, shot a tiger on the main Ooty road, next to the tank after the Bandipur check post. It took a while for such incidents to be taken seriously, but I never took a chance. I sold my tiger trophies to some people in America. I did not get involved in the paperwork; I just wanted them gone. I gave away most of my panther heads to Pat Watson, and I think he gave it to the Whitefield Club, and I distributed the rest to my friends and well-wishers. After my dad died, I sold all my guns back to Guncraft, who further sold it to some businessmen from North India. It was an unspectacular end to my hunting days.

Tribals of the jungle

Anyone who hunted in those days used the services of the indigenous tribes of the forest to help with the shikar. I too used my money, education, and ostensible social rank to my advantage to enlist the support of people from the tribal communities. This would be considered politically incorrect today and I may provoke disapproval for my actions, but I also had great respect for their traditional systems of knowledge, which served me far better than what is available now. They had such amazing skills passed from parents to children over centuries, and it is a terrible thought that soon there will come a day, not too long after I am gone, that those skills will cease to exist as well. I suppose during my time, I had a great sense of entitlement, and lorded it over them, having them at my beck and call. Although I always treated them with respect, in my mind they never had ambitions or opportunities to be anything other than trackers or shikari guides. Today, they have blended with the mainstream population and have the same aspirations as anyone living in a big city like Bangalore.

However, for half a century, I relied on them in various capacities, and I am most grateful for what they taught me. They provided me with priceless insights into the ways of the creatures of the forest, and what they taught me through experience, I consider my most worthwhile learning. Needless to say, they saved my life on many an occasion and for all this, I will always be thankful to them. I know that, today, if I meet one of the youngsters from any of the tribes whose services I had employed, he would know more about cell phones than me, and I would know more about reading animal tracks than him—that is the sad state of affairs.

When I was with them, I was often astounded by their abilities. Blades of grass turned in a particular direction, a loose stone or fresh gravel on a path, broken stems, none of these signs escaped their eyes, and all this helped them construct a story. Looking at pug marks, they could tell you if it was a tiger or a panther, whether it was a male or female, to some degree of precision the time elapsed since they were made, and based on their familiarity with the land, where the animal could be found, or at least where to wait to see it again. Some of these can be attributed to the power of observation, and, over time, I learnt how to identify some of these signs, though, in my opinion, no city dweller can ever match their skills. While there are many tribes I have encountered, I will describe a few I worked with the most frequently. They are the Sholagas from BR Hills, the Poojarees from Salem district, Chenchus from Hyderabad, the Irulas, Kurumbas and Kaatu Nayakans from the Nilgiris. I should also like to include the Lambanis, although technically they are really not native to South India.

All these tribes were extremely resourceful and had skills such as knowing where to collect honey and other forest produce, what berries to eat, and how to prepare remedies for simple ailments from the plants in the forest. Of course, their excessive beliefs in ghosts and spirits could often infuriate you, but that was the other side of the coin. They are simple folk, mostly honest, and extremely devoted if you earn their trust. Trust not only for the way you interact with or treat them, but also trust in your ability as a hunter, and their knowing that you would be able to deliver the goods when the occasion demanded it.

The Lambanis are supposed to be from the same brotherhood as Romany gypsies. They have a distinct appearance—the women wear bright ornaments and colourful skirts embroidered with mirror work and beads, and their arms are covered in bangles. They are quasi-hunters who live on the edge of the forests, never completely inside like the Sholagas and other tribes. As trackers, their skills do not come close to those of some of the endemic trackers from the Nilgiris or the BR Hills. However, they are very enterprising and crafty, and for the right enticement, they can be persuaded to get things done, as they are less constrained by superstition and beliefs, thus straddling the ancient and the modern world more effectively. They used to be found in Shimoga and surrounding areas but also had small settlements in and around Kanakpura and Sangam.

The Kurumbas from the Nilgiris, were originally shepherds, living in the jungles as hunters, trappers, and gatherers, who did basic cultivation. My dad had told me that he remembered seeing them in caves when he was a young boy, but ever since I can remember, I have seen them in small settlements where they lived in huts made of bamboo, mud, and grass, often deep inside the jungles. They are gregarious, engaging in a barter system, collecting honey and medical plants and trading with the other communities like the Todas and the Badagas. They have a unique relationship with the Badagas, who have a designated Kurumba man to act as a protector to their small community. There are five types of Kurumbas who live in the Nilgiris, namely, Paalu (milk) Kurumbas, Betta (hill) Kurumbas, Jenu (honey) Kurumbas, Mulla (net) Kurumbas, and Urali (village) Kurumbas, based on their profession or place they stay. I have had the opportunity of working with them, and their skills are remarkable, although nowadays I see that they have given up their old way of life and work for daily wages in plantations and resorts that have sprung up in the Nilgiris.

Irulas are another tribe that is found in the Nilgiris. They make their livelihood by collecting fruits, tubers, and other forest produce and exchange them for rice, salt, and even clothes. Their claim to fame however, is their ability to collect honey from places most people would consider inaccessible. Traditionally they worked as herdsmen for Badagas in the Nilgiris, and hence are always a good source of information on the movement of big cats. There is a different type of Irula found in other parts of Madras state, called Kadu Poojarees. Byra, my dad's friend, was one such Poojaree who is mentioned in my dad's books.

I recollect seeing Byra when we used to visit the jungles past Denkanikotta and Anchetty. He had matted hair and wore nothing more than a loincloth. He was much older than my dad, but they were quite inseparable when Dad used to go out into the jungles in and around Anchetty. He was even more basic than most of the other tribals, for he never even wore a shirt. I guess he was one of the last of his kind, a true blue tribal who refused to change despite the world changing around him. He passed away in the mid-1950s and my dad was inconsolable for a while. Ranga, on the other hand, was much closer to me and was my shikari guide and man Friday for years after my dad passed away. He was an opportunist, extremely lazy and unreliable but absolutely fearless. In fact, as time passed, he progressed into extortion and other rackets, and I had no choice but to slowly distance myself from him.

Kaatu Nayakans (translated as Hero of the Forest, no less!) or Shola Nakayakans are the shyest among all the tribes in the Nilgiris. They are dark in complexion and shorter than the other tribes in these areas. They are hunter-gathers who, in my perception, are in a way analogous to the American Indians, as they believe that all forms of nature have spirits, and worship them accordingly. They believe in sorcery and black magic and are believed to have spells to control other creatures, both humans and animals. They love meat, tobacco, and chewing betel leaf. Added to this, their unkempt appearance and their great reluctance to have baths can be a cause for consternation if you are seeing them for the first time. However, they are simple folk, extremely honest and always reliable.

Sholagas are found in Karnataka and Tamil Nadu, but their nucleus is the BR Hills. They are perhaps the best trackers I have ever come across, and I have worked with a lot of them during my trips to Hailstone's place. My famous tiger *mantram* (spell) was taught by a member of this tribe. Forty years back, they used to live exclusively off forest produce like wild tubers and berries. As they are non-vegetarians, they are partial to various forms of meat from the forest. They used to have this bizarre habit of washing their hair in milk, something that would result in a terrible odour, although I have seen that this practice has considerably reduced over the years. Like all other tribals, they love to smoke beedis and chew betel leaf. They pray to the two-thousand-year-old tree called Dodda Sampige, deep inside the forest. A trick they taught me was to imitate the cry of the jungle fowl, and the resulting sound when made correctly is marvellous. One needs a very thin leaf that has to be rolled, and then with a series of sucking and blowing motions, one can make a creditable call; of course, it is perfected with a lot of practice!

The Chenchus are an aboriginal tribe who live in the Nallamala forest of Andhra Pradesh. Armed with nothing more than a bow and arrow, they are experts of these jungles, and they gather food like roots, berries, and *mahua* flowers, or hunt animals. Their meal consists of gruel made from *jowar* (a kind of cereal), and tamarind is another key ingredient in their dishes. They are small made and of a lighter complexion than the tribes in the Nilgiris. They too have resorted to farming and agriculture or working for the forest department over the years. They pray to the Hindu god, Shiva, and Srisailam is an important temple for them. Although I never did much hunting in Hyderabad state, the only place I would frequent was Chamala. Dad became very friendly with the stationmaster at Chamala after he helped bring down a man-eater, and ever since, the Andersons got a very warm welcome when we were there. Not only did I find it easy to get bookings at the Chamala forest bungalow, but the stationmaster helped my Dad acquire a large plot of land quite close to the forest bungalow. Despite the preferential treatment, my trips were restricted because of the sheer distance. It was very picturesque and had wonderful game, but unlike the Cauvery river or even the Nilgiris, visiting this place meant a longer time travelling and slowly but surely my trips to Hyderabad state came to a halt.

Chenchu tribesmen

As I started spending time in the jungles, I quickly realised I preferred to do it alone, especially when hunting was on the cards. I have always been very choosy about the kind of people I took along. It meant extra food, luggage, and the added responsibility for another life. Most people do not have the discipline to survive in the jungle, or worse, to survive my rules! I was always a slave driver while taking people along, and only the ones who were genuinely interested came a second time. Leaving on time, waking up before the crack of dawn, and, of course, ensuring that the time during dawn and dusk was spent not in the confines of four walls but under the open sky scouring for something to happen, were imperative for a trip. My explanation was simple—we are there for the simple objective of enjoying wildlife. The analogy is the same as when you go to watch a movie—you are there for a specific purpose. Therefore we have to go by the animal's time, not ours. The average time someone needs to get ready is thirty minutes! And that is after spending ten minutes waking them up. People today are spoilt rotten. They want special kinds of food, they want mineral water and sunscreen, they want western commodes and insect repellants, they dress in garish clothes or try to ape some Hollywood stars by wearing shorts and sandals. They need soft beds and blankets. At the first drop of rain they stop in their tracks, they wear perfume, and despite having the most sophisticated watches, they do not know how to be punctual. At the first scrape, they need to apply Dettol, and often I am asked if tetanus shots need to be taken! Even the women of yesteryears were far tougher than the men of today. To sum up the situation, my dad would say that while we are losing wild animals, we are certainly gaining wild tourists.

I consider myself unfortunate to have seen the modern way of life. One would believe that every passing year brings in more convenience and comfort, but having seen the old and the new, I can say with much confidence that how we live today is not the way to live. Everyone is in a hurry to reach somewhere all the time. I remember a time when I would pass down a road and I would know so many people walking alongside me. People were courteous and kind, they were respectful and considerate, and these courtesies were extended even to total strangers. I would give up every single amenity we have today if I could just have my old life back.

Chapter Five

The Years In-Between

BY THE END OF MY SCHOOL DAYS, I KNEW THAT I JUST didn't have it in me to ever study again in a classroom. It was not a particularly revolutionary thought as a lot of Anglo-Indians didn't study beyond this phase. We were a fairly well-known family and therefore getting an odd job now and then was easy. It then occurred to me that a car workshop was something that would always have a steady stream of customers. Of course, I knew nothing about automobiles and had no money for an initial investment or for that matter to hire someone who knew how to repair cars. Luckily, my feeble effort to convince Dad to set up a garage for me miraculously worked. I might even say that his fascination for cars helped seed the idea in my devious mind! He agreed to an initial investment to build a small garage, which was within the walls of the Prospect House property, and I managed to convince Sydney Pocock who my Dad knew, to start this as a partnership. He wouldn't be paid a salary, but any income would be split fifty-fifty. He brought in the expertise, while I provided the real estate and capital. He was also given accommodation at one of our outhouses and we started in earnest. Pocock had an excellent reputation and soon we had a flourishing business. We worked on Standards, Vanguards, Austins, Fords, and Chevrolets. There were no Indian cars in those days—all cars including Morris Minors were imported—and each of us made about seventy five rupees every month, and for me, that was enough to finance a couple of monthly trips including petrol, bait, shikari guide fees, and other miscellaneous expenses. For a while it went off well, but then we got into arguments about money, missing tools, etc. and a little after two years of our partnership, we parted on bad terms. The reason was that I caught his son red-handed stealing and selling tools at the Gujj, and Pocock would never admit to his son being a thief, so it inevitably ended our business.

Pocock's Garage

It's strange but my parents never asked me to get married. During those times, it was an unheard of thing, not to coerce your children to get married, but somehow they never did, other than the occasional query. They knew about my insatiable passion for women and hunting and felt that I always knew the responsibilities and repercussions of my actions. Added to that, their marriage was going through a rough phase as well, so I suppose that they didn't want me to go through the same problems they did. Though we were a middle-class family, we always seemed to have money, and that in a way spoilt me, for I was never under any compulsion or pressure to go out and be the bread winner. Both the jobs my Dad had, paid well; first with the Telegraph Office and later with

HAL. In addition, his books did extremely well internationally and we led a very comfortable life. Therefore, all I needed to do was to find ways to ensure that my hobby of shikar had enough financiers, and I realised very early on in life that there are always people who have talent and those who have money. I clearly belonged to the former group, so it was a matter of finding people with similar interests, ideally richer.

I was not a particularly industrious person, but I had to find the means to go back into the jungles, buy a new rifle and ammunition, and all that cost money. So, although my first business had failed, I started doing odd jobs, and while it gave me a lot of freedom, the income was not steady and I had to find a job to fill the financial gap. Again, luck was on my side, and I managed to get a job at the Star Printing Press that produced a local newspaper and I worked there till some point in 1955. The press was located opposite my school and was owned by Merwan's dad. It didn't take much persuasion on my part to get the job. Bangalore was so small then that everyone knew everyone and people trusted each other implicitly. I don't think I had any qualifications to boast of, my grades were below average, but Mr. Chamarbagwala didn't think twice about giving me the opportunity. I helped with the machinery, doubled up as an odd job person and made about sixty rupees a month. While I was thankful for the money, it was less than what I made with my garage business. Adding to my expenses was the cost of having girlfriends. I had a voracious appetite and it was satiated by sleeping with a lot of women. Young, old, unmarried, married, divorced, widows, Europeans, Anglo-Indians, Indians, it really did not matter. I almost never had to chase them, I was so used to women giving cues, implicit or otherwise. Many would be one-night stands, others would last a couple of weeks, and there were a few that even lasted months. Although I never enjoyed the thrill of the chase, the danger of being with many women at the same time came with its own set of risks and rewards. I was always clear right from the start about the brevity of our relationship, and I made no pretence of being monogamous, but even then, juggling multiple relationships was not an easy task. Unlike the jungle where each minute promised a new adventure, with women, I quickly perceived that it became very boring. This phase made me realise that I could never settle down and get married; I couldn't imagine the drudgery of being with the same woman for the rest of my life!

When it came to variety, my craving was borderline delirious and the endless supply bloated my ego beyond permissible limits. Just when I would think that I had finally found the right girl, I would become aware that she bored me, and my eyes would stray to the next one. This phase further strengthened my belief that I was more at home in the jungles sitting over a waterhole without a weapon, than in the city with all its complications. In fact, the joke doing the round during those years was that I got a bigger hard on when I saw a tiger than when I saw a naked woman!

Binny Mills

Bangalore Woollen, Silk, and Cotton Mills, better known as Binny Mills, was one the premier organisations to work for in Bangalore in those days. Established in 1884, it was the oldest mill in the area, producing the best quality of cotton and woolen garments. In the early days, the mill was powered by steam, but Bangalore became the first city in the country to receive electricity in the early 1900s and soon the mills ran on hydro-electric power, and were probably one of the first few factories to run on electricity in Bangalore. The mill was then taken over by the Chennai-based Buckingham and Carnatic Mills (Binny & Co.) who ran it for almost a century. They had two large mills in Chennai and a smaller one in Bangalore. The unit in Bangalore was called the Binny Cotton Factory and was run by an American industrial engineer and a German who was in charge of operations. They had their sales office on MG Road, with sprawling bungalows for their officers in Benson Town, while their main office was near the city railway station in Okhlipuram.

Like composite textile mills everywhere, the decline of Binny Mills started in the late 70s. They stopped modernisation of their machinery and all of a sudden there was competition in the market that demanded higher outputs. That meant more work for the workers, and with that came the labour unrest. These unions were borderline militant and just wanted to create trouble, with no intention of working in proportion to their commensuration. The organisation then tried to offset the rising labour and running costs by increasing the textile prices, but that was another disaster. The consumers were not interested as they had cheaper and better alternatives available, so naturally sales plummeted and things went downhill from there.

I was very lucky to have got a good job at Binny's and it happened quite fortuitously. Although I didn't have a graduation degree—in those days it was really not a prerequisite—I managed to get a job through certain circumstances that were heavily loaded in my favour. I had been hunting for many years, and had a fair reputation both in Bangalore as well with many forest department officials. A lot of guys my age looked up to me and were always trying to get me to take them hunting. However, I was extremely choosy, having learnt the hard way that city chaps never do well in the jungles. Clive Greenwood, my friend, whose father was a senior executive at Binny's, was an exception. I had been hunting regularly with Clive from 1956. His entire focus during a trip was to bag a trophy, and I felt that at times he missed the sheer thrill of being out in the jungles, but he was a good partner to have on these jaunts. He was a crack shot, had sharp eyes, and nerves of steel. He realised that my job at that time didn't give me the financial freedom to go hunting as much as I would have liked to, and he spoke to his father about me in glowing terms. Greenwood Sr. did not find it particularly amusing that his son was spending time with me, a rotten apple, a bloodthirsty scoundrel and clearly not the cream of Bangalore society in those days. However, boys will be boys and sons will defy fathers, so the father relented to the pressure built by his son and I started off in Stores as an assistant clerk in 1959. My starting salary was one hundred fifty rupees a month, which was quite generous and I decided to stay on. The decision paid off because when I resigned after twenty-five years of service, I was a manager at the Garment Industries Division at Hebbal.

I still frequented the jungles, but I no longer had the freedom as before. My forays, and to a certain extent my love life, were often interrupted by my responsibilities at Binnys, although all my girlfriends knew that given a choice I would rather take a trip into the jungles than spend a weekend with them. Greenwood Sr was furious that I continued to take his son hunting, as he believed that the steady job at Binny's would dissuade me from my hobby. So, he tried to send a veiled threat through Clive that my job was at risk if I continued to take him along. I laughed when Clive hesitantly told me of this father's warning, but no words were needed from me. Clive knew where my priorities lay, and told his father,

"That's an easy choice for Don. He would give up any vice in the world, including women, but he will never give up hunting, and as long as he's going, I'm going with him!"

Sydney D'Silva, Donald and Clive Greenwood – BR Hills

I always managed to squeeze out a trip to the jungles over the weekend yet never missed the siren on Monday morning. Years passed, and I steadily grew in stature with frequent promotions. Coincidentally so did my girth, and far more seriously, the power of the worker's union at Binny's. By the mid-seventies, their single-minded agenda was to bring the factory to its knees. Communism was the new mantra for a set of people whose agenda was far more sinister than they would want the rest of the world to believe. Binny's had become a nightmare and everyday some bizarre demands would crop up. The union was run by Michael Fernandes, and although he was the union leader, sometimes I cannot even credit him with some of the demands made by the workers.

The manager before me had decided that all the workers had to be given a snack in the evening along with tea; in fact, he had even gone to the extent of prescribing the grammage for each item, one of the many examples of German precision there. This was taken out of context by an Indian communist, and every evening at tea time, there would be trouble. A crowd would gather and food would fly in my direction, where I sat along with the rest of the workers, accompanied by a string of abuses:

"You are cheating us, this vada is not seven ounces" or "Do you expect us to eat this dosa which is clearly not five ounces".

While I didn't have much to defend myself against those accusations, sometimes my understanding of the natural world helped me. They would sometimes put beetles or "*vandus*" in their food and complain that I used to encourage the kitchen staff to use that to add grammage to the food. I would retort: "Don't bullshit me buggers, these *vandus* come out only at night, not in the bloody day time!"

The women were no less. They probably had what my Dad would call "the sixth sense", only theirs was about an imminent strike, and in a matter of minutes a well-oiled machine would let out all the water in the fifty odd bathrooms for women. Then came the posturing: "How do you expect us to work when there is no water in the bathroom?" Those who are familiar with the underground art movement that mysteriously trash public property would have found themselves in familiar territory if they were to see the insides of the bathrooms at Binny's. And those who may have believed that there weren't enough women artists at that point in time, had to only visit the ladies bathrooms at Binny's to realise that their fears were unfounded. I'm not sure whether I was flattered or flabbergasted for I featured in some of these murals—I had to go and inspect these at times, that was part of my job—in often exaggerated, unbecoming and anatomically impossible sizes and positions!

Although I used to run a tight ship at Binny's and was well recognised for my ability to get work done, I was infamous for my womanising as well. I had a lot of people reporting to me, including many women, and although I gained notoriety, it never affected the way I treated anyone or my work. Before office started, after office hours, during breaks... I always found the time and the excuse to spend ten minutes behind closed doors. Condoms were an alien concept, so one had to be quick, and extremely careful; an adrenalin rush, akin to the feeling I had while delivering the coup de grace during my hunts.

Despite my good run at work and poor reputation with women, often I would get stuck in situations that unintentionally made things worse. There was once a welfare officer at our office, a Kancheepuram sari-type Brahmin lady who was highly educated but would run to me for every small issue. I was well-respected for my ability to find solutions to problems that I had no experience in solving, and soon she would come to me a couple of times a day to pick my brains. By then, I was quite senior and was the only Indian who had a glass cabin like the English and German big shots. One morning, I received a very disturbed call from the factory, "Come quickly sir, we are having major labour problems. And bring the welfare officer with you."

"Oh bloody hell!" I told myself. I didn't have my car; what was I to do? So, I asked one of my assistants if I could borrow his scooter; not that he had much choice, but he agreed. Mrs. V, who was clearly not used to riding pillion, put on a brave face and declared: "I'll sit behind."

I had a strong feeling that the fact that she had never been on a scooter before helped in her quick decision. I was used to riding motorcycles, and I was quite confident that I could figure out how to handle the scooter as well. I've always had women sit behind me on the back of my motorcycle with legs on either side, and I was wondering how Mrs. V would do that, considering her sari, but she hopped on sideways. Now, under normal circumstances this equation had too many unfamiliar variables, but it was an emergency, so off we went. If the gods wanted to have an extra chuckle, Mrs. V helped them by claiming that she did not want to hold me. The odds were never too impressive to start with and breaking point was 100 metres from the scooter stand. All of a sudden, a dog ran across the road. I quickly applied the brakes and saw that Mrs. V's grip on some part of the scooter had been non-existent at best. She was a tough bird and though hurt, she never uttered a word while we walked back to the office. I left her to tend to her wounds while I tried to make some calls for alternate arrangements. I was talking to someone when she walked in.

"Are you ok, Mrs. V?"

"Actually sir, this is where I've hurt myself," and she practically lifted up her sari to show me the spot on her thigh. Not that I minded, but it was a glass door and everyone was staring at us. The poor lady was in such a state of shock she didn't realise this.

"Put it down quickly," I said. "I'm in enough bloody trouble with the union as it is."

"Aiyyayyo sir!"

Indeed an "Aiyyaiyyo" moment, for I was ribbed about it by my friends for years to come.

We often had social gatherings for the board members and I was responsible for making all the arrangements. The visitors from abroad were encouraged to share their experiences while in India, and often there would be amusing "Indian stories" and the audience would have been warned in advance that they better laugh at these jokes and cheer at speeches if they valued their jobs. I recall an incident where a lady who had newly moved to Bangalore from England was explaining the nuances of Indian cuisine. "I must say that these chaprasis (peons) are not as light as they seem. Just two or three at night will leave you full and satisfied." She must have felt extremely proud of herself when her audience exploded with genuine laughter, although she wouldn't have realised why.

I believe I was a very fair-minded and hard-working manager. I never raised my voice or threw my weight around, and I always set an example of discipline and decorum. Promotions were common for me, and I got a very comfortable glass cabin where I managed reports and paperwork. Then the local management had this wonderful idea that we lacked training and other skills. So, they asked their British directors to send someone to train the staff at the garment factory. The first guy who came in for the training was fired by the board in a month. The second guy lasted longer but he was also fired. As with most challenges, they turned to Donald Anderson next. It was clearly not what I wanted, and my countenance was an honest reflection of what I felt. All this happened in front of a board, mind you.

"Why don't you look too happy, Mr. Anderson?"

"You see, sirs, I've seen what happened to the first two trainers, and I don't want to get fired, for clearly I have no prior experience in training people."

"Let me make it very clear and easy for you Mr. Anderson. If you don't take up this job, you will not have to wait that long, we will fire you right now."

I don't know if Germans have a sense of humour, but he wasn't smiling when he said it, and I really didn't want to take a chance. So overnight, without any warning or desire, I was made Training & Production Manager. I reached the next day and found that someone else had occupied my cabin. I stormed up to my manager's office and demanded an explanation, for was I not the new "Training & Production Manager"?

"Office? You're the bloody production manager, you'll be on the shop floor."

Thus, I fell from grace; from an air-conditioned office I was demoted to working in a hot, noisy environment with no one to run errands for me. I did eight-hour shifts and then stuck on for another four hours doing paperwork and supervision. It was bloody hard work. At its peak, in an eight-hour shift, we would produce two thousand shirts and eight hundred trousers, such was the commitment level of the unit. Standing on my feet for eight hours practically non-stop, I would be exhausted by the time I ended my day. And if you can believe it, on Fridays, I would head off to the jungles straight from work, drive for another six hours, start my shikar during the early hours of Saturday, repeat it that night and Sunday morning, rest during the day on Sunday, and if possible squeeze in a hunt on Sunday night and drive back to Bangalore on Monday morning to start the routine all over again. Of course, I didn't do the jungle trip every weekend, it would have been too much, even for me.

At Taj Connemara, for a Binny's conference

I ensured that my salary was stuck at Rs.1600 a month, despite many attempts to increase it. I always refused in good faith as the Binny's rule then prevented an employee whose salary was more than 1600 rupees per month from receiving gratuity or pension. Towards the end of 1979, Binny's Chennai had twelve thousand workers while Bangalore had eight thousand. Production and profits plummeted with the constant strikes by the unions and we reached a stage where we had to let go of a large number of employees. It was a no-win situation, for people would lose jobs, the union would erupt, and all this would cause further problems. However, it had to be done, and I was given the ignominious task of firing people. What made it worse was that they promoted me despite all my protests and gave me a salary bump to two thousand rupees a month. When I left in 1980, I got a huge amount as pension. Michael Fernandes came up to me and said, "Sorry to see you go." I think it was out of respect and not out of concern or sympathy. I was a hothead back then and retorted, "Let's see how you run the company now." It was a cataclysmic fall thereafter.

Food

Mum never used to cook, as we were quite well off and could afford to hire one. But she had taught our cook, Rosie, how to make some standard dishes that became an integral part of our house. Rosie was a

132

Tamil Christian, and she managed to add her special zest to what was already an atypical Anglo-Indian cuisine. Our kitchen borrowed heavily from various influences: some from my Dad's side which was British, some French and Ceylonese influence from my Mum's side, and then, of course, the unique flavours and recipes of the Bangalore cantonment. Making pickles was my Dad's responsibility and he would collect ingredients and recipes wherever he travelled and would give them his own twist. They were slightly less acidic than the typical Indian pickle and instead would be hot and sweet. While my Dad did not really set foot in the kitchen at home, he would often try and replicate some of the recipes he liked with game that we shot for the pot during our jungle outings. He would thus turn into provider and cook on these trips and Mum loved it, as it gave her a real holiday without any chores.

Vegetarian food was never popular at my house, but potato chapattis were something I always liked. Pickles too were popular, lime and brinjal topping the list. North Indian food was relatively unheard of, so things like *bhutta* [roasted corn on the cob] or boiled groundnuts were never seen when we were growing up. Chinese restaurants did not exist till a good decade after the war, and were usually run by immigrants from the Orient, sometimes third or fourth generation. Koshy's and The Only Place were great places to have steaks, and Breeze, on Brigade Road, was one of the first to have a jukebox in Bangalore. What we know as Thom's Bakery was a very popular café back in the 60s and 70s and it was started as competition to Koshy's on Brigade Road. At that time the bakery and department store existed but was just an extension of the restaurant and it was a very popular place for the young crowd of Bangalore, especially the Anglo-Indian families who lived that side of town. There was no ban on dancing in those days and for ten paise, one could start a song on the juke box at the cafe and the place always had a very lively atmosphere. Although I was older than the average crowd that frequented the place, I always got admiring looks from the girls from Jyothi Nivas College whose campus was practically adjacent to the café.

It would be a fair statement to say that in the city, the topic of food was only second to that of jungle stories. My dad had a great fondness for sweets and although coconut was an odd flavour for a family favourite, everyone in our family was partial to it. There were the standard ones like caramel custard, bread pudding, and dry fruit puddings. Among the restaurants, Funnell's on MG Road was very famous before the war, but my favourite was Imperial or Impys, whose *kushka* and mutton chops were to die for. The Taj restaurant on Infantry Road gained popularity among my circle of friends, and a big meal for three or four people came up to just ten rupees in the sixties. As I started working, All Saints Bakery, Crown Bakery near Catholic Club, and Fatima's became haunts where all of us would come together and have fun. The streets would be empty after a certain time, and my friends and I would all be outside the restaurant, drinking beer, and creating such a ruckus, but we were never unruly and never had trouble with the police. Among the other places that I used to frequent was the 3 Aces Club on MG Road. While I was never much of a dancer, there was always good music at the club, with a lot of talent from Calcutta. It was one of a kind and was a great place to meet women. While it was certainly seen as a place unsuitable for the gentry, it was still respectable (if that's possible) for many years, but in order to draw more business, it degraded to a strip club and then worse.

When we did get to the jungles, we would eat just about anything. And I mean anything. After our supplies ran thin, we would eat wild berries, tubers, jungle fowl and at times venison, although my dad vehemently opposed that. As for water, the nearest flowing stream would provide relief, but at times, our thirst would be so severe that we would drink from jungle pools, knowing full well that we would fall ill with diarrhea and other diseases.

Some of the best product brands that I grew up with have disappeared from the shelves at home today. Crosse & Blackwell were manufacturers of cheese, butter, jams, jellies, and pickles. Major Grey's Chutney was another favourite; it had raisins, vinegar, lime juice, onion, tamarind, and spices. Colman's Mustard and Polson's butter was present on every breakfast table, and Van Houten's Cocoa provided me with a hot chocolate drink in the evenings while Quaker Oats porridge was a regular feature at breakfast. Of the few Indian brands, I distinctly remember Venkatachellam's curry powder, which was ubiquitous in every household, be it English or Indian. There were just a handful of places you could buy all these items, the most sophisticated being Spencer & Co. on MG Road, founded by Mr. Oakshot, an Englishman. To the right of Spencer's was Liberty Theatre, where the Handloom House stands today. New Opera was another theatre that started off as a place where dances took place. Other than Spencer's, the other department store was Nilgiris on Brigade Road but it was not as grand as Spencer's. Despite the presence of these supermarkets, we led a very frugal lifestyle and never really visited them. We used carbolic soaps and home-made shampoos. We never went to a hospital, let alone saw a doctor unless it was something as major as broken bones. Hot soup usually cured most illnesses, a teaspoon of brandy gave us a good night's sleep, and, more often than not, cured all maladies. If that wasn't enough, we used to drink Virol, a tonic that helped children grow! At home, breakfast offered options like bacon, sausage, and fried eggs with bread, butter, marmalade and jam. This was followed with a cereal called shredded wheat or cornflakes. At times we had to have Marmite, which looked like black jam and tasted disgusting, but was supposed to be full of protein so it sometimes found its way to our breakfast table. Horlicks and Ovaltine were breakfast drink for kids then, while adults had Camp Chicory Coffee which is a lot like Bru.

Harry Black and the Tiger

In 1957, 20th Century Fox announced the film *Harry Black and the Tiger*, an adaptation of the novel *Harry Black* by David Walker. The initial plan was to shoot it somewhere in north India, but for some reason it didn't work out and they decided to move it to the Nilgiris.

Bhowani Junction had been released in 1956 and although that was shot in Pakistan, the success of the film encouraged Hollywood to make inroads into the subcontinent. The mysticism and romance of a similar story, complete with a man-eating tiger seemed to the studio, at that time, to have all the ingredients for a box office smash. Stewart Granger, an established star, had just finished *Gun and Glory* was chosen to play the lead role, while supporting him would be Barbara Rush and Anthony Steele. A film set in India needed Indians, and there were two roles for them. I.S. Johar played Bapu, the gun bearer, while the gorgeous Kamala Devi played a nurse, Somola. She got noticed for her smouldering good looks by Hollywood and went on to act in a handful of films in America.

The closest airport and big city was Bangalore and Bandipur became a natural choice to shoot the film. The producers had got in touch with people in Bangalore a few months before the shooting actually began and word was out that a body double was needed for Granger, for some of the scenes that had him face the tiger. There really wasn't much to decide, as to who would fit the role. It may sound as if I'm boasting, but in Bangalore, in 1957, there weren't many choices when it came to young men who were well-versed with the jungle, big built, and marginally foreign looking. The choice was almost unanimous, and the scouts met me at home. A chap by the name of Godwin met me much before the crew arrived in India, and everything was arranged. Bandipur was about hundred and thirty miles from Bangalore, too far to travel every day, so the crew pitched camp and stayed there for the entire time we shot the movie. There were just a couple of concrete buildings, the rest were thatched huts and the entire cast and crew stayed in these huts: Granger, the director Hugo Fregonese, and everybody else, including me. The distinction between the huts lay in the interiors, and Granger being the star that he was, was given the royal treatment. The dining area was common for everyone and that became the place where most people spent time when they were not shooting. The food was supplied everyday by Koshy's, from Bangalore, and they got publicity saying that Stewart Granger swore by their fare, but the truth was that Granger hated the food from Koshy's and would get someone from the crew to make him stuff he enjoyed. Anthony Steel and Barbara Rush, however, were more down to earth and had no airs about what they ate or who they mingled with. The day would start at five in the morning, and we would set off for different parts of the Nilgiris to get the shots, some of them as far was Gudalur, where we shot at some private tea estates for some select scenes in the film.

While the main crew was to get the prescribed shots, there was another group who worked on collecting sights and sounds that would embellish and attempt to give a real jungle feel to the movie. The producer, John Brabourne, who was also Lord Mountbatten's son-in-law, was keen on giving viewers the most authentic feel of the location and insisted on getting nothing but the best. So the team wanted original jungle men, and word was sent out to get the "real deal". Bandipur never had an endemic tribal population, so a makeshift arrangement was made to get a couple of Haki-Pikis. They are excellent trackers, trappers, and imitators, and to my regret, the only opportunity I got to work with them was for this movie. Hugo wanted to record some jackal sounds and as luck would have it we could not get any jackal sounds for two days. But on the third day, we got lucky and the Haki-Piki duo took us to a location where one could hear the jackals. The crew were a bit nervous going so far off the main road, so I went along with them for protection. We drove up to a point, and then walked for a fair distance. The two started an astonishing demonstration of jackal howls, and amazingly, within a couple of minutes, their cries were answered and we got some recording done. However, after we got back to camp, we realised that the recording was not as clear as we would have liked, so instead of doing the entire rigmarole all over again, we wisened up and simply got the pair to put on their vulpine act. It was so good that it was impossible to tell the difference!

Granger always maintained a distance with the locals, but we would catch up once in a while, when we both discussed our common love for hunting. In fact, he was keen on shooting bison, but the director put his foot down, saying that he did not want Granger to injure himself. There was a small tug of war, but Hugo got his way and Granger was forbidden to take part in any activity that would put the production at risk. He came up to me and we started talking about the guns we used. Granger, who was still in a foul mood and wanted an argument, started disagreeing with me, talking down the weapons I used. He mentioned a certain rifle that he believed to be superior and by then we had a small audience who had clearly seen this sort of thing before.

"Don, don't argue with me, I've been hunting from the time you were a toddler, so I know my guns. In fact, I've been to Africa and shot big game with Harry Selby, and here is a scar that a Cape Buffalo gave me."

He pointed out a scar on his abdomen, and although I wasn't convinced that it was made by a buffalo, he received the expected "ooh" and "aah" from the onlookers. I smiled and said,

"Do you know why I say that my bloody rifle is superior? Look, Jimmy, no scars!" and I lifted my shirt. The crowd broke out into a chuckle and even Granger had to smile. I was only twenty-three years old, but I was cocky enough to put Stewart Granger in his place. That did wonders for my reputation!

In fact, the next day, he approached me and asked me how much I was being paid for all the work I was doing on the set. When I mentioned that I was being given two thousand rupees in total, he was horrified. Apparently even the lowest crew member earned a lot more than me and he was determined to correct that. In those days, they had the spool type of recorders and as mentioned before, the crew were determined to capture sights and sounds from the jungles. That meant getting close to the animals and Granger exaggerated the dangers they were exposing themselves to.

"Do you have any idea how dangerous the animals of India can be?" he thundered. "Unless you chaps want to go home in wheelchairs or worse, I suggest you take an experienced shikari with you, someone like young Anderson here," he casually mentioned, with a twinkle in his eye that only I could see. Sure enough, my salary was increased three-fold, and all I had to do was accompany some men and hold my rifle while they did their recording. However, things didn't always go the way I wanted them to. Sometimes, even the most educated men will not listen to reason and Hugo was no different. For instance, the time they wanted to film a tiger beat and he insisted on using baby elephants in the shot. I argued that in real life no one used baby elephants but his argument was that people at the movies loved to watch baby elephants and eventually he got his way.

Stewart Granger with his stunt double

Soon the time came for me to actually contribute in the manner I had been originally hired—as a stunt double for Granger. The scene actually had a tigress, not a tiger, and she belonged to Mysore zoo. She had been part of a circus and hence was used to obeying commands, which made it easier for the crew to convince her to put on a show for the camera. For the shots that had me fighting the tigress, they had made an enclosure of sorts with a net outside to prevent her from running away. I was then put inside this enclosure and the cameraman sat outside and just put his camera in through the net. They got me and the tigress to do multiple takes of the scene where Granger is attacked by the feline. They forced the tigress to jump up over and over again, and each time I had to fall back as it did, thus giving the effect that it was actually falling on top of me. The camera man outside the net shouted and screamed while the blasted cat and I were inside, glowering at each other. It had been well-fed, but unlike a dog who loves to perform and do tricks, she wasn't too keen. In fact, the joke going around was that the tigress was more at risk than I was, and that I had to be thoroughly inspected before letting me into the nets, as my instincts would be to shoot her! Granger never even saw these scenes, he was too busy flirting with the women on the sets, impartial to age or nationality.

However, he was undeniably the star of the film and his reputation far preceded him. In fact, there were many women from Bangalore who would come to visit him, practically every day! They would disappear into his shack and the next morning, a glance would find his hut strewn with all sorts of ladies garments. My room was different—I made sure the women took everything with them and left nothing behind! He was a very handsome and virile looking guy and was used to having women falling all over him. However, I suppose like all movie stars he had his ego that needed to be massaged and he had to control everything around him. We were once shooting a scene that needed him to be shirtless and after the shot was over, he took off his pants as well, down to just his jocks, and made a spectacle of himself. This was right on the main Ooty road and sure enough a crowd of tourists had begun to collect like ants around honey. It was time to get back to the shoot and a European lady who got a bit more excited than anyone would have liked, made multiple attempts to get close to Granger. Despite the crew asking her to pipe down, she was quivering and made little squeaks, and then Granger lost his cool. "Hugo, unless you tell this red-headed bitch to shut up, I'm not going to act anymore." Needless to say, the poor woman vanished. What's impossible to believe, but true, was that that there was someone who had a bigger ego than Granger, and that was the guy who held the lights! He would throw the biggest tantrums and always had excuses when there was work to be done. It was amazing why he never got fired in the first place!

My dad was very excited with everything that was happening and one day he came to visit me. Like me, he too was a good eater, and we were having lunch with a few crew members, when one of them remarked,

"Old man, what's the matter, haven't you Indians seen food before?" An extremely racist remark, even for that time, and I remember seeing red, just jumping up and advancing to punch his daylights out! Luckily for me, we were separated even before the fight started. By then Granger had read one of my dad's books and was very impressed; in fact, he bought one from Bangalore, and signed it along with his co-stars.

When they finished shooting the movie, they left from Bangalore airport where hundreds of people turned up to bid them farewell. By then the news of their departure was all over Bangalore and the airport saw an unprecedented amount of traffic that day. I stayed with the crew almost till the gates, and as they were leaving, out of the blue, the cameraman announced that there was another star in their midst—Sabu, the elephant boy—and pointed me out. I was bamboozled but many people in the crowd who didn't know me very well and had a vague idea what Sabu looked like, surrounded me and started asking me for autographs. I tried my best to explain the misunderstanding, but no one would listen. From the corner of my eye, I could see Granger and the rest making a clean getaway, laughing their heads off! The reason for the confusion was that Sabu had acted in a film in 1948, made on the life of Corbett called *Man-eaters of Kumaon* and was perhaps India's best-known face in Hollywood at that time.

Licensed Hunting

In his youth, Dad may have shot a few tigers and panthers for sport, but as he grew older, he only shot when it was absolutely necessary—when he felt that human life was at stake. In the 1930s and 40s, the presence of a tiger or panther terrorising a remote village never made it to the local newspapers in Bangalore and it was only through an established informal network that he could hear about these cases and decide to put an end to the menace. I did my fair share of shooting tigers and panthers like he did, but I never could spend the kind of time he did in the jungles, and my network of informants were not half as good. So, a lot of my hunting was with a license, and while most people do not subscribe to that concept, it had its place in Bangalore those days.

If I look back at how jungles have transformed over the years, I can say with a fair bit of conviction that loss of habitat is the single largest cause for the wildlife we have lost. Next would be unlicensed hunting or poaching, but there was a time when poisoning added to the death count, and this is something most people are unaware of. By the early fifties, Folidol was being used to devastating effect by villagers all over India. It was an easily available and rather cheap pesticide and herdsmen used to apply this on the carcasses of the cows, buffaloes, and goats that were killed by large carnivores. While arsenic did not have a smell, most tigers, panthers, and even the scavengers would refuse to eat carcasses that had been doused with it. However, Folidol had a distinct smell, but somehow all the creatures ignored that, and would die painful deaths. It was extremely potent as it could be imbibed even through the skin, so even a creature that was sniffing a dead cow at close quarters could become a victim. It became quite popular among humans as well, often used to murder unsuspecting victims or to commit suicide, and it was banned in most countries across the world by the late sixties, but by then the damage had been done, and this is an often-forgotten era when a lot of India's wildlife got wiped out.

The Indian Wildlife Protection Act of 1972 sounded the death knell for licensed hunting. However, much like today, if you had money, anything was possible. I know of high-ranking government officials who shot tigers in the early eighties, from forest department jeeps, with huge flashlights. For the neutral, it would seem that the most destruction was caused by licensed hunters like me, but that's not entirely true. None of us went out with a machine gun and mowed down tigers or even deer. We prided ourselves on pitting our skill against that of one animal, and that meant spending days in the jungle, observing and interpreting signs, stalking the animal, and eventually getting it within our gun sights.

During my dad's hunting days, shooting animals was neither viable nor affordable for the average man. If he lived near the jungles, he would resort to shooting to save his crops, livestock or his family, and if he lived in a city like Bangalore, he would have to be well off to afford it. So, only a handful of people did serious shooting. The number of licenses handed out was strictly controlled, and the license itself was very clear about what was and wasn't allowed. Here is an example of what was declared under licensed hunting by the Nilgiri Wildlife Assocation in 1962.

- All animals are classified as either big game or small game and you have to take a license based on the animal you plan to shoot.
- Big Game includes tiger, panther, bear, bison, sambar, spotted deer, barking deer, nilgiri tahr, nilgai, four horned antelope and blackbuck.

The number of big game for the course of a season cannot exceed 1 each of the animals mentioned above except in the case of spotted deer where two are allowed and barking deer where four are allowed.

- Small Game includes jungle fowl, spur fowl, partridge, quail, woodcock, snipe, wood pigeon, hare and mouse deer. Migratory birds, wood cocks and pigeons are not allowed to be shot during certain months of the year when they are breeding and nesting.

Listed below is the list of rules that a licensed hunter had to comply with.

1. No hunting allowed from a machan or at a waterhole
2. Hunting is not allowed before sunrise or after sunset
3. Shooting of tiger or panther with 100 yards from a road or track is not allowed
4. Shooting of all creatures are prohibited inside a wildlife sanctuary and only allowed in reserved hunting block
5. The licensed hunter cannot carry more than two weapons at any time
6. The hunter must go hunting only with a licensed shikari guide registered with the Nilgiri Wildlife Association.

Prohibitions and restrictions on hunting

1. Elephants – Except a duly prescribed rogue or in self-defense of life and property.
2. Antelope or pea fowl except with the permission of the Chief Conservator of Forests.
3. Monkeys, Brahminy kites, parrots, birds of song and of bright plumage.
4. Tigress with suckling cubs.
5. Females and immature males of bison, spotted deer, antelope and barking deer designated as big game.
6. Mature males are defined as follows
   a) Bison – Animals in which the widest outside span between horns measures not less than 33 inches or the girth at the base of the horn measures not less than 18 inches or there are not less than 4 corrugations on the horn. For shooting bison only high velocity bullets can be used. The minimum bore shall be 333 H.V. and the bullet not less than 300 grains.

b) Spotted deer – In hard horn, longer horn, measuring along the outer curve, from burr to point must be greater than 28 inches. Sambar – In hard horn, longer horn, measuring along the outer curve, from burr to point must be greater than 24 inches.

c) Barking deer – At least one of the horns should measure 3 inches from the pedicle

d) Ibex – The saddle must be well defined.

e) Tiger – Males should be at least 9 feet in length and females at least 8 feet in length from the tip of the nose to the tip of the tail, along the back.

In addition, the following are prohibited

1. Removal of bird's eggs.

2. Setting up of nets, snares, traps and the use of poison or explosives.

   - Failure to comply with any of these rules could lead to a termination in license and further penalized as per the Madras Act II of 1879 and Madras Forest Act V of 1882.

This meant that licensed hunters like me not only had to be skilled marksmen, we had to be good naturalists. We had to understand animal behaviour and learn how to identify whether an animal was mature enough to be shot. Those who visit wildlife sanctuaries in vehicles today realise how tough it is to come across a predator, and those that have tried to attempt that on foot realise how the same scenario is next to impossible. This is because over the years, animals in these places are used to the sight and sound of a vehicle and recognise it as non-threatening. However, their instinct is much sharper and the sound of a human footstep or the smell of man will cause the same animal to scurry for cover, as centuries of evolution have wired them that way. So, finding a tiger or panther during my hunting days, leave alone shooting one, was extremely challenging.

Most of the trophies that Dad and I shot were mounted by Tocher & Tocher, who established themselves in the early 1900s on King's Street in Frazer Town. I believe they learnt their trade from the Van Ingens in Mysore, who had started their business in the 1890s. The latter were a class apart and catered to the Maharajahs, shikaris and gentry all over the world, and hence were quite expensive. So, the more affordable and closer to home Tocher organisation became our default destination to get our trophies done. Tocher was my dad's friend and taught both of us how to get the skin prepared for mounting, even coming with me on a couple of trips to show me how to do this. I believe he was not British, but had some east European connection, the family having migrated many years prior. They would take about two months to get each mount ready, and they were masters at their craft, producing some amazing specimens in various positions. The other taxidermist we used was Muniswamy who lived on Lalbagh Road. Although I would never entrust him with the cats, when it came to wild boar and sambar, I often used him to get the job done at half the cost of Tocher.

Kenneth Anderson skinning a porcupine

Tocher also taught me some basic taxidermy skills, and with a pair of scissors, a sharp knife, pliers, salt or alum with ash, one can dabble in some amateur skinning. To those who are interested from an academic perspective, this is how it is done. The first and foremost thing is to measure the animal, as quite often after it has been skinned and stretched, the resulting specimen is often larger than the original, and most shikaris prefer it that way! Firstly, with charcoal, spots on the animal must be marked out, after turning it on its back. Starting from the lower lip, all the way to the tail, the next cuts are from the inside of the fore and hind legs, through its pads. Now the skin can be taken off, although around the head, extreme care must be taken. It's not for the squeamish and many a time I have had friends who threw up on seeing this. Carnivora take a longer time to decompose but also give off an offensive odour and hence it's always better to have your nose and mouth covered with a handkerchief. The skin is cleaned to remove blood and then stretched out, with pegs if one has carried them, over a carpet of dried grass, and liberally mixed with ash. There should be extra support under the head and the ears must be turned inside out. It is then treated with an equal amount of salt and ash, to get the moisture out. This has to be repeated multiple times for the next forty-eight hours, after which it is ready to be mounted by your taxidermist. This is, of course, how my dad taught me, and he was a stickler for this sort of thing. In south India, there is always moisture in the air, hence parts of the skin, which do not feel the effects of the preservative at the time, will simply decompose taking the hair along with it, leaving unsightly bald patches on the skin. In places where the skin is thick, it must be thinned down with a sharp knife so that the curing agent reaches the roots of the hair and hardens the whole skin.

The best taxidermists are often praised for their ability to reproduce expressions like anger in animals but in my opinion, they are often inaccurate in their handiwork because in the real world, animals often combine their expression with corresponding body language. So, it's a common and comical sight, and something that goes unnoticed, to see a snarling stuffed tiger whose posture is rather staid!

Chapter Six

My Haunts – Part 1

LIKE ALL MEN, I AM A CREATURE OF HABIT, AND although in my youth I would try and explore new jungles and paths less trodden, every once in a while, I would return to those spots where I was comfortable. A habitual forest bungalow, familiar faces, established routes... there is a certain reassurance all that brings. In this chapter and the next I will attempt to tell you some of the jungles I favoured and frequented and some of the adventures I had.

If I were to compare the villages I used to visit and what they are today, perhaps the one that has seen the most change would be Hogenikal. Although it is in Tamil Nadu, the name comes from the Kannada words *hoge* (smoke) and *kal* (stone or rock), from the fine spray caused by the breathtaking waterfalls created as the mighty Cauvery river crashes on to graphite rocks. Called Marikottayam by the locals, it used to a sleepy village with friendly people, a great place for angling and a lot of elephants, panthers, wild dogs and the occasional tiger as late as the mid-50s. Then it just crumbled under the weight of population and human greed. Rampant poaching, dynamiting of fish in the river and chopping down of trees destroyed what was once a pristine paradise, a place my dad loved so much.

The Cauvery has many tributaries, and one of the smallest is the Chinar. However, from the Anderson family perspective, this was the most important one as we had many adventures in the forests that were sustained by it. Often, the Chinar disappears into terrain that looks

146

inhospitable but meanders and comes back to the main Gulhatty Road sixteen miles later. If you start walking from Anchetti to Gundalam, you would find yourself along the banks of the famous Secret River that my Dad writes about. This secret river is another tributary of the Cauvery and joins the main river about sixteen miles from Anchetty. Another twenty miles from this point would bring you to Sangam, where the Cauvery meets the Arkavathy. Beyond Sangam, of course, is Mekedatu, a tourist spot, and it used to be a wonderful getaway for people in Bangalore. The Secret River, being just a tributary, is often dry during parts of the year, which is perhaps one of the reasons that it's not easy to find. I'm not a romantic like my dad, and I've never found anything secretive about it. However, I can comment on the quality of water—as it did not pass along any major village, the water was always good enough to drink.

Although my dad was a regular visitor to Hogenikal, it wasn't until 1952 that I started visited it on my own. That meant going past Anchetty, Gerhetti, Mutttur, Pennagram and onwards to my destination. The Chinar river can be dangerous, especially during the monsoon, and one had to cross it twice en-route. The crossing at Muttur was particularly dangerous and there are times when I have broken my journey and waited for the river to subside, rather than taking the chance to cross it while in spate. Six miles from Hogenikal is a place called Uttimalai, where my dad had a small thatched hut. Parallel to the main village road was another road that snaked its way into the surrounding jungles, and this used to be one of my dad's favourite paths to walk on. On many an occasion, he would stay in his hut during the day and then, armed with nothing more than a lantern, would wander off on that narrow path, walking perhaps the entire night and would return in the morning. The forests were populated by elephants, but he firmly believed that all wild animals were scared of light and would avoid confrontation at all cost. Byra, his shikari who was often mentioned in his books, was his constant companion and they made a quaint but inseparable pair.

Every once in a while, there would be festivals celebrated at Hogenikal, and people from all the neighbouring smaller villages and settlements would come there to participate. I remember an incident in the early fifties when I visited the village shandy that was part of the celebration, and believe it or not, there was an Indian version of a coconut shy. As the day progressed, the original art of knocking down the coconut with objects like stones had been replaced by the local men trying their luck to knock down coconuts with their locally manufactured matchlocks. They kept missing and it was an amusing sight for the neutrals. I was never short of overconfidence and waged a bet that I could bring it down with my shotgun. They were reluctant as they knew that I had a superior weapon, but the compromise was that they would move the target further back to even the odds. I naturally brought it down with my weapon but then realised that those guys were poor losers. "*Dorai*, even a fool knows that you have a better gun, so that says nothing about your skill. If you want to impress us, do the same with OUR weapon."

To the amazement of the onlookers and mostly to mine, I managed to knock a coconut down with the first shot. Things started to get more interesting with stakes being upped with a lot of shouting and jostling and I beat a hasty retreat before my incompetence was demonstrated the next time around.

After Independence there was a significant spurt of nefarious activity in these parts. Although the British were still around, Indians started getting bolder in their quest to get richer. Locally made matchlocks and country bombs appeared on the scene and were mainly used for poaching animals. Summertime would be the worst, as they would sit up at waterholes for deer and pigs. They would also dynamite the waters and kill fish indiscriminately. At night, jungle paths that once were empty, not because the jungle was devoid of people but because the locals would be careful to avoid meeting people like my dad, now held the possibility of meeting a gang of armed poachers. While it was my duty to report them to the authorities, I knew that sometimes they were doing it to just feed hungry mouths at home. They also had the greatest respect for me, because I would often sit up alone, unafraid of animals or evil spirits that they believed clearly frequented these parts. They would often confess that they were astounded how lucky I was and ask me what *mantram* I had with me. I would patiently explain to them, that if they sat at a waterhole, with a blanket covering themselves, smoking their beedi, and often lifting the blankets and murmuring, no creature within five hundred yards would come near that waterhole. Despite my advice, there are times when they would get lucky, against all odds!

Another of my dad's haunts was Javalagiri, where he even shot a couple of man eaters. However, the popularity of the place lay in its proximity to Bangalore. Just forty-five miles away, it provided him the opportunity for a quick getaway. This was probably the first jungle I remember him taking me to. By the time I was a seasoned hunter, my shikari guide there was Muniyappa. He was not a tribal like some of the other shikari guides whose services I would use, but a Telugu-speaking chap who lived there. Despite not having hereditary skills passed on, as in the case of Sholagas or Chenchus, he was an excellent resource, and what he lacked in tracking skills he made up with sheer bravery and grit. He had a small piece of land and a tiny hut, located about half a mile from the village and bordering the forest. The forest bungalow had better living conditions, but it also meant reserving it in advance, paying fees, never knowing if you could be thrown out if some official landed up unannounced etc. Being so close to Bangalore, it was one place I could just reach in a few hours, and I could do that on the spur of the moment, and so, inevitably, I ended up at his hut. Five hundred yards from his hut was the fire line and then the forest began, and I had a clear view from the hut.

One afternoon, a panther killed his cow right on the fire line. Muniyappa had chased it off, but did not remove the cow from the spot. As luck would have it, I happened to be in the village at the time and saw this as a great opportunity. The cow was hardly touched and I knew that the cat would be back to eat to its heart's content. There were no trees close by, and I was wondering where I could hide myself, when a brainwave hit me. I called Muniyappa and got him to make a haystack as quickly as possible. Haystacks are common in villages and I felt that the panther would not consider it suspicious. With a few more helping hands, we created a reasonably big haystack close to the remains of the cow, and I squeezed myself into it. It was very good camouflage and I was sure that I could fool the panther. At that point in time Muniyappa had a flea infested cur whose sole job was to keep him company and the duo retired to his hut, not too far away, with strict orders not to make too much noise. It was about 6:30 and the sun was setting when I noticed a creature walking very slowly to the cow and starting to feed. I gripped my rifle, but on closer inspection I realised that it was Muniyappa's mangy mutt! Muniyappa would have had an apoplectic fit if he had seen it but what worried me more was the safety of the dog. The panther was due any moment, and it would have a double treat if it managed to get the dog as well. A steak as main course followed by doggy dessert! I had to get the dog back, so I made soft whistling sounds, hoping that they were close to the call of a bird and that the panther wouldn't notice. It was to no avail, for the mongrel was too busy enjoying his dinner. I made a slightly louder attempt and it seemed to work, for it started to run towards me. I was feeling rather pleased till I saw a large panther chasing it. I wasn't used to this sort of thing before; I didn't know whether to take the shot from the position I was sitting in, or whether I should stand up, because I sure as hell did not enjoy the prospect of me, the dog, and the panther, together in the haystack! The dog made my decision easier, as it ran past my hiding place, ignoring me completely. Missing me by less than five feet, it ran towards Muniyappa's hut. The dog's eyes, filled with terror, were fixed on the hut, while the panther's blazing eyes were focused on its prey. As this life and death tableau unfolded before me, I jumped up, turned around, and followed the pair with my gun. The panther caught the dog in no time but the grip wasn't very tight, and a small dust bowl of two bodies writhing, yelping, and grunting exploded in front of me. Perhaps I was insensitive, but I didn't care too much about the dog. I didn't want the panther inside Muniyappa's hut, which was just a few yards away, so I took aim and fired. To my good luck I managed to kill the panther. Muniyappa, who had the presence of mind to stay inside, peered out and was shocked to see a dead panther just a few feet away!

In the early sixties Javalagiri held an abundance of wildlife and it's shocking to see how it all disappeared almost overnight. In fact, I remember once I left Bangalore late and reached there past midnight. I didn't want to wake up Muniyappa, and the weather being warm, I decided to sleep somewhere in the village in an open area. I spied a hay-laden lorry parked in the middle of the village and thought that it was a perfect spot to spend the rest of the night. It was an excellent plan, till I was woken up at some point on hearing a very faint noise. I looked over and saw a bull elephant reaching out with his trunk and munching my bedding as if it was the tastiest thing in the world. That's how wild Javalagiri was!

BR Hills

Biligiriranga Hills, or BR Hills as they are more commonly referred to, have a special place in my heart, for like my father, I too have had some memorable adventures there. They represent the easternmost parts of the Eastern Ghats and they connect the Western Ghats with valleys and plateaus in between. They are constituted by two ridges that run in a north-south direction. These rich deciduous forests are home to the Sholaga tribes—some of the best trackers I have ever come across—and in this forest exists a large, thousand-year-old tree called Dodda Sampige that is sacred to them. These hills are heavily wooded and are prime elephant country and at the foot of these hills were where G.P Sanderson ran his *khedda* (a stockade trap for the capture of elephants) operations.

Relatively inhospitable and unknown, BR Hills became famous when Randolph Morris set up his coffee estates in this area. He was a Scot like my dad though much older than him. The story goes that Morris arrived in India penniless and worked odd jobs at different estates till he landed up here and then went on to establish the first large-scale coffee plantation at Attikaan. He was killed by a bison and is buried at a place called Bellagi in his estate. His son, Ralph, then took over the estates and was much more of a hunter than his father and a very secretive one, as most hunters are, including me! I had the opportunity of meeting him once when he was looking for a manager at his Attikaan estate and had placed an advertisement in the local newspaper in Bangalore. I saw this as a perfect opportunity to get away from Bangalore and settle down in a place that paid me well, and, of course, give a fillip to my hunting hobby, which at that time had been waning considering the frequent monetary investment it needed. Attikaan is located in a beautiful area teeming with wildlife and I didn't think twice. I applied for the post and he was very prompt in responding. He mentioned that he was eager to meet me, and sure enough in about a week or so I was invited to meet him at the West End hotel in Bangalore. We discussed a lot of things including my ability to speak local languages, my understanding of the jungles etc. After about thirty minutes, we were wrapping up and I felt that I had the job in the bag. Almost as an afterthought and perhaps with a touch of humour, he mentioned, "A planter's life is a lonely life. Are you prepared for it?"

And then I opened my big mouth. "Sure, that's fine, because I love the outdoors and hunting."

His ears pricked up but my senses did not.

"So, you like hunting eh?" came his nonchalant response.

I delivered the coup-de grace. "Of course, in fact I have a hunting license for parts near your estate."

Looking back, I think I heard him mutter a prayer of gratitude to the stars above.

"Oh, is it? Very interesting, we must catch up another time and exchange stories. I will get back you about the post by the way," and they were the last words I heard from Morris. He left India almost immediately after, selling his estates to the Birlas sometime in the mid-fifties.

I continued to frequent those parts and once came across a cluster of leaf huts during one of my trips. I asked my Sholaga shikari guide what they were. He mentioned that these were huts that Morris used to stay in when he came hunting in these parts. These huts were so basic, they offered nothing more than protection from rain, and that meant that Morris would leave the luxury of his estates and come and live in these conditions for days on end. The area was inhospitable, cut off from the rest of the world, full of leeches, and I started to admire the guy for living in such hostile conditions. It goes to show the kind of pioneers who lived back then. Interestingly, Ralph and I shared a common Sholaga shikari guide, whom I will talk about later.

Hugh Hailstone and his home, the Moyar Valley Ranch, were an integral part of my adventures in the fifties and sixties. Hughie was not just a top-class shikari, but an entrepreneur and a shrewd businessman as well. He was younger than my dad, but they were similar in many respects, and geniuses in their own ways. While my dad's intellect was focused on his writing, it was a shame that he never expanded his horizons. Hailstone, on the other hand, had many revolutionary ideas, all of which were successful. He owned and cultivated 180 acres of land in Mudiyanoor and was extremely successful. He started "Modern Gunsmith" in Coimbatore, and every self-respecting hunter in that city became a patron. He started some business connected to metallurgy and I recall that that too was a success. In the mid-fifties, electricity was not a commodity that many people had access to in these parts, but Hailstone was undeterred. With windmills, dynamos, and car batteries, he created electricity to power up his bungalow and it was quite a magical sight for all the people who lived around.

To reach Hailstone's place, you had to pass through BR Hills and go past Dimbum where a beautiful little bungalow used to stand atop the hill. From there, you started your descent, past Talamalai to eventually reach the little village of Mudiyanoor, where the ranch was on the left side. The road from Dimbum to Mudiyanoor was a horrible stretch and one had to cross many small streams on the way. I would go to the BR Hills mostly on my own, initially on my bike and later in Merwan's car and I have been charged several times by elephants. It is always a close shave when one is on a motorcycle, but I was young and all that brought tremendous excitement. Another road that I used to frequent was a road built from Talamalai all the way to the Moyar ditch, called the Tipu Sultan Road after the maharajah who commissioned it. It was lonely, desolate and not motorable back then. Things haven't changed today. As a matter of fact, it's virtually impossible to visit most of my haunts in the jungles, thanks to the restrictions imposed by the forest department.

I was about twenty when I first met Hailstone and I had an old shotgun I knew was not a very good weapon. For some reason, he took a liking to me and invited me over to start shooting in those parts. When I landed up at his place with my dad, he looked at my gun and spoke in a serious but quiet tone. "Son do you want to get yourself killed?"

I knew what he meant, but feigned ignorance.

"No, why do you ask?"

"Well, then I suggest you choose a different weapon."

There was an uncomfortable silence all around, and before I could come up with a smart retort, he asked, "Can I get you a rifle?"

I wasn't sure whether he was offering to gift me one, but I didn't leave it to chance.

"Mr. Hailstone, I don't know if you're joking or not, because it costs money. It's very difficult to get a license to buy the rifle, and then, of course, there is this small point of me not having the money for that."

He smiled. "Why don't you let me take care of that last bit, and go ahead and get a license?"

After I procured my license he told me about the gun shop he owned in Coimbatore, and presented me a wonderful weapon, a .423 Mauser - A grade. For those who think about what those numbers mean, it's the bore of the pipe that releases the bullet, and in this case, it meant 0.423 inches or approximately 10.75 mm. The Mauser was his favourite weapon and he told me that he had shot more than a hundred panthers with it. It turned out to be the best gun I have ever owned as well. It gave me the confidence to go to the jungle and always know that I was prepared to face anything. While a lot of people know that he gifted me his .423 Mauser, the weapon that I was synonymous with, they don't know the rest of the story. I went to Bangalore, thrilled to bits, and heard a week later that he was coming to Bangalore. He came home and gifted me a big box of cartridges—and a bill! Although a cartridge cost 1.50 rupees in those days, he had charged twice that amount. I didn't want to make a scene, as I was most grateful for the rifle, so I coughed up a hefty amount and got a mouthful from my dad who paid for it!

With the 423 Mauser - at Arsikere

I think I reminded Hugh of what he was like many years ago—adventurous and a go-getter—and he showered me with considerable attention, patience, and of course, access to his ranch. However, his behaviour could be erratic at times, and sometimes I would find myself in a spot.

Towards the last years that he was in India, he was living with an Indian lady who was about twenty-five years younger than him and, as with such arrangements, the age difference often caused insecurities for the older individual. Once he invited me over as he had to drop off one his cars to Coimbatore for repairs. We were to drive separately and then come back in one. I reached in the evening and knowing that I didn't have much time to do my shooting, picked up my gun and wandered off. Unfortunately, it started raining and I rushed back, soaking wet. I hadn't

154

brought a change of clothes, so I dried myself and sat down for dinner without a shirt on. I was talking to the lady, when he walked in and he blew his top!

"Is this how you dress in front of a lady?" he thundered at me, although his eyes were on her. Neither she nor I were guilty of anything that would have crossed his mind, but I knew better than to defend myself for it would have only made things worse. So, I politely apologised and borrowed a tattered shirt that probably belonged to one of the servants!

The lady who was staying with him had a son. Hughie was so fond of that boy that he legally adopted him, something that was not really done in those days because he was not married to her. They all left for England and he died there. The lady and the boy, Johnny, were not interested in coming back and eventually his empire was just usurped by some people who managed get most of the land transferred to their names and later sold it. It passed hands, and when I visited the place in 2013, it was called Tiger Farm, a dilapidated building with just a few acres around it.

Hughie had a house in Frazer Town and visited Bangalore often. He was therefore a frequent visitor at our home. He also had houses in Karachi and England, and of course Coimbatore, sixty miles away from Mudiyanoor. He also happened to be the financial advisor to the Maharaja of Jodhpur, and an ace metallurgist, travelling all over India offering his services to industries. He always came up with innovative business ideas and there was never a shortfall of financial support. For example, he was the first one to come up with the idea of making toothpowder with some jungle fruit. He also had this idea of making matches with the stalks of the elephant grass that BR hills were covered with, rather than cutting down trees.

If Hailstone was around I usually went alone but when he wasn't, I had the entire place to myself and took many of my friends there. The usual quartet that landed up at Hailstone's place was Sunny, Merwan, Willie, and myself. Sunny provided the entertainment, Merwan the food (and quite a bit of the expenses), I provided the gun and the excitement of shikar while Willie was the glue that held this motley crew together. At sunset, I would leave the group and go with my Sholaga tracker to sit up in a machan, while the others would stay at the ranch. This was an arrangement that was acceptable to everyone as in those days Mudiyanoor was infested with elephants, and despite the gun I carried, it was quite dangerous to walk about after sundown. If I managed to shoot something by 8:00 or 9:00 p.m., I would just cover it with my jacket and walk back with just my two-cell torch for company. My guide would have gone home or would stay at Hailstone's place. No one wandered the jungles in those days, so if something had happened to me, no one could find me, certainly not my friends who had no idea in which direction I had headed out. And as for my guide, if he was sober he would only come after the sun had risen in the sky. Unlike my dad who would sit the entire night atop a machan, I could never inculcate the virtue to sit still, that too way up in a tree, unless some dire circumstance forced me to. So, I would do my Cinderella impression and be back home before midnight. I must say that rather than sitting on a machan all night, I prefer sitting on the ground, and my dad got the reason spot on—I would always fall asleep while waiting!

Varghese was hired as Hailstone's driver but was one of those people who did far more than his designated role. Always eager to try new things, and full of enthusiasm, he was a total failure at everything he attempted, and we tried to discourage him from a lot of "super ideas" that often plagued his mind. He believed he was inherently brave and would have the occasional bouts of courage, usually brought on by imbibing an eye-popping amount of brandy in a relatively short time. One on such occasion, and this was before I knew him well, he came up to me and asked me for my shotgun. Usually I never give my gun to anyone, but for some reason I complied, ensuring that I had removed the shells. He sat on the verandah at my feet and proceeded to scout the darkness through the sights, killing dozens of ferocious beasts that roamed the grounds. By then a hot bath was prepared and I left him unattended. Right in the middle of my bath came the unmistakable sound of my gun going off. I grabbed a towel and burst out, fearing the worst. It was a small towel and I had to run quite a bit, so when I arrived at the scene I felt a mix of relief and embarrassment. True, I was not aptly covered, but there was Varghese, unharmed but looking distraught.

"*Aiyyo, Saare, Aiyyo.*" (Oh no! Sir! Oh no!)

Apparently, he had loaded my gun, taken my torch and wandered out into the vegetation just beyond his house. The torch beam picked up a pair of eyes, and he instinctively aimed and fired at a tiger. He bagged his first cat—which unfortunately turned out to be his own pet!

Varghese by my side, at Moyar Valley Ranch

Let me tell you of a man-eater I shot in the BR hills. This was sometime in the late fifties, after Ralph Morris had gone back to England. A tiger started killing coolies and there was absolute mayhem in the coffee estates. The workers refused to work, and before the situation got any worse, the management had asked the forest department to get rid of the man-eater. The man-eater had a nasty reputation for being absolutely fearless and would attack people even during the middle of the day. Naturally, none of the forest officers were particularly keen to go on this suicidal mission. Luckily I was a licensed hunter with a permit, and they figured if they could get me to kill the beast, they would get two birds with one stone. Of course, I was not told the full story, especially about the man-eater's lack of fear, and a letter landed up at my house, specifically asking if I would be interested to shoot a troublesome tiger. I was delighted and made plans immediately.

With a prayer of thanks on my lips, I started off on my Norton motorcycle in the afternoon on a Friday, feigning some sort of illness at work. There are some trips when even the most un-superstitious shikari knows that something will go wrong, and this was one of them. I had a puncture even before I left Bangalore city, and nearly had an accident outside Mysore where I skidded on some gravel, while trying to avoid an oncoming vehicle. I wasn't hurt, but the bike suffered a dent, and the corned beef sandwiches in my food packet decorated the highway. I stopped at the Dimbum check post for tea and refreshments and that's when I pieced together that I was actually called to kill a man-eater. A familiar rush of adrenalin pumped through my veins as I kick-started my motorcycle. I was soon on flat terrain and zipped through the muddy road, skillfully navigating the pot holes. To make matters worse, it began to rain. Torrents from the sky lashed down and I was looking for a place to stop and let the deluge die down. I turned a blind corner and nearly crashed into a herd of bison that were standing bang in the middle of the road. I was a few feet away when I realised their presence, and as I tried to avoid them, my bike skidded for the second time that day. I yelled instinctively and as I fell off the bike, I felt a shooting pain in my shoulder. The headlight broke and the bike careened off to some distance away. After a few seconds of silence, pandemonium broke loose as the herd bellowed and scattered in all directions. Bison are probably the last animals one needs to worry about in the jungles, but here was a herd of twenty or so in pitch darkness roaring blue murder and playing the bovine version of Russian roulette. They were just trying to get away and protect their young, but it certainly was not a very pleasant experience. After a while the stampede subsided and apart from the occasional snort of derision, peace reigned again. The rain had subsided, and I tried to find my bearings. My bike seemed to be ok, and apart from the broken light, things didn't look too bad. I started my bike and attempted the relatively easy task of driving a bike with no lights on a forest road without illumination of any sort, in an area that certainly had a man-eating tiger lurking around. I couldn't drive fast because I couldn't see more than a few feet ahead, yet I certainly did not want to be riding at a pace easy enough to interest the man-eater.

Luckily, I reached my first destination, a Sholaga settlement, where I called for Resha, my shikari guide. With his help, I immediately set out to find baits to tie up, but the nearest owner of a cattle *patti* (pen) was extremely unhelpful for he refused to sell any of his buffaloes. I informed him that I was buying bait to kill the man-eater, which cheered him up, but he still wouldn't sell me bait. Vexed, I decided to wander about a bit, hoping to meet people who might give me clues about the man- eater. I met a group of coolies who were waiting for a vehicle to take them somewhere. I was informed that this was the same road where the tiger had carried away his last victim. With that bit of encouraging information, I walked on. I had walked for about two miles and had started a low descent down a ghat road when I saw the tiger. It was sitting on a parapet on its haunches and we were both equally shocked to see one another. I slowly raised my rifle and the tiger somehow sensed that I wasn't his typical victim, for it jumped off. I knew that this was the heavens throwing me a line, and I didn't want to lose the opportunity. I ran across the road and jumped off the parapet, not even checking how high from the ground I was. It was such a stupid thing to do, for I landed onto a lantana bush, and even through the drop wasn't much, I made a very clumsy attempt with a lot of noise and the man-eater had me completely at his mercy. In those days I had complete faith in myself and my .423 rifle even though it had fallen down during my accident earlier. As I got my bearings I looked up and there was the tiger some distance away, looking at me with some sort of bewilderment. In a trice, it had flattened itself to the ground, ready to spring. Narrating all this has taken time, but when it happened, it was in a matter of seconds. I pulled the trigger and the bullet went past its gaping mouth. I stepped aside to escape from its final charge and fired another shot at almost point-blank range. I started to shake violently and followed that with a severe case of retching. I often had this reaction after close shaves in the jungles; it was perhaps nature's way to bring down the adrenalin levels in my body. Resha soon appeared on the screen and erupted in joy. This was one adventure that ended almost as soon it began, not that I minded!

Resha was my tracker and apart from paying him handsomely for his services, I also taught him to shoot jungle fowl and spur fowl to provide for his family. There was no agricultural work in those parts, and money was hard to come by. A lot of the locals relied on working for shikaris like me to help with their livelihood. The Sholagas are simple folk, and don't have any weapons such as bows and arrows like the Chenchus or the Hakki Pikkis. They are excellent trackers and meat is obtained through ingenious ways of trapping small mammals and birds. They grow up with the knowledge of what produce from the jungle is useful to them, and sometimes their singlemindedness about things like that would surprise me. Occasionally they would ask me to stick my hand into a small hole in a tree as we were walking. Although I trusted them, I certainly did not want to put my hands into an orifice in case there was a tiny chance that they would be wrong. They would laugh at my discomfort and then reach into the cavity and pull out a small honeycomb, which they would then proceed to share with me. A few bees would sting, but they would just slap them away, more or less impervious to the stings. More often than not, the average Sholaga will stand by your side and face whatever danger you're facing, elephants being an exception, of course.

Contrary to popular belief, I did not always have an agenda to shoot. Sometimes a walk with my trackers would end up with some amazing discoveries. Once, Resha and I came across a bull bison and a huge male tiger lying dead practically next to each other. We heard from one of the settlements that the fight had gone on for the entire night. Grievous wounds had been inflicted on both and I was curious to know why neither adversary had run away. Tigers were not very common up in the grassy parts in those days, so perhaps it was a new experience for both to see their opponent. I started using Resha's services in the heavy jungles where the hills would start, but over time, he became my default tracker for all over the BR Hills.

Resha was not my only tracker and guide, there were others, like Jeddia, son of Doddathoddy Madda. I never met the father, but I've heard my dad talking about him. He was also a tracker for Randolph Morris. Jeddia, incidentally, had the distinction of working for both Ralph Morris and me. He was a Sholaga tracker and lived near Mudiyanoor village. Although I knew him before I met Hughie Hailstone, I talked about his skills to him and he was often called upon whenever Hailstone had guests who were keen on hunting. Although he continued to work for Hughie, whenever I landed up he would excuse himself from all other commitments, devoting his time exclusively to me. Although he's not mentioned by name, his photograph appears in one of my dad's books *Man-eaters and Jungle Killers* captioned "the extent of a tiger's meal".

Sholagas are amongst the bravest trackers I have ever had the privilege of using. Whenever we were tracking dangerous game, they would walk in front, and when the going got difficult, they would literally crawl and look for tracks. Their diet mostly consisted of wild mushrooms, honey, and bamboo shoots, and so the occasional deer or pig when shot by me would be most appreciated. However, their meat supplement was not entirely dependent on shikaris like me. They were masters in creating snares to catch smaller animals like jungle fowl, partridges, hare, and even mouse deer, if they were lucky. The Sholagas are often small built, full of energy, can walk for miles through thick jungles without stopping, and are always sure of the tracks they came across.

As I mentioned earlier, I knew Jeddia before I became friends with Hughie and a frequent visitor at Moyar Valley Ranch. So, in the early days, I had no choice but to spend the night in Jeddia's hut when I reached Mudiyanoor. Like many Sholagas, he would often wash his hair with buffalo milk and leave it to dry, and it would stink to high heaven. Now imagine that in a thatched hut that had no windows or any sort of ventilation and where the only entrance was a two feet by two feet opening one had to crawl through. There would be no candles or any form of light. I would lie on the mud floor, and have insects climb all over me at night. I remember once I had reached late in the evening, and when I woke up the next day I realised that the entire village had contracted chicken pox! It did not cross Jeddia's mind to inform me about something like that. Sure enough, I started to itch by the time I reached home a few days later. It just goes to show how these people don't fuss about something like a disease—if you got it, you either got better or you died. They didn't associate any sort of stigma or abhor diseases like we do. I often thought about sleeping in the open, but this was elephant country and my tired and aching body would shut down my olfactory senses when I subjected myself to Jeddia's five-star treatment. Our roles and rituals were perfunctory. He would wake me up an hour before dawn, a notable feat considering he did not have a watch or alarm of any sort. He must have been in his 60s and I in my mid-20s, but he was a tough old codger. Nothing ever bothered him and he had endless energy when we were out in the jungle.

Jeddia

Sometimes we would walk to a lake that was situated between Hailstone's property and Mudiyanoor village and sit on the banks of the lake at a slightly elevated position where we could watch the boars coming back after their nightly raid into the cultivated fields. A must-stop spot for them was the lake, to quench their thirst and eat the bulbs of the water hyacinths. The sky would be filled with the early streaks of light in the horizon as we circumvented a portion of the lake and reach a point where I could shoot the boar. Based on where they fell, I would either stay on the banks or wade into the freezing water, switch on the light, pick out the animal and knock it over, while the rest would flee. There has been more than one occasion when I did not notice an elephant in the water and the gun shot woke him up. He would splash his way through the water, hurrying away into the undergrowth, disgruntled at being interrupted.

After I shot the pig, Jeddia would get help to take the meat back to his village. For me it was adventure, but for the village, it meant food for an entire week, so our little caper was equally satisfying to both of us in different ways. Talamalai and Talavadi have a lot of marshes and lakes with thick vegetation all around and that in turn meant that this was perfect bison and elephant country. The Sholagas are also amongst the most honest of all village folk, very simple and very loyal. Polygamy was quite common though, and Jeddia had his brood. Despite his age, he ran a tight ship, with designated tasks for each member of the household. There was some arrangement where each wife did some chores and I think the shift changed weekly! Without any sort of education, they managed to keep the system going. They were not just adept at this system but at everything they did, and despite their poverty were always happy and good natured. Now all that has changed and they have been spoilt by people from cities like Coimbatore and Bangalore.

Let me narrate an incident with Jeddia and a narrow escape I had. I was out hunting late one afternoon on the Talamalai Road when we came across a party with some bullock carts. It was a marriage party returning after the function, about twenty of them, and they were relieved to see me. They explained how they had been chased by a bull elephant and had multiple casualties. It had injured an old man who was slow to run and then attacked one of the bullocks as well. The other bullock has run off into the jungle, and they were waiting for some miracle to happen, knowing fully well that the creature could return. I knew this area well, and Jeddia agreed that the rogue would likely be at a certain waterhole about two miles away from where we met the party. So, I took Jeddia and we proceeded towards the spot. In those days, we used to get three kinds of bullets—soft nosed, split nosed, and hard-nosed or solid bullets. Most people shot deer, boar, panthers and tigers, depending on the risk you wanted to face, with soft-nosed bullets. Elephant shooting was strictly prohibited and hence the shops in Bangalore rarely stocked solid bullets. So naturally, I too did not have any at that time. But I was young back then, adventurous and cocky, so I didn't think twice about the risk I was taking, stalking the elephant. Jeddia went ahead and returned shortly, confirming that the pachyderm was at the waterhole just as we had predicted. The easiest path to the spot led through a game path, and even though there was a greater risk reaching directly, I preferred that to the alternative where I would stalk it through the tall grass and have it smell me and have me at its mercy, much before I saw it. Unfortunately, things didn't go as planned and though we were walking on the trail, we saw it almost as soon as it sensed our presence. Like a sprinter who braces himself for the starting pistol to go off, it held its head high and curled in his trunk between its tusks. I could see its cruel eyes staring in rage. As if the mayhem it had caused was not enough, the bull trumpeted and charged like an express train, screaming with hatred and covering ground fast, an exhibition of unyielding power. I knew that I stood absolutely no chance of stopping it if I was looking at a frontal head shot with a soft-nosed bullet, so I did what I had to do. It was not my proudest moment, but I aimed at its left knee and fired. Sure enough, it broke the momentum as its left front leg gave away. It was a horrific sight as the elephant nearly somersaulted because of the speed at which it was running, and the bull stumbled to a standstill amidst a huge cloud of dust, not too far from where I was standing. Ensuring that I stayed away from the trunk, I walked alongside and behind it. The pachyderm was screaming with pain and anger, clearly dazed and confused, and didn't really see me. The jungle was filled with its cries as I, at almost point-blank range, put a bullet into its temple. It wasn't enough as it still kept moving, and I fired another shot into the shivering body and brought an end to its suffering. All this was too much and I had a severe case of retching, something my dad used to experience as well. As I sat down I looked for Jeddia, but I could not see him. I was wondering what had happened when there was a shout. It was my faithful tracker and he was up a tree! "*Buddhivantha, Buddhivantha*" (Genius, Genius) he shouted, and I afforded myself a watery smile.

The name stuck and I became the "Buddhi" hunter of BR Hills for a while, and certainly for Jeddia, as he called me that for the rest of his life, switching over from "*Devare*". That day, a lot of people from nearby villages came to see the dead rogue including my friend Hailstone, who was very proud that it was his rifle that had killed it. I have been chased by tigers, panthers, bears, and wild boar, but being chased by an elephant is the scariest, given the sheer size of the adversary, and this episode I must say was probably one of the most terrifying I have had in my entire life. In fact, since that day, I've always believed I would be killed by an elephant during one of my escapades in the jungles.

Maaka was another tracker I used often. He was a Sholaga who was originally from Bailur and had settled down in Mudiyanoor. Now, Bailur had a forest bungalow atop a small hill and offered a lush verdant view from the top. If one acquired a hunting license, the accommodation at this bungalow was a given, and I spent many nights in this picturesque dwelling. This is on the opposite side of the BR Hills and used to be one of my favourite haunts. The road from Lokkanhalli leads to Bailur and eventually takes you to Dimbum and then Coimbatore. In those days the entire area was covered with elephant grass that grew about six feet in height, and that dictated the kind of animals that lived there. Carnivores were rarely seen but the place is etched in memory for the massive herds of bison that used roam in those parts. On many occasions, I have seen bison herds of more than two hundred, a sight unimaginable nowadays. However, a double blow—of rinderpest and the introduction of lantana—obliterated their population and the entire topography of that area changed. Not only were there large herds, but this area also produced the largest bison I have seen. Perhaps it was the fact that it was secluded, perhaps it was the vegetation and the cover the grass provided, but the bison grew to mammoth proportions and I did shoot a few, the horns of the largest measuring seventy inches tip to tip (around the outer curves). While they made good trophies, there wasn't any particular skill or adrenalin rush when you shot one. It was just like shooting a cow. Also, the Sholagas don't eat beef, so that's about a thousand kg of meat just going waste and I didn't want that.

Slowly the elephant grass in these parts got replaced by lantana. While both types of vegetation sound difficult to navigate, one could still walk through the grass, but with lantana it was impossible to navigate, for you would get tangled in it. Lantana was introduced in India in the early 1800s, and slowly found its way all the way to south India. It is truly a scourge for none of the herbivores will eat it; cutting or burning it only seems to make it grow back even faster, and unlike many forest plants, it is of absolutely no use to either man or animal. It was always prevalent, especially on the right side, while driving to BR Hills, but towards the late 1950s, its growth proliferated and soon large grasslands of the BR Hills were overrun with the weed, partly due to the large amount of bamboo that was extracted from these parts.

Getting back to Maaka. I was visiting these parts on the trail of a man-killing tigress. Another shikari from Bangalore, by the name of Gardner, was also in the same area. He had sat over a kill and had fired at the feline, wounding it, while my night of vigil resulted in nothing. Gardner was severely ill by daybreak, having spent the entire night on the machan as he did not want to face a wounded tiger in the dark. Pneumonia was suspected and he begged me to finish the job he had started. Under normal circumstances, I would have refused, for I firmly believed that it was his responsibility. However, looking at his condition, I changed my mind. I left him at the bungalow where we were staying together. Enlisting Maaka's services, I decided to trace the path of the big cat. It was mid-morning by the time we reached the machan. In no time at all the Sholaga picked up the blood trail. From the huge bouts of blood, it was evident that the soft-nosed bullet had hit a major organ and that encouraged me. Surely, it wouldn't have gone very far. After another fifteen minutes of crawling on our hands and feet, we reached a small clearing. The closest bushes were some distance away and I thought this was a good place to catch our breath. Both he and I were fairly confident that the feline had moved away, and I stood with my rifle half-raised while Maaka walked towards my left to relieve himself. He had hardly gone twenty yards when a horrible all too familiar roar was heard and in a flash the tigress had launched itself through the air and latched on to Maaka. We had underestimated the animal—instead of crossing the clearing it had almost doubled back and lay waiting for us to clear it, planning to attack us from the rear. Maaka had practically walked into the jaws of the beast and it had leapt in the air to kill him. Considering his skill, it's hard to think that he had not realised what the tigress was up to, but this cat was fiendishly clever. Instinctively, he side-stepped the charge so it was not able to strike or grab his neck, but its claws raked his body and that caused Maaka to fall over with the tigress on top of him. It wasn't a large animal, and was rolling about the ground with Maaka pinned underneath. All the while he was screaming at me to shoot it, but I could not bring myself to do it for fear of shooting him. I tried to get a better shot and moved to a different angle, but they were locked together, the big cat unable to bite him as he had thrust his little axe in front of its mouth. I screamed and shouted to distract the tigress, hoping that it would turn away and provide me the window of opportunity I needed. In a split second it twisted double and leaped off Maaka—a spectacular acrobatic effort—and was upon me. I didn't have time to aim, I shot it with my rifle almost from the hip, a ridiculous shot considering the weapon I had, but the bullet entered its neck while it was in mid-air and stopped it in its tracks. It might have died with that shot, but I followed it up with another one, just in case. I ran towards Maaka who lay in a pool of blood. I left my rifle there on the ground and carried him on my shoulder to the village. It was a long way and, despite my strength, carrying a dead weight with blood streaming all over my body in the sweltering heat was an excruciating journey. I had to get him to the hospital, there was no other choice. We reached the village and I then drove him to Satyamangalam, forty miles away where he spent more than four months, recovering. I paid for his treatment; it was the least I could do for saving my life. His recovery was partial, he had damaged one of his legs, giving him a permanent limp and that practically ended his livelihood as a tracker. The mutilation of his forearm was the most grotesque, for it resulted in an actual hole in his arm, through which one could pass two fingers. It was not painful for him, after it healed, but it never ceased to amaze anyone who saw that injury.

Another incident at Mudiyanoor, which involved a tiger, was not as scary, as there were two tigers involved and one was made of wood! This was during my earlier trips to these parts, long before I knew Hailstone. I had shot a tiger that that was declared to be a nuisance by the Forest Department as it was attacking both people and cattle in that area. As luck would have it, the cowherds had been working for a rich landlord and his joy knew no bounds when I ended the life of the feline. So, unlike the usual scenario where I would get a couple of helpers from the village to skin the animal, this was a lavish celebration. They took me around the village with drums, trumpets, and a lot of fanfare. Then they took me to witness a strange sight—a wooden tiger that was kept under a tree. I asked them about its history or even the significance, but they didn't know much. All they knew was that they had been worshipping it for years and would perform a pooja every time a tiger's life was taken. The ceremony was a way of asking for forgiveness and to ensure that they were spared retribution from the gods, a tradition that had been handed down from generations. For years I wondered about the origins of that wooden tiger and then in 2008, I was given a book by one of my friends titled *Call of the Tiger*, written by Col. A.E. Powell. He talks about his exploits in these parts and mentions seeing the same wooden tiger, dating the tiger to a hundred years before him. I used to think that I was the first white man to have seen it, but here was Powell shattering my illusions. Powell mentions that an English captain had frequented those parts to hunt tigers and rewarded the locals by giving them money to make a wooden tiger in his memory, dating it back at least two hundred years. The tiger still stands today, although it is now placed inside a temple in the village.

The other person worthy of mentioning was my regular skinner, Muthu. Muthu was not a Sholaga like the others, but a Tamilian who had moved there. He therefore did not have the jungle skills like tracking, but was a master skinner. He worked in tandem with Maaka and his show started after an animal was shot. All the tricks my taxidermist Tocher taught me, such as skinning and curing pelts, I taught Muthu, and soon his skills were in great demand in Mudiyanoor as the resident Sholagas did not have this particular talent. However, he was killed by an elephant on the pathway between Moyar Valley Ranch and the lake nearby. Maaka, too, had a very short life, although I don't recollect how he passed away.

Instructing Maaka and Muthu

Now, let me tell about another reason why Mudiyanoor was one of my favourite areas to frequent. I'm a hot-blooded male and although I never had any dearth of attention from women while in Bangalore, I was always on the lookout for some fun when I went to the jungles. Those days, it was impossible to find such arrangements in villages that bordered the forests, Mudiyanoor being perhaps the only exception.

In the late fifties, I used to visit the village frequently with my Irish partner, Captain Keeler. He was in charge of getting business while my responsibility was taking the clients on shikar. The guests would be accommodated at Moyar Valley Ranch and I would take them hunting around Mudiyanoor, along with my tracker. I knew people in the Forest Department and they helped me acquire hunting licenses, and everything seemed to be going well. Although we had a good start, our partnership began to show signs of breaking.

Mudiyanoor village was for some reason the beacon of the Christian conversion movement in that area. In return for converting to Christianity, the locals, especially a lot of Sholagas, were given clothes, food and, of course, basic education, and who in their right senses could refuse that? So, while the older generation stuck to the beliefs they grew up with, the younger ones were easier to tempt into conversion. At that time, the catechist was a chap by the name of George Fernandes, whose influence I heavily milked, to get access to live baits for my hunting. He was quite well known in these parts and quite powerful because he held the purse strings of the conversion kitty, and I used his sway over the villagers to get what I needed to make my hunting safaris a success.

International hunters – with Captain Keeler

Although I did not realise it at first, when I took my clients out hunting, Keeler would have fun with the women in the village, and to my horror, I later discovered that the supplier of women to Keeler was none other than Fernandes! Flesh could be traded in return for all sorts of material wealth, and Fernandes knew that all too well.

Keeler was much older than me, but his penchant for women started becoming a problem. He decided to get smart and cut out the middleman, Fernandes, to save money. Trust a non-Tamil speaking, crooked, miserly Irishman to pull off a stunt like that. I won't get into the details, but there were complaints about Keeler's behaviour and if it wasn't for my intervention, Keeler would have got into serious trouble. I had to spend quite a bit of money to quieten the whole thing down. Anyway, Keeler and I parted ways and George Fernandes moved to another village, but the seed had been sown in my head and I spent many nights with different women from Mudiyanoor. There were no condoms in those days and heaven knows the repercussions of my actions.

Now let me tell you about the last time I shot anything in this place. It must have been in 1969 or so. I invited myself to Moyar Valley Ranch, and it was late in the evening and I was lying in my cot on the verandah. My mind was beginning to wander, and I began to think of many of the adventures I had when I was young. It was the first day of my week-long trip and I couldn't help feeling excited, but there was a lot of nostalgia, perhaps a premonition of sorts that I quickly brushed that aside. It was soon after the April showers, and the mayflower trees had changed from a dull green to a bright red. The damp jungle smelled sweet of jasmine and eucalyptus that grew in the estate. Hugh was sitting in his favourite chair next to me and we were having a smoke when suddenly there was an anguished cry from one of the estate dogs outside. We both looked at each other and exclaimed "Panther". I rushed into my room and picked up my .423 Mauser on which a lighting arrangement was always fitted. I ran out of the front door and reached the row of out-houses from where I believed I had heard the cry. I switched on my torch and swung it around. I saw a pair of yellow-green eyes reflect in my light and I recognised the unmistakable form of a panther. It didn't seem particularly disturbed as it slowly began to drag the dog away. I took a quick shot at its shoulder blades (a shot that has paid me dividends in my days of shikar). A second later, I heard a roar and the sound of the panther crashing through the coffee bushes. I knew that I had hit it, although the bullet had missed its intended mark. I'd done this before, so I decided to wait till morning, for stalking a wounded panther in the darkness is as good as suicide, a painful one at that. Considering that I shot him from quite close, there was a good chance that he would be dead the next morning. Or the shot would have caused enough damage to cause profuse bleeding and leave it too weak to attack me. However, I knew of exceptions, like the time in Ramnagaram where a panther with its bottom jaw blown off, charged me, full of life, and almost got the better of the duel.

On my way back to the bungalow, I heard the coolies mumbling and I went across to them and gave them the details of what had happened. I gave specific instructions that not a soul was to go near the spot till I gave the orders. I informed Hughie that I would take Kuppa, an ace tracker, at dawn, to go and finish the job. Despite all the hunting that he has done, Hughie's eyes gleamed when he heard about my next day's plan. Maaka was no more, but I was confident that Kuppa was as good as his predecessor.

I had a restless night, tossing and turning, as all shikaris do when they have a wounded animal that has to be followed up and brought down. I'm yet to meet an honest shikari who can say that he isn't edgy while following a wounded panther or tiger, a task no young shikari should underestimate. While following panthers in thick shrub (which should be done only by experienced shikaris) I recommend a 12-gauge shot gun with SG in both barrels. Also, an unswerving man should walk behind you with a reliable rifle in case the wounded animal is seen at a distance.

I was awakened at the crack of dawn by my faithful Kuppa. I checked my ammunition, loaded the guns and took extra ammunition just in case. Lastly, I said a small prayer. The sky was beginning to shed the covers of darkness as I left the bungalow with Hughie's best wishes. We soon came upon a blood trail, which at first led in a semi-circle. Following the trail was not easy as the coffee bushes were chest high and it would be impossible to spot the panther unless we were on all fours. So the two of us got down on our knees and moved infinitely slowly, ensuring that we were absolutely silent. The first rays of the sun picked out small pools of clotted blood and I guessed that the panther had been hit in the lungs. It had lain down every now and then, showing that the injury was serious. The trail led for about half a mile and entered the forest skirting the plantation. It had taken us more than an hour or so as we tracked slowly and very carefully. We entered the forest and inched forward for about two hundred yards, and then the blood trail stopped. We motioned to each other that it had perhaps gone another way and we needed to rethink our strategy. The logical explanation didn't enter either of our minds and we kept scouring the ground. I could see Kuppa about ten yards away, eye peering into the undergrowth. In a split second, even before I could collect my wits, there was a half roar and cough, a sound that petrified me. I saw a flash of ochre at bullet speed flying at Kuppa from a small tree between us. A horrific sight greeted me—Kuppa and the panther were rolling on the ground, and clearly the feline had an upper hand, having buried its teeth in Kuppa's shoulder. I could see it repeatedly clawing him with both its fore and hind legs. I could see that Kuppa was striking the panther with his sickle, but it seemed to have no effect on the animal. I raised my gun but could not shoot as each SG cartridge has nine slugs and I was almost certain to hit Kuppa. It was déjà vu as I had had a similar experience with Maaka. The panther left Kuppa and turned its hate filled eyes towards me. I could see blood all over the animal, some of it from its injury, but most of it was Kuppa's. I saw nothing but teeth and claws as the panther made it final charge with its tail ridiculously up in the air. My gun spoke first—with a deafening roar as my left barrel spat fire. It tumbled over and landed near my feet and I gave it the second barrel in the ear as it lay twitching but that was unnecessary. I could see it quiver, its legs kicking spasmodically. I controlled my urge to throw up as I turned towards Kuppa, and a very sickening sight greeted me. He was badly mauled, his chest had been torn open, and his lungs were probably punctured. He tried to get up, but I asked him to lie still, and that I would return with help. I ran back to the bungalow and got a few men to carry Kuppa. But as we reached the spot we realised that it was too late. He was already dead, his eyes still open, looking at his nemesis who lay a few yards away. Tears came to my eyes as I was extremely fond of Kuppa. He was so young! I blamed myself for his death, but I knew that Kuppa would not hold it against me, for wherever he is, he would know I did the best I could. I closed his eyes and promised him that I would see him again and talk about all our shikari experiences and especially about this day. That incident with the gallant little panther, who incidentally was only 5' 8", changed me forever.

Chapter Seven

My Haunts – Part 2

ALONG THE EASTERN AND WESTERN COASTS OF INDIA, also called the Coramandel and Malabar coasts respectively, run a range of mountains, parallel to the coast line. They are called the Eastern and Western Ghats respectively and for most people in Bangalore, the Nilgiris, a locale in the Western Ghats, was a favourite destination. The verdant Nilgiris can be envisaged to be a plateau bounded in the north by Mysore, in the north-west, west, and south by Malabar, and in the south-east, east, and north-east by the district of Coimbatore. On the northern side, the Pykara river tumbles through wooded ravines and continues as the Moyar river, running along the base of the Nilgiris, creating the famous Mysore Ditch.

If one were to travel from Bangalore, along the Mysore highway, there are two routes to Ooty, the first through Gudalur town, and the second through Kalhatty, and the decision has to be taken at a spot called Theppekadu inside the Mudumalai forest. The Kalhatty route played a more frequent part in my exploits, for my dad owned land on this road, and he and I have had many adventures in those parts. We would take a bus to Ooty, spend the day there and walk down to our hut located in Mavanhalla, a tiny hamlet at the base of the ghat. Eight miles from Ooty, and before Mavanhalla is the Kalhatty bungalow in a place called Segur. Let me tell you of a strange incident that happened there.

Jeffrey Davis, a British chap in the army, was stationed at Segur in the 1930s and led a poor social life while all his friends enjoyed the excesses that Ooty provided. So, he would ride his horse to Ooty on a Friday for a booze up and come back after the weekend. On one such journey back, it started to rain, and visibility was so poor that he decided to stop at the Kalhatty bungalow for the night. In the middle of the night he woke up and heard noises on the verandah of the bungalow. He was in a state of drunken stupor, and in near total darkness, he thought that there was a bear at the front door, not an unfair assumption in those days. He quickly ran back for his shotgun, and taking aim, let the old bruin have it, peppering the walls of the bungalow in the process.

"Aiyyo!" came the frightful scream.

Unfortunately, it wasn't a bruin but the caretaker of the bungalow, who had covered himself with a dark *kambli* (blanket) to protect himself from the biting cold. Davis' aim was abysmal, and the weapon's discharge hit the poor watchman but did not kill him outright. His screams seemed very bear-like to Davis, who, eager to the task, reloaded and finished the being at almost point-blank range. It was the next morning when his actions were discovered and he was charged with murder, but the story goes that he although he did not go to jail for the murder, he was court-martialled.

Decades later, my Dad and I used to walk down the Segur Ghat Road through the night, armed with nothing more than a two-cell torch. There were hardly any vehicles on this road and on more than a dozen occasions, I have seen tigers walking past. Anyway, we were on one these walks, and it started to rain so heavily that our torches proved to be ineffective. Rather than taking the risk of running into an elephant, we sprinted to the Kalhatty bungalow, and as it was locked, we decided to stay on the verandah till the rain eased up. We were drenched, and there was no way we could start a fire, so we removed our jackets and lay down in a spot away from the wind. We were both quite tired and fell asleep almost immediately. At about two in the morning, it got bitterly cold, and hearing a creaking sound, I woke up. I could see that my dad was already awake, and he was trying to listen carefully to the sound; there it was, the unmistakable sound of an ungreased pulley at the well. The hair at the back of my neck stood up; I am not easily scared, but this was spooky. There was no way that some villager would be drawing water at that time of the night, so the only other explanation seemed to be something I did not believe in. My dad on the other hand seemed to welcome the idea of meeting a ghost and shouted out asking who was there. Immediately, the noise stopped. So, we took our torches and walked towards the well, but when we reached the spot there was no one there. The rope didn't seem like it had been moved, so we figured that it was perhaps collective hallucination and we walked back to the bungalow. No sooner did we reach there, than the noise began again and this time we were fully awake. There was no way that it could have been our imagination. We went to the well again to check but there was nothing. The next time it started, we just ignored it and went back to sleep!

Four miles from the Kalhatty bungalow is Segur and another six miles takes you to the tiny hamlet of Masinagudi. The road from Ooty travels downhill till it reaches Theppekadu, a distance of twenty-two miles from Ooty. My dad had three plots of land in this area: One in Ooty, very close to where the Shinkows restaurant stands today; one in Mavanhalla along the main Ooty road; and the third at Segur, at a place called Chadapatti. The last one was the grass hut mentioned in his story "What the thunderstorm brought", the one he took his editor Malcolm Barnes to, and is the same shack mentioned by ERC Davidar in his books. In fact, there is an interesting story about the property. Reggie Davidar, Mark Davidar's father, was working at the law firm King & Partridge at Ooty, when he was requested by my dad to scout for land at the foothills, as this area was famous for game. Davidar was smart and managed to secure the land that became Chital Walk and famous for Mark Davidar's elephants, by paying nine thousand rupees for nine acres, while my dad only managed to secure the adjacent property, which unfortunately did not have a stream running through it. I think my Dad believed that Davidar had cheated him, as it was he who had discovered the property and entrusted Davidar with the job of buying it, but I think it was just a case of sour grapes! Behind the Mavanhalla property is "Wild Heritage" that belonged to Captain Jonklass, a Dutchman and is mentioned in my dad's book. This property was later sold to a chap in the Air Force by the name of Mendekar. It used to have thatched huts but was very well maintained and run like a proper resort; a regular haunt for my friends and me to spend the weekend. It was a bit expensive but ahead of its time for the rooms even had refrigerators filled with food and drink, and my most vivid memory is of tinned meat, butter, and cheese to accompany the bonfire and barbecues! The shikari guides and licenses would be arranged by the resort, and we would go for our hunting trips. In the evenings, the occupants of these huts would get together and talk about their exploits around a bonfire and a grand barbecue, memorable times indeed! Mendekar sold the property to the Church in 1971. What was then a row of thatched huts is now called "Quiet Corner", made of bricks and concrete, and the old-world charm has disappeared. I sold the three acres of land that belonged to Dad in Mavanhalla, for five thousand rupees in 1980. The Ooty property was perhaps one of the last properties of my dad that I sold, and this was sometime in the mid-eighties for about eight thousand rupees. It was prime property but owning properties was becoming a nightmare with government regulations about foreigners holding property in India.

Another place that my dad and I used to frequent was a plantation called Succoth estate, five miles from a settlement called Vazahithottam, just off the Ooty road. There were no roads to the estate back then, and we had to leave our car at Vazhaithottam and walk the rest of the way. Both Vazhaithottam and Succoth estate were owned by an Anglo-Indian by the name of D'Roza, who lived at the top of the hill with his wife and two sons. He had a tin shed at Vazhaithottam, which he had rented to an Englishman by the name of Collett. Though English, Collett had gone native and had picked up all the immoral habits from the locals, including not paying rent. He lived with a local woman, and made money by selling venison and other meat at the Masinagudi market. He was a crack shot, and with his rifle, affectionately called "Shorty Bill", led a very lazy and comfortable life. Meat from one sambar would get him twenty rupees at the market, and that would keep him going for a while. When I was a young boy, I was fascinated by Collett and his lifestyle. Although he never shot anything dangerous, I secretly hero-worshipped him as he had all the comforts he needed and earned his livelihood with his gun. He claimed that is brother was killed by a panther in Gudalur and that's why he never went after big cats, but the truth was that he had a limp and was a heavy drinker, and in an inebriated state one could never attempt shooting dangerous animals. In fact, he was so lazy that he would not even buy his own cartridgess but would send local men to go to Segur ghat and buy two at a time from Peyore & Sons. Dad's initial reason to meet D'Roza was to buy both estates but the deal never went through. However, Dad found a good friend, and more importantly from his perspective, a place to stay without having to pay rent, in the middle of the jungle! Collett was supposed to pay a rent of one rupee a month to D'Roza, but he never did. So, every alternate month, on the first day of the month, D'Roza would send his son, Henry, on a pony down to Vazhaithottam, and Collet who was perpetually drunk would fire his rifle above the poor boy's head and make him run back in fear. After Independence, D'Roza fell on hard times and sold his property to multiple buyers. Vazahaithottam hamlet became bigger with the numerous plantations that sprang up while Succoth estate fell into shambles. It still exists today, and the horse track that Henry used is now overgrown, although it remains the only route to the ruins on top.

D'Roza, Collett, Blossom and Donald

Even before the Wildlife Act came into being in 1972, there was a clampdown on tiger shooting for licensed hunters, although panthers and wild dogs were considered vermin and shooting them was allowed. There were specific rules framed for shooting any animal and any mistake meant that one had to pay a heavy fine. More than the actual levy, an embarrassing story would emanate from the local shikari guide that his *dorai* did not know enough to shoot as per the prescribed rules and that was not something to be proud of. For those of you who are not familiar with the subject, the local shikari guide was someone designated to come along with you when you went licensed hunting. He had to be paid as per a printed rate while tips etc. were extra. The guides were all excellent trackers but their skill depended on the alcohol imbibed at any point in time. So even if you had the best tracker in the village, his slow unsteady gait and horizontal demeanour did not always mean that he was looking closely at the animal tracks on the ground.

Konmari was one of the best shikari guides in this area, and I decided to take him along on a particular trip, along with my friend, Clive Greenwood. We were staying at Mendekar's place and had crossed the Ooty road as dawn was breaking in the eastern sky. We walked for about two furlongs and crossed a small stream. As we rounded a corner that had a clump of bamboo, we heard alarm calls from spotted deer. Both Clive and I had already shot a tiger each on our respective licenses, so I didn't have to tell Clive what the alarm calls meant—wild dogs, a panther, or an un-shootable tiger! It was still dark, but there was enough light to see for some distance ahead, and we treaded carefully. At one point I signalled Konmari to stay put, while Clive and I tiptoed forward, almost shoulder to shoulder. We came out of a small patch of vegetation in an area that was open except for some thorny trees and there we noticed a herd of deer. They were all standing alert, with their tails up, looking away from us. There were almost fifty of them, and the air was peppered with their periodic "aiow" calls. We crouched down and got our guns ready. The next minute it was pandemonium as the herd broke and ran straight at us. I had been chased by many animals before but a not a herd of deer! Before we had time to react, I saw the reason why—a tiger! It had been caught out, before making the final charge. The deer ran straight past, ignoring us completely. The cat saw us and in an instant changed from a gallop to a jump-and-squat that almost looked practised. It had seen us, and unlike its breakfast, had no intention of running past or over us. This tiger was not a morning person, especially now that its prey had disappeared and it seemed determined to have a quick bite or two. It was so close I could see its whiskers quivering. It flattened himself and its tail lashed from side to side, and it growled as he got ready to deliver the coup de grâce.

What was worse, to be attacked by an angry tiger or face the authorities and explain why I had shot one? Neither option seemed pleasant. From the corner of my eye I could see Clive raise his gun and it was only a matter of time before something regretful was about to happen. So, I did the first thing that came into my head. Screaming like a madman I ran towards the tiger. Arms flailing and head shaking, I ran straight in the direction of the crouching feline. The poor beast had probably never experienced something like this; it jumped to the side and ran off, muttering obscenities. As the adrenalin started to wear off, I started to laugh uncontrollably. I think it was just relief that I had survived, and soon Clive joined in. We were lying on the ground laughing so much that we forgot about Konmari. We looked at him, and there he was, set in stone. I approached him, and tapped his arm. Almost like a delayed replay, he acted out what I had done. He ran away from us, screaming, "*Aiyyayyayyo dorai, paithya pidichirukku*! (Oh no! The dorai has gone mad)" he kept screaming that over and over again, and I didn't have the energy to catch up with him. So the entire village came to hear about what a mad chap I was and for a very brief period none of the shikari guides wanted to accompany me on my trips.

Ramnagaram

Ramnagaram, also called Closepet after a British officer, was one of my favourite hunting spots for decades. Movies such as David Lean's *A Passage to India* had some scenes shot here, but its claim to fame was much earlier, through the film *Sholay* in 1975. It was a very small town and survived primarily on the silk and granite industry. The area is covered with hills that start at Magadi, cross Ramanagaram, and go all the way up to Kanakpura, a distance of more than forty miles. This place is absolutely devoid of any real forests, all it has are small bare hills, covered with boulders and caves interspersed with thorn jungle, which is perfect for panthers and bears. There are many hillocks in this area and Kuppa Gudda, my favourite, lies about seven miles from Ramnagaram and forty-six miles from Bangalore. At its base lived my shikari guide, Chowdiah. Compared to some of the other men I used for my hunts, he was very young, about my age. He could converse in a little broken English and was very prompt in sending me postcards whenever an opportunity arose. There was no question of a telephone from Kuppa Gudda back then, so he would cycle to Ramnagaram town and send me a postcard that would reach me the next day, the fastest means of communication possible. Any panther that became a nuisance to his village by lifting dogs or goats and started to lose its fear of humans would feature in his postcard and I would promptly land there to allay his concerns. The cost of the postcard including his tip was twenty-five paise, and I'm sure he made a lot of money. However, he was reliable, and I didn't want to disturb the arrangement. There was no concept of traffic in those days, so if I applied for half a day's leave, I could come home, take my stuff and still make it to the hillock by about four. I could attempt to bag the trouble maker, either a panther or bear, and then drive all the way back. Sometimes I would stay the night if I was not able to shoot a panther, and that was usually in Chowdiah's hut if the weather was cold, or under open skies, next to my motorcycle, in the summer. I would lay a tarpaulin down on the ground, and unlike in the thick jungles of the Nilgiris, I would sleep in the open, watching the twinkling stars in the night sky. I occasionally hunted in Savandurga as well, but that was more inaccessible and I never had a person like Chowdiah to help me, so my visits there were limited.

For its sheer proximity to Bangalore, Ramanagaram was unique as it provided panthers, bears, and wild boar. At short notice, I could go for a shikar and get back, with minimal planning required. I started hunting in these parts by the time I was seventeen or so and have shot sixty-three panthers from Ramanagaram and Magadi alone. Kengeri, on the way to Ramnagaram, was another haunt of mine, and unlike the latter, was quite lush and fertile, with hundreds of acres of coconut plantations. My friend Sydney D'Silva and I would come here often with our catapults and barring the odd elephant herd that we strayed upon, this area provided us a much-needed escape from the city. I started off with a catapult and slowly upgraded to a 12 bore shot gun. I used to bring down spurfowl and partridges that we cooked and ate. It was like living a real adventure. Instead of saying "bang bang" and pretending to cook and eat imaginary food like most boys our age, we experienced it in real life. We escaped elephant herds, swam and fished in the reservoirs, and once nearly got mauled by a pantheress defending her cubs on the way to the big banyan tree at Kethohalli.

There are two types of panthers—there is the forest panther, a large animal that lives in dense jungles, and then the village panther which usually raids villages at night to carry off a stray dog or goat. The latter is quite common in Ramnagaram and often come right into the villages, to enter goat pens and drag away an unfortunate victim. They are used to seeing villagers and are therefore not as shy of human beings as their bigger cousin.

While hunting in these parts, the choice of baits was limited to goats or sheep. The trick here was to ensure that the goat did not see you as you settled in, waiting for the panther. Only if it believes that it is alone will it start to bleat and attract the attention of the panther. I would usually tie them near a cave or a nullah where I had noticed panther tracks. In all my years of shooting panthers here, I have lost my bait goat on very few occasions. Don't get me wrong, it was not concern for the goat, but the fact that each goat cost me fifteen rupees by the end of the 1960s. If it died, I lost the entire money, but if I returned it without a scratch, I would get back ten rupees!

In some cases, I didn't need live bait, but when I did, Chowdiah acted as the middleman to procure the same. He had no skills to follow animal tracks or tie a machan and his role ended when he took me to the area where he had seen the panther. One day, fuelled by either curiosity or bravery, he asked me to take him along. I abhor taking along people who have no patience for this sort of thing. One has to be motionless, cannot smoke beedis, cannot belch loudly, or worse, cannot talk about how the crop will turn out or how fed up one is with one's wife's cooking. I have set high standards of qualification, and they are mutually agreed upon before anyone decides to accompany me on a trip; that's why a lot of my hunting trips were solo. But in this case my refusal fell on deaf ears. "Sir, you go - I come" followed by a dozen "please-please". So, with great reluctance I decided to take him along only after he took the "Don Anderson oath of waiting in silence".

Despite his apparent lack of skill in tracking, the information he had received was fairly accurate and we easily found the half-eaten remains of a goat that had been killed in a nullah. With a little help from him, I made a hide with dry branches about twenty yards from the goat, on the eastern slope. There were no trees close by to tie a machan, so this was the next best plan. This meant that both of us had to fit into the hide, a most discomforting prospect indeed. Threatening him with dire consequences if he broke the rules, we settled in for the evening. I had taken note from its pug marks in the soft sand that the panther had walked past the nullah and taken a right turn, and I had no reason to think that it would come from another direction, so I faced the course in which it had walked away. Chowdiah faced the other way, and it was agreed that if he noticed something, he would not talk, or even whisper, but just nudge my arm gently. He sat waiting, on his haunches like all people from rural India. Unfortunately, the moon was barely visible that night, making an embarrassed appearance once in a while, peeping from behind the murky clouds that threatened a downpour. At about 9:30, I sensed that the panther had arrived. Contrary to my presumption, he had come from the opposite direction, the one that Chowdiah was facing, and I don't blame the chap for not alerting me as it was impossible to see beyond a few feet. Unfortunately, it discovered us much before we realised its presence. Extremely vexed at having a voyeuristic duo spoil dinner, it made its displeasure as vocal as it dared, with short angry growls, hoping to scare us away. It wouldn't come any nearer and continued to vent its frustration with the universe from the comfort of its concealed position. I thought that I would get Chowdiah to distract it while I sneaked up from the other side. I carefully turned around and lay my hand on his shoulder to explain my plan. I could feel him shivering with fright. Clearly this was not what he had signed up for. He had realised that the difference between a dead panther seen the morning after I shot it and an angry one at night was far greater than he had ever imagined. The next thing I knew, I was hit with a strong smell of ammonia as the dry earth received some rather strong fertilizer! Considering that I was at less than arm's length, I did not wait to see what would happen next, so I whispered a warning in his ear, and then fired a shot in the air. Needless to say, I never bagged that panther and my fellow piddler never accompanied me on another trip.

Over the years I spent hunting them, I learnt that panthers have a habit of sunning themselves outside their caves when the sun is mild and my practised strategy was to look for them at these specific times, always climbing above their caves and tracking them from up above. I also noticed that they would never look up, especially behind, and I used this trait to my advantage. Despite these advantages, there are times when I have not been able to finish the job and have had to follow up wounded panthers to put an end to their misery. Ramanagaram has no skilled tribes, and therefore, quite often, I would have no shikari guide to help me track, an extremely difficult task when you not only have to track the animal but also be ready to shoot it if it charged. You have to be infinitely slow, absolutely silent, at times crawl on your knees, scan both the immediate surrounding as well as look into the distance, cross out every place that the panther could be hiding, yet have your finger literally on the trigger, and its only God's grace that kept me alive. I guess I was foolish and the risks I took were borderline suicidal at times. There are times when I would actually walk into caves knowing for certain that the panther was inside. From bright sunlight to the inky darkness inside a cave, the human eye takes a while to adjust and for that reason I would switch on my torch. No animal will tolerate an intruder in its home and panthers are no exception. There were plenty of instances where the panther rushed out and I wouldn't hear it till it had actually passed me by. Again, I can only say that Providence smiled on me, for if the panther had decided to go for my throat, my life would have ended at that moment.

There was this one instance when I observed a pair of panthers sitting outside a cave late in the evening. I shot the male first, as they are more aggressive. I didn't know whether I had missed completely, but both panthers ran back into the cave, and knowing that their senses would be alert, I did not venture in that day. Next morning, I reached the cave and peered in. The cave was absolutely silent, and I carefully crept in. I was in a half-crouched position for the cave wasn't really big. All at once, out charged the female, snarling, but it was just trying to escape and before I could raise my gun, it had disappeared. I was shaken up, but walked further in. The cave wasn't very long either and where it ended lay the male, frozen stiff. What was shocking was that he was half-eaten. His mate had clearly found the concept of bed and breakfast a little too appealing!

Ramnagaram is also home to a large population of sloth bears that are frequently encountered by the villagers as they tend their goats or crops. The best times to see them are early in the morning or late evening, when the weather is milder, as the days in these parts are un-bear-ably hot! This is largely because of the dearth of large shade trees, and the absence of a river or other large water bodies, making this quite an arid environment. In my experience, when wounded, the adrenalin produced in bears is more than any other animal in the jungle. He is belligerence personified and there has been a time when I had to use four bullets to bring him down. The other noteworthy creature in these parts is the jackal, but they have all been wiped out, along with the vultures, by the villagers who poison the meat of the goats and cattle that are killed by panthers, thus completely destroying nature's critical element in the food chain—the scavengers.

A brace of bears – Ramanagaram

The only time my dad came to Ramanagaram after I started hunting was because of a peculiar incident. This was during one my early days there. I must have been in my early twenties, wet around the ears, and I believed that I didn't need anyone to help me. I ignored the fact that I had Dad's shikari, Nanjiah, at my disposal and decided that I would do this hunt solo. I spent the morning of the first day observing a panther sunning itself on a rocky outcrop, and made a mental note of how to find that location. At about 4:30 p.m., I started my ascent. Perspiring profusely in the oppressive heat, I was sure that no self-respecting cat would be out then, but I was keen on climbing to a vantage point and observing my target from there. Suddenly from the corner of my eye I noticed a slight movement. There on a rocky ledge at some distance was my panther, and it was looking away. I waited for my nerves to settle down and, exhaling slowly, I fired my shot. It disappeared, but I knew that I had hit it. I slowly started my way up. A while later, at one point, I looked up to check my progress and I saw a bizarre sight—there was the panther looking right back at me. It looked to be in fine condition, almost curious, and I could not believe that I had missed. I waited to catch my breath, then aimed and fired. I saw it somersault and vanish; I had certainly not missed this time. By now I was determined to find it and figure out whether I had hit it the first time. Night was falling, and I switched on my two-cell torch. I was flashing it about, very close to the spot, when I heard a hiss. Instinctively, I shone my torch towards the sound while my left hand braced itself to fire the shot. Unbelievable, but there was the panther again, not too far away, its eyes looking back at me with fear and confusion. There was no way I could miss from that distance, and it stood almost patiently waiting for the final bullet to end its misery. I didn't have the heart to do it, and it was one of the shots that provided no excitement as I pulled the trigger. The panther collapsed in front of me. After I had rested for a while, I lopped off a few branches and covered it, for I did not want vultures to find it in the morning. In the darkness I found my way back to the village and slept under a haystack. My sleep was constantly interrupted by mosquitoes and that was not the only reason I longed for the sun to come up. I managed to get a chap from the village to help bring down the panther, and we walked up to the spot. The panther lay there, stiff with rigor mortis, and I was puzzled as I could see just one spot where my bullet had killed it. I heard a shout; my new friend was excitedly pointing to something. I reached there and to my amazement saw another dead panther about thirty feet away. As my eyes swept the area I noticed something lying

183

under a cactus bush and there was another panther! I had actually shot three panthers with three shots, thinking all the while that it was just one. On closer examination I found that one was a pantheress while the other two were males. Putting two and two together I realised that the female must have been in heat and the two males had arrived to make an impression. There was no way I could carry all of them back, so I managed to get word to my dad to come with a jeep to fetch me and the rest of my baggage. He was flabbergasted to see three pelts and although he gave me a dressing down for killing three panthers, he was quite proud of that story and went on to often narrate it to his friends.

By the mid-sixties Dad had stopped carrying a gun and had become a conservationist. He abhorred my cruel hobby and we never saw eye to eye on a few topics, this being one of them.

Sangam

Although I visited Sangam in the fifties and sixties, it was never with the same fervour as after the Wildlife Act was passed. It was not just because I had promised my dad to never hunt, but I was past forty and my passion for hunting had abated considerably. However, my unceasing love affair with the jungles was something I just could not give up, and angling became a new hobby out of sheer necessity. Sangam thus became my weekend home. Sangam is sixty-two miles from Bangalore and sixteen miles from Kanakpura or Kankanhalli as it was once called. It's sad that today the beautiful scrub jungle all around Kanakpura has all but disappeared due to indiscriminate mining of granite in these parts.

Sangam is the name given to the place where the Arkavathi river meets the mighty Cauvery. It has a beautiful forest bungalow right at the edge of the water, and I remember that as the only large building in those parts. As Dad and I would make our way, the sun would have disappeared, and in the distance one could see the glow of a single lamp lit on the balcony by the caretaker, the only light for miles. Although there were two rooms on the first floor, the balcony was our favourite spot, and unless it was raining, we would sleep out in the open. He would sit on a chair, at the edge of the balcony, smoking his pipe, staring into the gloomy darkness. The sound of the cicadas and the gurgling rivers would be occasionally interrupted by the soft plop of a fish or the mournful hoot of a fish owl from one of the giant trees that grew on the river bank. Not a soul around, apart from the caretaker who would have consumed his "quota" and fallen into a deep slumber.

Tiny Seddon was, in my memory, the first person I came across who frequented Sangam. He was closer to my dad's age and introduced us to the place in the late forties. Tiny had a Model T Ford, and unlike my dad who loved to walk, would be delighted to cast a line from the vehicle itself, if given a chance. In the summer he would drive over the shallow parts of the river at Sangam and on to Mekedatu for angling. When the water levels were low, we would sleep in the sandy river next to the gorge with hurricane lamps kept at regular intervals to keep away mugger crocodiles that were common in these parts. A further two miles from Sangam, across the river, is Mekedatu or "goat's leap" where the Cauvery flows through a narrow, terrifying channel of whirlpools, caverns, and gorges. Extremely dangerous, and practically inhospitable during the rains, it's a deathtrap for many people who come there every year. Depending on the month of the year, you could walk, drive like Tiny, or hitch a coracle to the other side and then walk the rest of the way to Mekedatu.

Tiny Seddon at Mekedatu

Since Tiny's days, forests were cleared and farms have mushroomed along the Sangam Road, organisations like W.A.S.I were established, and Sangam became a tourist spot, where people came for picnics with their families and friends. I never went there after the late nineties, and by then it was filled with noisy, unruly people during the day, and shady characters who came there to indulge in all kinds of activities at night. Shops sprang up, adding to the garbage strewn over by the tourists, and the face of Sangam changed forever.

It was not just the tourists; the other change that the place witnessed was the surge in poaching. My Dad and I had been seeing poachers since the early fifties, but from the mid-sixties, they started growing bolder, their insatiable greed knew no bounds, and dynamiting on the river became extremely common. Unlike shooting a deer or wild boar, where only one animal is killed, detonation in a river multiplies the effect of the explosion ten-fold and the collateral damage is mind-boggling. Any living creature within a certain radius of the epicentre will be stunned or will die, and rise to the surface to be scooped away by the waiting fisherman. Most of them are too small to be of value and are thrown back into the river only to rot or be eaten by larger fish and crocodiles. Earlier they would do this at dawn or dusk, but they started getting bolder and we started hearing them even during the day; the booming sounds carrying over the water, as we were angling. Rampant activities of this nature were responsible for Sangam losing the wildlife it once held.

Sometime in 1973, Eric Boesinger, Arthur Greenwood, and I decided that we had to do something to stop the carnage, we just had to do something to stop these poachers. The existing government machinery couldn't care less, and we knew that our asking them to deploy resources to monitor a river and prevent indiscriminate killing of fish would be laughed at. I recollect one such instance where we met a senior forest official. His understanding of the new law was very lucid—hunting of land animals was an offence—but he just could not comprehend what the fuss was about when it came to fish. According to him "wildlife" meant anything on land; what was in the river was fair game for anyone who had the means to get it out. While Arthur and I lost our enthusiasm, Eric's Dutch genes gave him the doggedness to keep at it, and he was instrumental in laying the foundation of a remarkable initiative. He was not just a keen angler, he had the foresight to see what would happen if things went on the way they were. He knew that he had to protect Sangam, the last bastion of the mahseer in south India. So, with the help of the Myrada group, he helped set up W.A.S.I or Wildlife Association of South India in 1976. They took over a twenty-eight km stretch on lease from the government and started a conservation project by paying a small group of guards to prevent poaching along this stretch. Angling was allowed only with permission, only between dawn and dusk, only with a rod and reel, and all captured fish had to be released. These were some of the guidelines that W.A.S.I introduced. Despite all his efforts, Eric never got the recognition he deserved and it is unfortunate that most anglers at Sangam don't even know that such a person existed. W.A.S.I was eventually taken over by Jungle Lodges & Resorts and they set up resorts at some of the erstwhile fishing campsites like Doddamakakali, Chikkamakalli, Bheemeshwari, and Galibore. Today, W.A.S.I no longer has control over the entire Cauvery stretch, but only over the Sivanasamudram area.

Called Basti by the Muslims and Doddi by the local Hindus who lived there, Sangam was anything but a secret spot. In fact, it was used extensively by the Mysore Maharajah who was very fond of angling and hunting even during the forties and fifties. The royal entourage would pitch camps by the riverside and stay on for weeks at a time, with specially invited guests. I don't think they did any serious shooting; they may have shot wild boar or the occasional panther, but angling was the main reason for the camp. Sangam was restricted, to a large extent, to people from Bangalore or Nawabs and other royalty from Hyderabad state. International fame arrived following the effort of a Britisher called Paul Boote. He was a keen angler who chanced upon this place through some friends who lived at Shivasamudram. After visiting Sangam, he went about Europe, weaving stories about the El Dorado for river anglers, deep in the jungles of mystical and mysterious India. Through word of mouth, select anglers trickled into India, including a certain gentleman who went on to become a TV phenomenon years later. The big break came when Boote went to Sweden and convinced AB Urfabriken or the ABU angling company to come down in 1978. The ABU team spent close to two months there and camped in their waterproof tents, living with just the bare necessities, but did they know their onions! They are the ones who understood the feeding habits of the mahseer and taught the locals better ways to catch bottom feeders like mahseer. Till then the people would use small crabs and tiddlers as bait, but the ABU team realised that *ragi* worked better. *Ragi* was twenty paise for a kg back then, and easily available, so soon it became the default bait for all the anglers who came to Sangam. During this time, team ABU met Boesinger and they were so impressed with him that they actually had a rod created for him and sent him the first ever "Cauvery Panasonic Boom", a beautiful piece that Eric treasured and would guard with his life.

Sangam became known as a definitive place to catch mahseer in south India, the common ones being the golden mahseer, the silver mahseer, the black mahseer and the giant humpback (also called the orange finned) mahseer. Mahseer belong to the carp family and were the prized game for the Britishers all over India, a superior substitute for the trout they would catch back home. It's unfortunate that blue-fin mahseer introduced to the Cauvery has displaced the native orange finned humpback almost to the point of extinction. In addition to the prized game fish, you also had the minnow, barbs, and other carps like grass carp, common carp, karnatic carp, rohu, catla, murrel, mullets, eels, and tilapia. The best months for angling are January through March; by April the water starts to recede with the onset of summer. At this time of the year, one can even sleep out in the open and see game right at the water's edge.

The loss of habitat at Sangam is not restricted to the mahseer alone. Another animal that seems to have disappeared from these parts is the otter. They are extremely shy creatures but if you were lucky you could get to see them very early in the morning along the river banks where they would have small dens. But by the early nineties, I stopped seeing them altogether. Once a big bunch of us arrived at Sangam much later in the day than we would have liked to, but still managed to catch an impressive number of fish, although none of them were very large. We put the fish in plastic buckets we had brought along, but then realised that we had packed so much biriyani and kababs that we really didn't want to cook fish to add to that. So, what could we do? A simple trick that Tiny taught me came in handy. We took a fishing line and passed it through each fish and out through the gills, thus stringing them together and then tying both ends to sticks that were firmly planted on land, while the line was let loose in the water. Perhaps a cruel method, but we strung about ten fish like this, which was about ten kgs, and looked forward to a fresh catch the next morning. Much to our dismay, when we woke up, we couldn't find even one, and the few floating fish scales were the only tell-tale signs of what had happened at night. A pack of otters had raided our live larder and had a feast. What's incredible is the fact that although we were sleeping less than ten feet away from the water's edge, none of us had even heard a squeak while the marauders did the damage.

While in the jungles, I never slept well at night, for over the years my senses were conditioned to stay alert for the smallest noise, as it could mean the difference between life and death. Even if everyone at camp was drinking, I would limit my quota to just a single glass of whiskey that I would nurse all evening, just to ensure that I was in my senses should danger present itself. So, as someone who prided myself on having a superior sense of hearing, I was astounded how the little creatures had managed to sneak up and carry out their foray so close to our camp without being detected.

One of my cardinal rules when camping, especially in a place like Sangam was never to sweep the leaves from the forest floor to make the bedding. For most people from the city, it's a natural reaction to remove dirt and insects but it can often have disastrous consequences and I learnt it the hard way. Insects like scorpions make nests on the forest floor within the carpet of dead and rotting leaves and they will attack anyone whom they see as a threat to their home, much like bees. They are drawn by the light source at camp, like a petromax, and from the mounds of leaves that have been swept aside, they will crawl out by the dozen and invade camp, practically invisible because of their colour. So, the best solution is to just let the leaves remain as they are, and you will be safe. Similarly, when it comes to bees, the natural instinct is to swat them away when they come close, and it's ok to do that provided that you don't injure or kill one. Usually they are just soldiers doing a reconnaissance, checking for threats to the hive. If you squash one of them, it releases pheromones in the air, and soon you will have a swarm after the people in the camp.

Catching a mahseer is in some ways equivalent to spotting a tiger in the jungle, but gone are the days when one could dream of fish bigger than 100 pounds. In fact, the record is 125 pounds, and I am listed amongst the record holders at W.A.S.I for a humpback that weighed 104 pounds. Legend has it that fish weighing as much as 180 pounds have been caught, but I don't believe that's possible. Then again, if someone was told today that a 125-pounder was caught twenty years back, they wouldn't believe that either! Till the mid-seventies, only serious anglers would come to Sangam because angling was not the first choice for the people who wanted to get away from the city. Hunting was a much more popular pastime, and many homes would at least have a. 22 in their collection. All that changed after the Wildlife Act was passed and for a lot of people, including me, angling became a requisite; a reason to go back into the jungles and get away from the city.

In and around Sangam there were select spots where anglers would prefer to cast their lines. One was opposite the spot where the Electricity Board station stands today. I'm sure all explorers love having places named after them and anglers are no different. Like most of the people who fished at Sangam in the early seventies, I too stake claim to having discovered the best spots in that area, including Mosaluhalla (Crocodile Rock) that people later came to earmark. However, my lucky spot was under a massive tamarind tree about half a mile from Galibore and my friends very generously named it Don 1. After Don 1, the most frequented campsite was Ontigondu; (One Rock) right after this spot is where the current in the river picks up pace and it starts to get dangerous.

Despite all the luck I had at that spot, the most famous incident at Don 1 was not an angling story. One of the Van Ingens was a frequent visitor at Sangam, and for some reason he professed his affinity for this particular spot. On one such occasion, he was there with just his chokra. After a particularly satisfying day of angling, he went to sleep in his tent quite early as he wanted to be up and ready before the break of dawn. After a good night's sleep, he woke up before the sun was up, but didn't think it was necessary to take a lantern as he walked out. His chokra was getting some food ready and was some distance away, and as van Ingen went into the bushes to do his job, he stumbled upon a very irate elephant that charged with absolutely no warning. The animal just rushed out of the darkness, and its heavy footsteps got the taxidermist running in a trice. He tried to get back to his camp, shouting for help, and that seemed to infuriate the elephant for it trumpeted fiercely and continued to chase him. His chokra burst on to the scene and tried to distract the elephant by screaming, but this was one determined animal and it caught up with the fleeing man. A violent smack of the trunk was all that it was able to execute, perhaps it lost its courage or interest, but that was enough to send the puny human flying to one side. Van Ingen suffered from a couple of broken ribs, but nothing more serious. If the elephant had decided to inflict more damage, it could have, but it just ran away into the jungle.

In fact, elephants were frequent visitors to Sangam and although it would be an exaggeration to say that they were bad tempered, they were always curious and to a great degree fearless, which caused a fair bit of discomfort for many people who stayed there. One of the bravest incidents I have ever seen happened here. During the summer, Sangam gets extremely hot and the Arkavathy river slowly loses its velocity as it enters the Cauvery. During one such season a farmer had grown watermelons along the side of the Arkavathy, a few miles before Sangam. I had gone there with my friends, but they were at camp while I went angling on my own. It was getting late, and I was wearily walking back to camp when I heard the sound of someone shouting on the opposite bank. It was obvious that someone was in trouble, so I started a jog trot, veering away from my path and on to the river's edge. An astounding sight greeted me. A massive bull elephant had walked into the watermelon patch and was about to start an all-you-can-eat watermelon buffet! The only hindrance was a small puny farmer with nothing more than a loin cloth standing between him and his feast. The elephant would put a step forward and the man would shout and clap his hands, upon which it would take its foot back. It would then attempt to move in a different direction, only to meet with the same problem. I knew that this had only one logical conclusion—sooner or later, the elephant's greed would triumph over its quasi-fear of the human, and in the darkness one more brave soul would lose his life trying to protect his livelihood. I cursed myself for not getting my gun; I did not want to shoot the elephant, just scare it away. The little farmer knew he had to do something quick and effective. What followed was an act of desperation, brilliance, and something I had never seen before. The farmer picked up a burning branch from the embers of the fire he had going and charged he elephant, screaming. If the elephant was surprised, it didn't end there. The man kept getting closer and closer, and both the elephant and I were waiting for him to stop. Then, with a wild swing of his arms, the man threw the branch on top of the elephant. The ensuing shock and the pain from the burning branch made it scream and run off. Unfortunately, the bough somehow got stuck between the fold of its giant ear, and that must have been excruciating as it ran off into the jungle. Under normal circumstances a running elephant would melt into the undergrowth but in this case I was able to observe the path, lit by the falling embers from the burning log, a remarkable sight indeed. I felt sorry for the elephant but I had to salute the farmer whose brave act could have so easily gone horribly wrong.

In those days elephants were suspicious or scared of lanterns and this kept us safe most of the time. A strange incident happened sometime in the late fifties, when I had gone angling at Galibore with my friends Gene, Bunty, and Thangavelu. At that time, to protect us from elephants, my modus operandi involved pulling down pliant branches of trees and tying hurricane lanterns filled with kerosene and releasing the boughs so that the lantern would burn from a height, throwing ample light in all directions. The ropes attached to the top of the branches would be pulled down the next day and the lanterns would be recovered. I would place these lanterns a hundred yards away from our main tents and cots in four directions. The only animal that would dare come close to camp were bull elephants and the lights were placed to discourage them from being too inquisitive. My friends were heavy drinkers and by midnight we had finished two bottles between the three of us, and had dragged ourselves from our chairs to our camp cots. Though it was summer, it was a bit nippy in the jungles, and we had a small fire going as we fell asleep. I am a light sleeper, and at about one o'clock in the morning, I woke up with a start. There was no mistake, I could hear stones being thrown, making a loud thud as they fell. It was so bizarre, I couldn't for the life of me think who would be doing so at that time of the night. Listening to the sounds, I figured that these were fairly large stones. I took out my torch and slipped into my shoes. Other than the occasional snore from one of my friends, the jungle was silent. The most powerful weapon I had carried on that trip was my fishing rod—I had not carried my gun—and I felt that it wouldn't really be of much use in this situation. I was still sitting on my camp cot and shining the torch in the direction where the noise had come from when I saw some bushes moving and from behind a tamarind tree stepped out an elephant. It was a semi-adult and that perhaps explained its curiosity. It ignored my torch light altogether and walked towards us. From my prone position on the camp cot, I could see the bull coming closer. The shadows made it look enormous, but I did not panic. I was a bit surprised because at fifteen feet away the elephant could surely smell us and yet it did not run away. All my life I had firmly believed that I would die in the jungles and that too under the feet of an elephant, and here it was about to come true. Since we were all about to die anyway, I thought I should let my friends see what caused their death before it actually happened—sort of like granting them a last wish—without their permission of course. I leaned over and nudged Gene and Bunty who were sleeping on the ground. They were quick to wake up—spending time with me in the jungles had prepared them to wake up without too much effort from my end. The elephant was not facing them, but they could see its profile. The view was not really comforting, for they both started to shake with fear. I don't think they could fully comprehend whether it was a dream or reality. Luckily, the bull had had enough of the investigation and moved away into the bushes. By this time Thangavelu was also up and he quickly added more kerosene to the flames and lit a sufficiently large fire to ensure there would be no more visitors that night. Gene declared that the incident had left him with no option but to relieve himself, and so wandered into the bushes. A deafening trumpet ensued; the elephant couldn't have been more than ten feet away from Gene! He ran back, and in the process we got to witness two males running towards us with their respective trunks out. The pachyderm swerved away from the fire and ran off, trumpeting vociferously. It's interesting to note that this bull actually came close, investigated, then moved away, yet kept observing us from a distance. I am grateful to it for not attacking us, for it had all the avenues to do so, but did not. I was curious to find out the source of the sound I had heard the previous night, and in the morning I tried to figure out this for myself. It was bizarre, but the bull was irritated with the hurricane lanterns that were hung on the tree and was shying rocks to get rid of the irritant.

The first set of people I started going regularly with to Sangam consisted of Tiny Seddon, Baba Cariappa, and Chippie Briggs. I learnt angling from Tiny and I was a fast learner. Like all beginners, I used a spinning reel to start with. I learnt through trial and error, and after losing a lot of the bigger fish, particularly the mahseer, I switched over to the bait casting reel. I felt that this gave me more flexibility and control, especially while flipping and pitching—while trying to catch larger fish that were found in deeper waters.

I must have caught more than a hundred fish in and around Sangam, that were fifty pounds and over, the largest of course being the 104-pounder I mentioned earlier. Like all self-respecting anglers, I too claim that I have fought bigger fish, just that I was not able to land them! In terms of skill, I know that I am far inferior to many of my contemporaries like Eric, whose skill was extraordinary. However, as with hunting, I have been extremely lucky. In fact, at the risk of sounding pompous, I've also been extremely lucky for a lot of people who have gone angling with me, especially at Sangam. The first time I took my friend, Sudhir, angling, he caught a forty-seven pound mahseer. Angling is made up of two different sets of skills. The first comprises handling the bait, how you cast your line, and of course your patience, and over time this can be learnt. The second and tougher part is "playing the fish" or what you do when you get a fish at the end of your line, and that's a true test of one's skill and endurance.

Angling record at W.A.S.I.

Over the years, I developed a schedule for the angling trips. Sunrise and sundown are the best times for fishing, in my opinion, and hence we planned the day in that manner. We would start very early with a cup of tea, and then head out. We would come back by about 10:00 a.m., have breakfast, and relax for a couple of hours. Then at 1:00 p.m. we would go to spots that had murrel like the one I discovered at a place above Mosaluhalla with a lot of small rocky islands. We would bring back about ten kgs of murrel to be fried, and it would accompany our piping hot lunch that would have been prepared by our cook, Thangavelu. This was then followed by a nap for an hour, after which we would have tea and head out again, to get back by 7:30 p.m. or so. The routine was then repeated the next day. Thangavelu and the other cooks also served as some sort of security against miscreants and monkeys who would often raid our camps.

We didn't need W.A.S.I. for setting up regulations for angling for mahseer, as we always released them after weighing and photographing them. The ones that ended on our plate were usually the smaller carp, murrel, tilapia, and all the tiddlers. Every campsite would have their own recipe to cook fish. We would clean the fish of its scales, fillet it, and smear it with onion and green chilli paste. This would then be wrapped in a thick layer of soaking wet newspaper which would be placed on a small platform of twigs, and then a small fire would be lit underneath. It had to be carefully monitored as the newspaper was not supposed to get very dry. It would be turned over a couple of times, taken out, and the fish would be lightly smeared with oil. Then, the newspaper packet would be soaked again and the process repeated. Fish cooks quite fast, and you could get a very delicious fish bake, slightly fried on the outside. Of course, this was only possible with slightly larger fish; the tiddlers would be deep fried whole and they made for some tasty snacks along with our alcohol. Catfish is a good choice for frying and my friend, Mukherjee, would in fact fry them and put them into a curry he would make—it was delicious! Fish fry or curry would accompany some of the food we brought with us. Rice and dal would be cooked by Bolaiyah and I would bring the pickle. Although I enjoyed eating the fish we caught, occasionally I would shoot something for the pot. Jungle fowl and spur fowl would find a place on our menu. The meat would be shared amongst the villagers we knew and also be given to the families of Chhota Subhan and Bolaiyah.

Before I started angling at Sangam, we would visit those forests for a hunt and also enjoy the remarkably serene environment that the place provided. Thangavelu would be in charge of cooking, and he also doubled up as the single largest consumer of alcohol on these trips, the two roles being inversely proportional. Sometime in the fifties, we were on a trip to Sangam with my dad and Sonny Leonard and a couple of others. We had settled in camp and were nursing our drinks, when Sonny got inspired to show off his death-defying stunts, jumping across the bonfire we had set up. To his credit, he was pretty good, and soon he was joined by Thangavelu who, after his quota of brandy, felt he was a circus acrobat. If we were waiting for an accident to happen, we were not disappointed. The two idiots had timed their jumps to such perfection that at one point they met each other while airborne and then crashed into the embers below, suffering burns. We unanimously agreed that this was perhaps the stupidest way to get hurt, and in honour of this infamous incident, coined the phrase "Don't do a Thangavelu" to warn each other on future trips when we felt that someone was going to scale the glorious heights of idiocy.

While Thangavelu was a good cook, he was not quite the master when it came to preparing fried partridge, a dish often coveted by my last Sangam gang that consisted of Sudhir, Jimmy, and Ravi. Although we shot them when we went to the jungles, to get them at short notice meant we had to rely on the stock at Russel Market, and Sudhir took his job of cooking them very seriously. The partridge was cleaned, and pressure cooked with salt for some time. It was then taken out, drowned in Amul butter, and then fried on a low flame along with onions and pepper.

Whether it was groceries or anything else, it all needed planning and only someone with an eye for detail could do this. Everything had to be in grams and millilitres and I kept track of it all. How much each person paid, what the cost per head was, everything went into my book and I was always ridiculed for going to the extreme of even including the cost of a matchbox. Of course, the tough part was when we broke camp. I would argue with my friends about leaving the leftover stuff for Subhan and the others. If I could convince them, came the excruciating but necessary job of dividing the leftover items amongst everyone. It was a source of great amusement for everyone, but I took my job very seriously.

Sangam attracted a lot of people, but the most important person I took there was the former Chief of Army Staff, Rodricks and his wife. This was after Operation Blue Star and he was on a hit list, therefore the security precautions during the trip were unimaginable. He was staying just off MG Road, and there was a huge battalion all the way from MG Road right up to Sangam. When we reached there, I found that there were at least fifty commandoes already stationed who had landed up the previous day to scout the area and set up posts at different points all over Sangam. Then came the royal treatment—they got excellent cooks, with a barbecue, and we were served by a bearer who wore white gloves and used expensive crockery, clearly not what I or anyone else was used to at

Sangam! Rodricks was a great angler, as was his wife, and on the first day she caught a twenty-pound mahseer.

There would be multiple angling groups at Sangam during the weekends but we never had issues with the others and were always civil to each other. However, there was an incident that I'm not very proud of, as it involved my gang. We had all driven to Sangam on our motorcycles and had camped at Mosaluhalla overnight. We had quite a bit to drink and it was almost three in the morning when we retired. I was keen on angling, unlike a few of my inebriated friends, and was up at the crack of dawn. I informed the cook to make us *uppiitu* at 4:00 a.m., and went back to sleep, with strict instructions to wake us up when the food was ready. After a couple of minutes I could hear Thangavelu pottering about in the darkness.

I cursed the blighter: "*Yenna achu?*" (What happened?)

"*Saar kathi illa.*" (Sir, the knife is missing)

A minute later I heard "*Saar yennai Illa*" (The oil is missing). Apparently, the whiskey bottle that held the oil was missing. My first thought was that some of my friends had drunk the oil by mistake, but I knew that they were not that drunk.

"You're the once in charge of all the stuff, so why are you asking me?"" I retorted, irritated.

Feeling very indignant, I tried to settle in, but I could hear him muttering to himself. Cursing the cook, I woke up and tried to help him find the stuff. To my astonishment, I realised that he was speaking the truth and all our stuff had disappeared. Our fishing equipment, our cameras, our cooking vessels, practically everything. The only thing that I could find was my torch which I had next to me on my cot. I was livid. The audacity of the people who stole it from right under our noses!

We waited for the sun to rise, and started looking for footprints. I immediately came upon them in the sand. Someone had walked into camp and had stolen all our stuff. We walked for a bit and suddenly the bare feet were replaced with shoe imprints. He had even stolen a pair of shoes that belonged to Sudhir and worn them at this point. We decided to head back to camp and inform WASI, but Jimmy was adamant. He wanted immediate justice and decided to follow the perpetrator. An hour later there was no sign of Jimmy, and we had no idea where he had gone, so we decided to walk to the nearest cattle patti and ask for help. We saw him just as we were reaching there. Evidently, he had landed at the same place after tracking the perpetrator along the river all the while. We then joined forces and started looking on the nearest hillock. We didn't have to go very far, the tell-tale shoe marks led us to a fox hole that had a lungi with all our stolen stuff in it. We went back to the patti where someone identified the owner of the lungi. We brought him out of his house but he was adamant. "*Gothilla, gothilla, gothilla*" (I don't know, I don't know, I don't know) was all that came out of him.

He refused to admit to the crime and after a point we realised that this method of questioning was not going to get us any results. I am not proud of what we then did—we gave him a jolly good whipping. In fact, at some point I vaguely remember the sanest member of the group shouting, "Stop it man, you'll kill him." We left him in a crumpled heap, and needless to say, we monitored all the newspapers continuously over the next couple of days.

Old man Jaleel was synonymous with Sangam for anyone who visited the place in the sixties and seventies. For most people of that generation, especially uneducated folk, age was not important, and they could give you the most bizarre numbers. Jaleel, who worked for the Mysore Maharajah, would insist that he was over eighty but I pegged him to be about a decade older than me although he certainly looked closer to the age he claimed. Although he was not originally from Sangam, he settled there with his family, serving dozens of anglers. He knew every rock, crevice, and tree in those areas and passed on that knowledge to his son Chhota Subhan and others. For Chhota Subhan, who was encouraged by his father to find some sort of work to support the family, the growth of Sangam as a destination for anglers was a godsend and he made a name for himself, becoming very popular with the visitors. Then there was Bada Subhan, who was the cook at the campsites and Bolaiyah completed the quartet. They made up a motley crew of highly skilled people without whose help angling at Sangam and Mekedatu would not have been so memorable for hundreds of anglers from all over India and even some from across the world. Initially they were the ones who were hired by W.A.S.I. to patrol the twenty-five km stretch in view of their absolute command of the land. Sangam was unique because there was just one way in and one way out, so it was impossible for anyone to sneak into that area unless they came from the river. During the early days these guys were suspected to be hand in glove with some of the poachers but gradually they understood that there was lower risk and higher return if they gave up their reprehensible ways and instead worked on salaries, not to mention the huge tips if they worked as *ghillies* (helper) for the licensed anglers. However, during the initial days, they did go on strike till their salaries were raised from two hundred to four hundred rupees a month, a sharp increase for those days. Jaleel grew old and could no longer work in his earlier capacity and would often visit the houses of many of the people he helped at Sangam, only to be turned away. Every couple of months he would visit me as well, and we would sit and talk about the wonderful times we had had.

With old man Jaleel

From the locals like Chhota Subhan, we would hear about legends that fished at Sangam, and John Wilson is credited with being the best angler that visited the area. Although not known for his stint at Sangam, the most famous person who fished with us there was Jeremey Wade, who is now a very popular television star. Call it beginner's luck, but Wade caught some really big fish that summer and he co–authored a book called *Somewhere Down the Crazy River* with Paul Boote.

Getting cars to transport everyone was difficult, so more often than not, we would go by bikes. The disadvantage of bikes was that you really couldn't carry a lot of supplies, so some of us would take the 6:00 a.m. bus from Majestic bus stand and reach Sangam by 10:00 a.m. They would carry the supplies while others like me would come on bikes. I had a Suvega Super 50 that served the purpose. I would ride it while my pillion rider would carry a fair amount of provisions piled up in huge gunny bags. We weren't getting any younger, and while all this was a lot of fun, we realised that we needed to have a car to cart people and provisions for our trips. Opposite my friend Meru Saldhana's home lived a guy called Dev Mukherjee who had an Ambassador car, so as part of an elaborate plan, we decided to make him our "*bakra* (scapegoat) of choice". We left it to Meru to cast the line and reel him in. He first tried the approach by dangling the "famous Anderson" bait, but Mukherjee wouldn't bite, as he had never heard of my dad. Meru knew that like all self-respecting Bengalis, Mukherjee too would respond better if the topic was about fish recipes.

"Do you like river fish Mukherjee?" he began.

"Are you serious?" retorted Mukherjee, his eyes clouded, while he dreamily mentioned his exploits. "Why, when I was younger, I would catch my own fish in the Teesta River with double hooks."

"Mukherjee, I have been guilty of hiding something from you. There is a place near Bangalore where aficionados like yourself can fish all day long, and apart from some great tasting fish, you can also try your hand at hooking 100 pound mahseer."

Mukherjee's eyes grew larger, part distrust and part excitement.

"Do such fish really exist?" he asked incredulously.

Well, we just had to take him after that, and we conveniently got ourselves invited in his car. Meru, Syed the Turk, Santa Maria, Robert Watts, Mukherjee and I went for the first trip and it was a spectacular success. Although at first glance Mukherjee contemptuously dismissed it as "not as big as the Teesta", he caught about four small carps in the first hour. Poor Mukherjee! He was snared hook, line, and sinker. Of course, we were devils really, praising him no end for his skill, and all that helped seal a long-term partnership of car borrowing with our Bengali babu. He was a businessman and not always around to come with us, but was kind enough to let us borrow his car. All he was interested in was to check if the petrol had been filled up to the same point as when we had borrowed it!

I remember a trip with Meru and his family, Mukherjee, Dr. Ansari and two of their friends. Usually the newcomers who were not used to the rigmarole at camp were victims of most of the practical jokes and in this case the two unnamed gentlemen mentioned were marked targets. We enjoyed a good day of angling and had settled in for the evening. Dinner was being made, and Meru and I had ensured that through the day there were sufficient hints dropped about us encountering elephants as it was the season of wood apples. We convinced the two gentleman and our driver that when it came to wood apples, elephants would not let anything stand in their way to get to them. While Bada Subhan took over the kitchen, we motioned Chhota Subhan and Bolaiyah who promptly announced that they had to run some errand and would not be back for a couple of hours. For once, we didn't mention our prank to Mukherjee or Ansari, and ensuring that everyone heard me, I warned Subhan and Bolaiyah to "be careful of elephants" as they walked away from camp. A while later, we heard the distinct sound of branches breaking. Elephants! I spoke to Ansari in hushed tones while Meru approached Mukherjee. "I think we are in a spot of trouble," I casually mentioned. "The elephants seem to have discovered our camp, and see it as a source of food. Perhaps they didn't get enough wood apples, they must be ravenous. We must be careful, but let us not cause alarm and worry the newcomers."

"We perfectly understand," murmured the two, clearly feeling chuffed that we had decided to confide in them, a possible indicator that we felt that they were as tough as us in the jungles. I could see them straining their eyes in the hope of finding the elephants. It certainly would have been fun if they had managed to spot them, for the branches were being broken by Subhan and Bolaiyah, whose errand was nothing more than to collect dry branches and break them at intervals! However, the noises, though frequent, were some distance away, and Mukherjee, Ansari and the other two seem unperturbed. Although it wasn't discussed in such detail, Subhan and his companion felt that the reactions from the people at camp were an insult to their efforts, so they decided to make things a little more interesting. One of them made the sound of an angry elephant, which shook up the camp. To make it more dramatic, Meru and I acknowledged that the trumpet was indeed one of anger, and the result was hilarious. As panic set in the camp, the branch-breakers upped their efforts and, if not for the inexperience of the four victims of our prank, it would have sounded ridiculous. Branches were being broken with an urgency that bordered on maniacal. A few more elephantine sounds pushed it over. One guy jumped up as if he had been shot and landed under the van that had brought them. The other guy created a lasting memory in my mind, for he managed to find my helmet from the bike and then attempted to climb a tree, holding a glass of whiskey, and promptly fell down. The driver fell on his knees and started wailing "*Cauvery Amma, kaapaathikko*" (Godess Cauvery, save us) over and over again. Dr. Ansari was too scared to do anything, so he just sat there shivering violently, but the funniest was Mukherjee, who kept telling Meru's wife, "This could be dangerous, hold on to your kids" as he positioned himself between the elephants and them, armed with nothing more than his torch, which he kept flashing in all directions. Meru's wife had to cover her face as she knew what was going on, and Mukerjee's antics had her in convulsions.

"Don't worry dear, we have to be brave now," reassured Mukherjee, seeing her head in her lap, shaking. I decided that we could have some more fun. I gave hope to the crowd: "The only way to scare them off is to show them that we are many in number. I've learnt this trick from the locals over there, everyone take out your steel plates and bang them with your spoons."

For the next few minutes, we had the entire camp banging way on their plates to scare away the elephants. Subhan and Bolaiyah came back and added that they couldn't go far and that the entire camp looked like it was surrounded by elephants, and they increased the frenzied clanging. After a while we asked them to stop and explained the joke, and boy, did we all laugh!

As the tourists started pouring in, we had no choice but to change our plan as they cramped our style. Whenever possible, we would leave Thursday after lunch, spend the night there, and take the day off on Friday, breaking camp by Saturday before the crowd came in. We then figured out that there were others who were as clever as us, especially a Channapatna gambling gang who followed the same pattern. Although they were non-interfering buggers, it was an uneasy feeling, knowing that they were around, as at times they numbered thirty or more. Sometime around 1984 or 85, they started to sell beer at Kanakpura and that opened the floodgates Gangs would come there with their bottles, drink themselves silly, get extremely boisterous, breaking bottles on the rocks, getting into fights and generally disturbing the peace of the area. They didn't care about angling or the wildlife; they were not interested in anything other than drinking and making merry and I knew that this spelled the end of Sangam as a haven for us.

It's uncanny that like my father who had some sort of connection with Mumptyvayan the brigand, I had a vague and almost non-descript association with Veerappan. Although the S.T.F (Special Task Force) was formed only in the early nineties, he had been causing trouble in these forests right from the mid-eighties. On one occasion I was at Sangam, returning from Ontigondu, when two men appeared in front of me. They carried firearms while I had nothing other than my fishing rod with me. One look at them was enough for me to comprehend that these men meant business, they were no greenhorns.

"*Dorai*, do you know who we are?"

It was a statement, not a question. I affirmed, although no names were mentioned. Word travels fast and I knew that the legend of the Indian Robin Hood was no myth. Just as his informants kept him up to date about developments, my gang at Sangam had also warned me about the presence of such a gang and what they were capable of doing.

"We need some raw materials," they stated. It was not a threat but I was in no position to negotiate and after all they weren't asking for much, so Bada Subhan and I shared a secret we promised to take to our graves—abetting the dreaded bandit! I don't know why they trusted me, but I was approached on multiple occasions for small requests like oil, chilli powder etc. although I never met him. Their observation system was excellent, for I would be approached only when I was alone. Despite their roughshod ways, they would always approach me first, and I would then instruct Bada Subhan to hand over whatever they wanted. No questions asked, no money exchanged, no promises, nothing. I didn't sympathise with them, yet I didn't want to notify the authorities. Perhaps they were desperate or maybe they had gained confidence, but one day towards the end of '89, I was at a camp with my friend Meru and a few others. We had all settled down for a quick nap after a heavy lunch when I noticed a bare-bodied man at camp. Most people were asleep, but I heard him far away. I knew that he had swum across the river but to walk into a camp was brazen, especially at that time of the day. He must have swum up behind Mosalahalla and walked right into our campsite. I didn't want a conversation, so I gave him the slightest of acknowledgements and as I turned my eyes away, I noticed Meru sitting up and staring at the proceedings. He was practical enough not to intercede, but I could hear the questions whirring in his head. The man went over to Bada Subhan and took away dal, chilli powder, and some other stuff, tied in his shawl. I covered my face with a hat, and pretended to sleep, but Meru walked over and began quizzing Subhan. He was a terrible liar and I could see him give contradicting answers to Meru's questions, but luckily the matter ended there.

The S.T.F were no fools. They knew that I knew those areas inside out, and they sent the police to my house in Eejipura on a couple of occasions, asking for my suggestions on a whole host of topics. They were really fishing for information about Veerappan's gang members. Luckily, they always sent someone who did not speak English very well and I always used the language barrier as an excuse not to divulge any information. I truly didn't know about Veerappan's whereabouts, but I felt that whatever information I gave them would only cause more trouble. Veerappan was too smart and there was no way my information would help the S.T.F or the police. They would not just hold me responsible for their lack of success, they would spread the word in the jungles that I was the one who gave them the information. So, I refused to get involved. I am extremely cautious about what I say, and the joke doing the rounds in those days among my Anglo-Indian friends was that "one could get water out of a rock, but one cannot get information out of Don Anderson."

Chapter Eight

Kenneth Anderson, My Dad

MY FATHER, KENNETH DOUGLAS STEWART ANDERSON, was born on 8 March 1910 in Bolarum, a railway colony in Hyderabad state. He was baptised at the Holy Trinity Church and was known by many names including KD, KDS and "Snake Charmer Anderson", but he was called "Jock", the Scottish version of Jack, by his parents, a name that stuck, and by which most of his friends remembered him. It wouldn't be inaccurate to say that he grew up in the company of adults, as he didn't have siblings. His cousins lived far away and his only friends were the few children of his father's fellow officers in the army, none of whom shared his interests.

His father, Douglas, got posted for the second time in Bangalore and the family moved to the city when Dad was about seven or eight years old. He thus knew a fair bit of Telugu, Urdu, and Hindi by the time they came to the city where he would spend the rest of his life. The domestic help in Bangalore, a bevy of ayahs, chokras, and malis, in the early part of the last century were mostly from Madras State and he thus grew up learning to speak fluent Tamil as well. He learned to fit in with both the European and Indian worlds from a very early age, and this comfort level would prove useful in the years to come. Like me, he too was taught by his father to handle a gun at a very young age.

He studied at Bishop Cotton's Boys School and later at St. Joseph's European High School, two prominent educational institutions for a British family in those days. Tamil remained his favourite verbal arsenal and he was known to spout some extremely vulgar Tamil songs much to his mother's disconcertion. Although not a particularly wayward child, his fascination for pets often led to minor skirmishes at home. During his childhood, the pets at the house were restricted to dogs but Kenneth's constant fascination with snakes and other creepy-crawlies was a constant strain on everyone's nerves. They soon realised that Dad's fascination with animals was not just a passing fancy. He genuinely seemed to connect with animals and they with him, and so his demands for exotic pets were often entertained.

Reptiles, especially snakes, were a source of endless fascination for him and apparently, he used to spend quite a bit of his pocket money on snake charmers, without informing his parents. Keeping pet snakes was out of the question, but for a small price, he could play with the snakes that the snake charmers would bring, and they would spend hours together, away from the prying eyes of his mother. In fact, what was fascination during his early years turned into a thriving business for him when he started selling snake venom to some hospitals in Bangalore in the fifties and sixties. I had a major part to play in this venture, and although unlike my Dad I never liked snakes, my pleas would fall on deaf ears.

"Don't make excuses, you don't have to relish the experience, just do as you are bloody told," was a common response. Holding down hissing snakes made me perspire, and clammy hands are not exactly an advantage when extracting snake venom. But it brought in a fair amount of money, so I helped him anyway. Unlike today, where snakes are kept in glass cages in herpetariums, in those days we just had pits dug in the ground, one for cobras and one for Russell's vipers He would pull out a snake with a curved metal snake-stick, catch its head with one hand and force it to bite on a membrane that covered a small bottle that he held in the other hand. After that he would hand over the snake to me and it was my job to release it back into the pit.

Although he had been bitten when he was young, there are only two occasions I remember it happening to him and the first time I was at home. He had pulled out a particularly angry cobra from the pit. It was remarkably agile and kept lunging at him repeatedly while on the stick, so he called Thangavelu Jr to grab the tail of the snake. By then he had caught hold of the snake's head but the tail was still flailing fiercely. No sooner did the boy touch the snake than it wrapped its tail around his arm. He screamed and pulled back and Dad suddenly lost control of the head he was holding, causing it to bite him in an instant. We came running on hearing Thangavelu's screams and saw Dad sitting on the ground, ashen. We cut the area around the bite and tried to squeeze the poison out, and decided to take him to Victoria hospital, without even knowing whether they had anti-venom for cobra bites. He declined, insisting that we contact his friend, a railway station master somewhere in Hyderabad state who supposedly had a special *mantram* to cure him. We followed the instructions given over the telephone and true to his word, my Dad survived, while the cobra that bit him was caught and placed at the foot of his bed in a basket and ended up dead!

We provided a never-ending source of venom to hospitals in the city and this became a good source of income for us, but with the implementation of the Wildlife Act in 1972, the government changed laws and banned individuals from owning wild animals, and that effectively ended our business. Also, by the early seventies, my Dad's energy levels to continue this sort of thing had considerably waned.

After my grandfather moved to Bangalore during WWI, he came across two tiger cubs while hunting in Shimoga. For some reason, their mother was nowhere to be seen, and the cubs were seen gambolling without a care in the world, so they were picked up and brought to Bangalore. Dad got one while the other was given to one of my grandfather's fellow officers. Dad's first and only tiger cub grew in strength and size and was quite the centre of attention at Prospect House. Despite the reputation Bangalore had for European oddities, a pet tiger was pushing the envelope, even for those days, and many people would come to see it. "Stripes" was a very affectionate pet, probably because it was very young when it arrived. Unfortunately, it didn't live for more than a few months, for it developed some sort of illness and not even the best vet in Bangalore in those days was skilled enough to treat let alone diagnose a tiger! Dad was inconsolable and despite his father's valiant efforts, getting a replacement was not as easy as he thought it would be. Among another pets, he also managed to buy a mongoose and a cobra off a snake charmer who ran an entertaining act involving the duo. A cruel sport, for the mongoose's teeth were filed down and the fangs of the snake had been removed. They would be brought in separate baskets and once released their instinct would get them to attack each other, and that was a source of revenue for the owner, and entertainment for the crowd. However, this was a stunt with limited long-term potential as, after a while, both the snake and rodent realised that neither could inflict any sort of harm and would end up just ignoring each other completely. One such lackluster demonstration was at the Anderson residence and he ended up buying both creatures for a song.

Kenneth Anderson's first tiger – 1912

An infamous incident that involved "snake charmer" Anderson was at Imperial Cinema, opposite Imperial Hotel on Residency Road. This was during his school days, and Dad and his friend Leslie Bartley decided that they would have a bit of harmless fun. They carried half a dozen snakes and released them as soon as the movie started. The audience had no idea till a few of them started to feel slithery objects against their legs. While the first few instances were ignored, a few viewers in the crowd started growing fidgety. All hell broke loose when someone put their hands down and touched what was apparently a very lost serpent.

A single scream triggered pandemonium. Some people pushed aside their chairs while others jumped on them and the atmosphere was akin to a horror show. Dad also stood on a chair and shrieked, but during a recovery drive after the lights were turned on, people noticed that the gentleman who was screaming the loudest had a snake peeping from inside his shirt! He was promptly thrown out and banished from there.

At school, he was a master chess player, and that was the closest he got to play any sport. However, he was very good at writing articles and performing in the theatre. He was a voracious reader as well, and his room would be piled from floor to ceiling with books of every possible subject and interest.

An overachiever at school, he completed his Senior Cambridge in 1926. His parents had great hopes for him and sent him to Edinburgh to become a barrister. Their decision was reinforced by the fact that Forbes, his uncle, was in Scotland at that time. He was given the responsibility of being Dad's guardian. Despite his familiarity and comfort with the East, especially India, Forbes was clear about the divide that existed between the countries, especially the difference in race, and he did not want to be someone who patronised or made friends with Indians. This, according to dad, was hypocritical, considering his uncle was born and raised in India. He refused to comply with his uncle's pretence and spent all his time with the small Indian population in Edinburgh. However, the real problem was that he missed India, the climate, his pets, and of course the people. Despite his accent, he could pass off as a British boy with his blue eyes and light hair, but Dad felt that everyone was stand-offish, selfish, and did nothing to help one another. I suppose it wouldn't be unfair to say that perhaps he was a little spoilt as well, having a multitude of people at his beck and call when he was in India. After about eight months in Scotland he made up his mind to come back home but he never mentioned it to anyone. In fact, the miser that he was, he sold his first-class ticket to someone on the ship in exchange for cash and a downgrade. He broke his parents' hearts when he came back in 1928, but he was their only child and they had no choice but to be resigned to the fate that he was destined to live in India all his life. If that wasn't bad enough, he eloped with my mother when they were both just nineteen. He met her at Bowring Club and a whirlwind romance ensued, culminating in marriage in April 1929 at Sorkalpet, Cuddalore. They spent the next week at Pondicherry where Mum's family lived. All this was considered blasphemous in the Anderson household and the relationship between my grandfather and my father soured after that.

At Edinburgh – 1918

From my earliest memories of him, without any sense of exaggeration, I would say that he had a certain gift to able to communicate with animals of every kind. His words were not very different, neither was his tone, but somehow animals could sense that he understood them, and vice versa. This ability manifested in different aspects of his life, and he always referred to it as his "sixth sense". In the modern world, one would scoff about the existence of such an ability and laugh if someone claimed such a power. I can't give an explanation, but I've seen many instances where he would visit someone's home, and all the pets at that place would be all over him, completely ignoring the calls of the owners.

When he was with the Telegraph office, he started to buy land in the states of Hyderabad, Mysore, and Madras. He never considered it an investment that would appreciate over time, merely a piece of land he could stay on when he wanted to get away from Bangalore. In the 1930s and 40s, it was very easy for a British citizen to buy land, and despite being tight-fisted when it came to anything else, for buying plots of land adjoining forests, he could be ever so excessive. He had over twenty such properties in places including Pondicherry, Mamandur, Pulibonu, Yelagiri, Javalagiri, Hogenikal, Santaveri, Wodappeti, Segur, and Ooty.

Mind you, he led a very frugal existence when he was out in the jungles, and all he wanted was a roof over his head to protect him from the sun and rain. He almost always slept under the stars, ate the most basic food, and with his fluency for languages, had acquaintances everywhere. He thus became the anti-thesis of the "*dorai*" in those days, a strange and uncommon experience for the village people who knew him.

One such place he owned was in Uttamalai, where he had a one room house in the middle of the village, maintained by a rascal by the name of Qasim. He was an unscrupulous chap who wouldn't think twice about selling both his wives and their kidneys, as separate deals of course. He was enterprising enough to maintain the place like a bed-and-no-breakfast option for travellers who came to the village. The problem was that he was open not just to renting it out for a night, but also for a few hours, and although my dad never realised it during his lifetime, the property gained notoriety.

When Dad passed away, he bequeathed all his properties to me. However, the landscape changed with alarming pace after the early seventies, and the locals started getting more aggressive, often stating that we had overstayed and that we should go back to England. They had some information that foreigners were not entitled to hold properties in free India. They were correct to a certain degree as I had a British passport, and I felt that it was better to lose some of these properties than get embroiled in a situation where I would get extradited to another country. My visits became more and more infrequent as the sheer number of properties made it impossible to manage them and most of them were "*maaroed* (usurped) away" by the people who were entrusted to look after them. I lost some of the properties, and in an attempt to salvage whatever I could, I made quick deals and never got a fair value for the property I was selling.

Dad also bought land in the Nilgiris including a one-bedroom cottage at Ooty and the bamboo hut in Mavanhalla mentioned in the story "What the thunderstorm brought" in one of his books, which was adjacent to ERC Davidar's place. I sold the bamboo hut and the land it stood on in 1977 for about two thousand rupees. He also had a thatched hut on the Ooty main road, just after the Mavanhalla bridge, which he sold to

Davidar again, and today a bakery stands in that place.

As evident from his books, he was fascinated by the supernatural. He was someone whose beliefs were based on scientific reasoning and logic, yet he was inclined to believe in the paranormal because of what he saw around him. A lot of this came from his upbringing, having been raised in the company of Indian servants, for whom superstition, ghosts, black magic, spirits, gods and goddesses are all ingrained in their culture. There was never a phenomenon that could be classified as unexplained, everything had a reason, was bound in karma, and as a young boy, he perhaps grew up with a predisposed notion towards these beliefs. In those days, a European child's constant companions were his ayah, and other spokes of the domestic machinery that ran the house, and their beliefs rubbed off on to the children they looked after. As a child, he was fascinated with the swamis and fakirs who visited his house, and he would be seen conversing with them, much to the alarm of his mother. It would be perhaps unfair to attribute all his preternatural notions to the people of India, for he was a voracious reader even as a small child, his favourite subjects being haunted mansions, ghosts, banshees, and other things that go bump in the night. He was trying different methods to see ghosts or at least communicate with spirits and of course all this is evident in his writings—from believing in the sixth sense to having encounters with the supernatural.

Over the years he collected objects that were in some way connected to the occult and he had a room just for this, quite a sight for the unprepared eye. It was filled with skulls, crystal balls, planchettes, grotesque figures, religious symbols, myriad coloured gems, spells written on sheets of paper etc. I never believed any of it and my explanation for all this was that when one is on their own, the human mind is capable of wandering and will see things it wants to believe in.

He believed in gem therapy, where sunlight is passed through specific gems to transmit a unique frequency. This is absorbed by the body of the person wearing the stone or gem and over time, the person's system resonates in sympathy with this new stimulus and the healing process starts. The healing could be for issues ranging from simple maladies all the way up to attaining nirvana, or so was the claim. An offshoot of this was chromo-therapy or the use of lights to complement energy levels of the individuals. Among his other fixations was naturopathy. For a good ten years, he invented his own medicine to treat his baldness with hibiscus flowers. He used to rub his head religiously with a slimy concoction. Unfortunately, like most of his self-taught diplomas, the result was a total failure, as not a single hair grew!

Inventions were not limited to drugs to combat hair loss. He also believed in making his own medicines as cures for all sorts of disorders. Perhaps the catalyst was the interactions he had with local mystics and other people of the same cadre, but he improvised on a lot of them, and invented many medicines on his own. Curing of ailments with magnets was part of his repertoire for many years. At that point in time, I used to have severe pain in my lower back, and Dr. Anderson promptly offered me treatment where I did not have to waste money on doctors and medicines, a most compelling reason if there ever was one! He would place a large magnet on my back and move it clock wise one day and anti-clockwise the next. Of course, there were times when we would have to skip a day's session, and then both of us would forget which direction the magnet had to move the next day. No surprise, it didn't cure my aching back. He was not just a physician, he even treated psychological problems in which hypnotism played a big role.

He was an inventor too, a pair of spectacles to look at people's auras being among his note-worthy inventions. He believed it was the third eye or something to that effect, and that when perfected could be used to see energy levels that outlining people. Like the story of the emperor's new clothes, a lot of people admitted to seeing these auras, but I never gave in to that sort of pressure.

Most of his theories, inventions, and ideas were met with much amusement and derision at home, but he always seemed to take it rather well. He would quote a verse from the Bible: "No prophet is accepted in his hometown", implying that however great a person is, he is never appreciated by those who are close to him and only an unbiased person could truly see his greatness. Of course, that would lead to more laughter in our house. He was a no-nonsense person, never one for small talk. He had no qualms about coming straight to the point during a conversation, even with strangers.

"Bullshit baffles brains," he would say, looking one in the eye!

A lot of the man-eaters he shot were before I started going into the jungles with him, but he continued to go after them even after I had grown up, and occasionally we did that together. Although not his first, the Jalahalli panther is the one that brought him recognition, particularly because of the geographical proximity to Bangalore. In the late thirties, Jalahalli had a lot of scrub jungle and was visited by people like my dad who occasionally hunted for partridge and spur fowl. Hugh Plunkett and his brothers were good friends of my dad's. The family had a small farm house near Jalahalli and was therefore familiar with the area. Hugh, who had accompanied Dad, made the vital mistake of walking up to the panther after shooting without throwing stones at it and checking if it was alive, an error of judgement that cost him his life. He was clawed and bitten so badly that the doctors told him that the only solution was amputation, but he refused. Eventually gangrene set in and took his life. He lies buried fifty yards from my dad's grave in the Hosur Road cemetery. While Dad managed to put an end to the animal, he was filled with remorse after that, and that was not an uncommon thing. He loved all animals and taking their life always led to some sort of compunction.

He was particularly moved by this incident and wrote a poem, called **"The Panther's Requiem"**. Though this poem is written from the panther's perspective, I believe that the message is universal, implicitly echoing his lament that humans are responsible for creating situations that make animals appear as villains.

To all people ye who gaze on me,
That ye behold a skin unique in history,
Which clothed a creature quite as brave and free
As any living in this vast country.

Alone I faced five scores of scared men,
Armed as they were rifle and spear,
Swords, hatchets, staves coupled with human ken
Availed them naught, for they were stung by fear.

With Nature's sole defence, my fang and claw,
Thirteen I seized in my determined maw,
Not one would stand to face my fierce bound,
But scattered wide as dust blown from off the ground.

My beauteous body streamed blood from a torn side
Blasted and shattered, through cruel men's cupidity,
For they did covet my once glorious spotted hide,
Though their courage to mine was mere insignificancy.

They did wish to rob me of my own,

214

My very life, God's gift they should have known
To one who had a right to live, eat and enjoy existence
As much as they, who dared question this inheritance?

Think not hard of me, because I was
The destroyer of two brave human lives;
T'was mine or theirs, the best to win
Their greatest gamble only the brave play in.

While my victims did with advantage gain,
Such relief as modern science could afford
In my fierce agony or excruciating pain
I did bite the living flesh from off my rotting bones.

Alone and starving I did face the foe,
Sheer cowards who shot from a far distance,
While the burning heat of fever fast arose,
To torture me quite beyond endurance.

My parched tongue in vain did lick the gaping sore,
In which the cruel worms did their fell task
Poisoning my life-blood, while saliva denied its healing power
For want of water, one cool drink was all I asked.

'Tis over now, my sufferings are no more,
I died as I had lived, fierce and alone,
Brave, unconquered; the boast of no human foe
Could claim me as its own accomplishment.

By no machan, spot light, goat or beater
Was I brought low; cowardly ingenuity!
With four wounds I was far quicker
Than the crowd of men who lacked my indomitability.

Perhaps fate may ordain that I should meet
My two victims, if so I shall with pride
Respect them as they will me, we being the only three
Of a hundred breathing things, who stood their ground
and died.

One of my dad's favourite hunting stories was about Hugh's brother,
Arthur Plunkett. Arthur and his brother George, who were older than
my dad, were constant companions on a lot of our trips after Hugh

passed away. The three brothers looked at Dad with great respect, as he was a hero to them for his fearlessness when it came to hunting man-eaters, and they would often be tempted to sit up over baits to emulate similar feats. However, at the last minute their courage would fail them, and inevitably the bait would be sold back to the owner at a considerable loss.

Arthur, the braver of the two, felt that since they frequented places like Anchetti that were close to Bangalore, they didn't have the courage to shoot a tiger or panther, and so begged my dad to make arrangements in Hyderabad state, far enough from home to give him the shot of courage needed to get the job done. So, Dad arranged everything with his friend, the station master in Chamala, and Arthur landed there feeling very excited. However, as evening advanced, he realised that perhaps he needed to bolster his courage just a tiny bit with a small drink.

"Just a teaspoon," he cautioned himself as he hastily gulped down the potent Mahua liquor. "Maybe just one more, for the road," he added an hour later. He was feeling deliriously happy by the time he and his Chenchu tracker set off for the machan. Soon it began to get dark, but Arthur was focused, his steely resolve hardened by the powerful concoction. In about five minutes, they heard a rustling sound just under their tree and Arthur couldn't believe his luck. He was so confident that he did not even have to shine his torch; he confidently fired away and the dark shape fell into a heap, lifeless. Arthur was jubilant, and the heady mixture of the liquor and shooting his first tiger was so much that he fell into a deep sleep. He was not the only one, for his companion who had been suspiciously quiet all evening, too, fell into a deep slumber. However, the Chenchu was up at day break and awakened his master to show him the tiger that was killed the previous night. Arthur woke with a start, and realised to his horror and embarrassment that he had shot his buffalo instead!

Dad got married when he was just nineteen, so Mum was a constant companion on most of his trips. June and I were then added and it became a family affair. We would travel by car or train up to a point and then by bullock cart. I don't know how my dad managed to find those remote obscure locations but he would weave these wonderful stories about these places and it was all very exciting for us. The train or car journey would be made during the night and at the crack of dawn we would cover the last stretch by a covered bandy drawn by two bullocks.

This simple vehicle was nothing more than a broad platform on very high wheels, completely covered with mats. Blankets were placed on a bedding of straw which covered the platform and the boxes were kept on the periphery and tied down. The large wooden wheels were hardy but even a small stone would cause a terrible jolt and the ride was not exactly comfortable. The driver sat within easy reach of his bullocks' hind-quarters, and I would always beg to sit beside him, as it made me feel important. His repertoire of talking to the bullocks consisted of a complicated system of "hoh-hohs", "tock-tocks", and other odd sounds with his tongue combined with whip-flicking, slapping, tail-twisting, toe-poking, and, of course, verbal abuse. It would appear that the bullocks had no idea what to do until their master subjected them to some sort of corporal punishment. These unintelligent but hardy beasts have surprising endurance and a fair speed of about three miles an hour, and with breaks, can cover a fair bit of distance. Among the many changes that have taken place over the years is the colour of the milestones on the roads—in those days it used to be black, as opposed to the dark green ones that exist today.

Bullock-cart journey – 1937

Pulibonu was a favourite place of my dad's when we were growing up. I suppose this place was marginally less risky for there were no elephants in this part of the world, and that gave us considerable courage to roam about in the jungles. We would leave from Bangalore early in the morning and change trains at Bowringpet as it was on the link between Madras and Bangalore. The trains would be very crowded and one sat on wooden seats in the third class compartments, as travelling by first class was unheard of. So, we took cushions with us that served us on the trains as well as in the bullock carts for the next part of the journey. We would spend practically the entire day at the station, and then catch the train to Tirupati, alighting at Chandragiri at 6:00 in the evening. The station master at Chandragiri was a good friend of my dad's and would have made all the arrangements for us when we alighted. We would then begin the last leg of the journey by cart to Pulibonu which was about ten miles further, or sometimes even to Mamandur, another of Dad's preferred destinations ten miles further away.

As with most fathers and sons, after a certain age they treat each other as adults. Till that age is reached there is a clear line of control, and it was no different in my case. Visiting the jungles was what we did together and that's how I grew very close to him. Spider Valley and Devarabetta were particular favourites for these jungle walks. Sometimes he would pick me up from school on a Friday evening, we would drive for three or four hours, walk for another couple of hours, pitch up our camp, watch the wildlife, sometimes do a little bit of hunting, and repeat the same on Sunday. We would then leave late Sunday evening, be back early morning in Bangalore, and I would get ready and go to school. It was very hard, especially when I was quite young. Although he was a mild-mannered person who almost never lost his temper, he could be very tough when it came to things like this. I was about eight or nine when we started walking in the jungles, just the two of us, and I was expected to rough it out like him. I had to carry my own knapsack, and although it was considerably smaller than the one he carried, after a while my back would begin to ache. I wouldn't say anything but would then transfer it on to my head and then different arms, till I just could not carry it anymore. We would start walking before dawn to ensure we didn't run into elephants, but soon it would get unbearably hot, and eventually our water would run out. Initial complaints would soon be replaced with torrential tears, but none of this ever seemed to make a difference to

218

him or the speed we were walking at. I don't ever remember him losing his temper at such times but my protests were met with logical queries.

"I just can't walk anymore, Dad. I've had enough."

"What do you mean you can't walk anymore? Are you going to spend the rest of the day sitting in this spot? There is no one around for miles, and I am not going to sit here waiting for you to feel better. I have an adventure ahead of me, do you want to be a part of it?"

He would walk off, and I had no option but to drag my tired feet after him. And so, I would walk on for another hour or so, till the whole process repeated itself. There was no mollycoddling or praise. He never raised his voice or beat me, but he was incredibly tough in so many other ways.

Father and son at camp

As I got older, we started to walk during the night, and we would often encounter elephants but the two-cell torches we carried were good enough to scare them away. We often stopped at river banks, dug three feet in the river bed for water, filtered it about four times, and that was usually good enough to drink. Often in the mornings during summer, we would find tracks of elephants quite close to our spot, attracted by the scent of water.

You must be wondering why I subjected myself to this time after time. The answer is quite simple. I hated school and anything to do with studying. The thought of Monday morning, the drudgery of going back to school, arithmetic, and geography just seemed so painful. I just had to fill my head with thoughts of school and I would find instant energy to start walking again. Considering my attitude my dad also should have known better than to drag me out each time. However, he was very keen that we did this together. In fact, my dad would write leave letters for me to present at school, wherein it appeared that I would suddenly contract terrible diseases that lasted for about three days and then mysteriously disappear. With his amateur command over medical matters, he and I ran perhaps the longest running scam ever to go unearthed in the history of Bishop Cotton School.

In the jungles Dad never used a compass or the stars to find his way. Instead he learnt what he was taught by his jungle friends—to notice and remember landmarks like trees, rocks, landscape patterns and so on. It's not easy and if one is doing it for the first time, it can be quite scary as it's very easy to get lost. If you're travelling on flat terrain you cannot see ahead for more than ten or fifteen feet and so he taught me to interpret visual, auditory, and olfactory signs.

I learnt to build endurance, to walk over long distances, to live on a meagre and ever changing diet, and above all, to have a positive attitude. His military-like training forged the way that I conducted myself in the jungles as I grew older and I can say with conviction that it helped me immensely, not just to save my life on numerous occasions but to also appreciate everything I saw or encountered. In the jungle every possible waking moment is spent as an attempt to enjoy as much as possible of the time with the creatures of the forest.

Dad had a distinct walk—somewhat in the style of Charlie Chaplin, so if one saw footprints in the jungle, with the feet splayed out, one had a fairly good idea of who was responsible for them! In the jungles, his two favourite activities were walking and sitting over waterholes, especially on moonlit nights, and as he got older, he even stopped carrying his gun. I would accompany him on a lot of these trips, and while he could sit up practically motionless the entire night, I would be extremely fidgety, only stopping when I fell asleep.

Dad did not look like an Indian, yet his demeanour could be intriguing for someone meeting him for the first time. He was not tall and became stocky as grew older. His blue eyes would stand out against his tanned countenance and he always had a ready smile. It would be an exaggeration to say he had a strong British accent, but when he spoke Tamil, Hindi, or Kannada, he certainly had one, although he spoke with confidence. He looked like a sunburnt European, but dressed in the most appalling manner. He never cared about what people thought or spoke about him, he was very clear about his convictions and his priorities. When it came to learning about new things, his pursuits were insatiable. Once a particular topic caught his attention, he would be relentless in his search to understand everything about it. As with all brilliant people, he was eccentric and always looked to understand subjects most people would not attempt. To say that he was eccentric is putting it mildly. He was far ahead of his time and understood most things about most subjects. Be it engineering or medicine or religion, he could speak about that topic like a professional. He was just fourteen when he qualified for university, which was a good two years before his peers. There was no MENSA at that time, but had he been tested, I am sure that he would have qualified to be in their list. He could converse about any topic under the sun and with anyone who was interested to listen to him. As a father, he was neither very encouraging nor particularly involved with our school life. Although I was very good at sports, it never seemed to make him proud. June, on the other hand, with her academic brilliance, was the apple of his eye. We used to turn to him with all our problems because Mum didn't know much about the subjects we studied, especially as we grew older.

People who knew us would say that I inherited a lot of his traits, not the brains of course but his keenness for detail, and of course his love for the jungles. Over time he realised that I shared a common interest with him, or maybe I inculcated that habit so that he could be proud of me, or maybe he got me hooked on to it, but he and I finally had something to bond over. Irrespective of how it happened, he was the single largest influence on me and he taught me everything he knew when it came to the jungles. There was never any theoretical lesson. Each minute detail about the jungle was taught to me while in the wild and we were almost always on foot. He knew the behaviour of every animal and the song of practically every bird. He could converse with most tribes in some manner or the other and was in his element when in the jungle.

He spent fifteen years with the Telegraph Office and then worked with

HAL till he passed away. Everyone from the Anglo-Indian community knew him well, especially those who lived in Whitefield, although he was not the most popular person considering his eccentricities and his preference for animals over human beings.

Yet, he was a very kind and good-hearted person, and while he was capable of getting angry, I can never remember him ever resorting to using a cane—that was Mum's department, as she was extremely temperamental and strict. He loved all living creatures, not just from an academic perspective but genuinely. For Dad, the creepier the crawly, the happier he was, and he was almost like a defender of the underdogs in the animal kingdom. While June and I never picked up this trait of genuinely liking cold-blooded creatures, we handled baby crocodiles, iguanas and various kinds of snakes, and lost our fear of reptiles by the time we were four or five.

While he had no time for grown-ups, he loved animals and children, especially friends of June's and mine. When we were very small, we used that weakness of his to take us all for movies. However, he was such a miser that he would inform us that we could get just two friends of our choice and he would take us all for a matinee show. He would carefully count his money, keep the exact change and would always be flabbergasted when unexpectedly another three or four kids would land up, out of the blue. Not to be outdone, being as thick-skinned as he was, he would ask everyone to pay for their own tickets. And then the kids would chorus: "Mr. Anderson, we don't have any money" and inevitably he would have to pay up, but he would keep repeating loudly the fact that he had paid for everyone. This was not restricted to the movies alone, he would end up paying for many children when we went out for *dosai*, ice cream, and other snacks.

A funny incident that highlighted his tight-fistedness was one day when a cobra bit Dad during venom extraction. I wasn't at home. They tied a tourniquet and my Mum sucked and spat out the infected blood. If all this commotion and excitement wasn't enough, in the midst of it all, Mum ran off, came back with a revolver, and shot the cobra before anyone could even realise what was happening. My Dad was extremely upset, not because he loved the serpent but because it would have continued to be a source of income for us if we had caught it instead of killing it! They took him to a hospital where a dose of anti-venom cured him. However, it was not a very efficient method and the doctor had no idea how much to administer. He was given a very powerful dose and although it saved his life he was violently ill for almost a week. Soon enough, he was back to his venom extraction business!

For many years, while working for the Telegraph Department, his salary was 100 rupees a month. I suppose it was a good amount for we had a luxurious lifestyle. A multitude of hired help, a menagerie of pets, most of them with their own dinner plates, and all the other domestic expenses were run on that income. In 1956 he changed jobs and started working for the British Aircraft Company in Bangalore in the drafting department and later as a factory manager for planning. After nationalisation it became known as the Hindustan Aeronautics Ltd. He worked there till he was diagnosed with cancer in early 1974.

Like most of those people who held a British passport and were living in India, he too had to make a choice in 1947. While a large majority of them felt that they would be subjected to retaliation or, at the least, ostracised by the Indian people with their newly received freedom, Dad had no such misgivings. Though a *dorai*, his heart belonged to India and its people and he would openly talk about it. On the day of Independence, all the white skins were boarded up, and were given strict instructions not to go out. There are always mischief-mongers who use these situations to some other advantage and no one wanted to take a chance, after all it was freedom after about 200 years.

"Bugger all if I'm going to sit inside like a coward," was his vociferous statement and out he went causing much consternation amongst all of us. He was gone a long time, and my Mum was constantly looking outside, half expecting someone to bring her news of her newly acquired status as a widow. And then he was back, covered with garlands! Apparently, he was *gherao*ed by a group of people, who asked him what he thought about India getting Independence. Dad replied in chaste Tamil that this was the best decision that the British ever took. The crowd broke into rapturous applause, covered him with garlands and carried him around on their shoulders on MG Road!

While most Europeans felt it was better to leave the country, fearing retribution, the Anglo-Indian community was in a dilemma. Even amongst those who wanted to leave the country, getting the right documents proving their lineage was a challenge and they had no real choice but to stay on. Then there were cases like my dad, who, despite holding a British passport and having the finances to move abroad, chose to stay back in India. We had heard of McCluskieganj somewhere in north India, a Shangri La for Anglo-Indians, but I think it catered to the communities in Calcutta and other pockets in north India, and in Bangalore no one took it seriously. In fact, my dad vehemently opposed any sort of racial segregation and always believed in living in a homogenous society, and I would attribute that to the way Bangalore was in those days.

Every generation censures the one after theirs, often basking in their rectitude of judgement and lamenting the disappearance of the "good old days". I'm sure that my grandfather did that to my father, who did that to me. I don't have progeny to spew on but the change I have seen in the last thirty years is beyond permissible belief.

At every turn I am confronted by the monstrosity that we have created in the name of progress. Places, people, and priorities have undergone such a profound transformation that I am happy that Dad is not alive to see it. It would have broken his heart to see what the jungles of today feel like. In his books he writes about the metamorphosis he was witnessing, often expressing pangs of sorrow and regret, but I don't think even he, in his wildest imagination, could have envisaged the situation we see today. Don't get me wrong, even in his days there were poachers, corrupt officials and opportunists. In my opinion the difference is that today the genuine love for the jungles and its denizens is not imbibed in the souls of those who have been given the opportunity or responsibility to do so. Take a forest official for example. His job today is mostly administrative, and perhaps that's the need of the hour. Perhaps the multitude of roles he is designated to fulfil, leaves him no time to understand and appreciate the piece of paradise he has been assigned to. Back in the day, every official would know every bend in the road, every nullah, every rivulet that traversed his kingdom, and I attribute that to two reasons. The most obvious one is the advancement in science and technology; nowadays one can cover large areas quicker, with better roads and vehicles, thus making the official more efficient. A daily round, something that used to take a whole day, can now be done in a couple of hours, releasing time to ensure that his work-life balance is ensured. In my time, this chore was not a race. The only way to do it was on foot or horseback. My second and more accurate explanation is that for the people in the old days, the fascination to understand habitats and its constituents lay somewhere between pride and love. And I am not restricting this attitude to the forest squad alone. Today that's all but disappeared. People visit forests nowadays only to take pictures of tigers, and are always in a hurry to shoot the picture and rush back to their computers. They don't appreciate the time they spend in the forest or any of the lesser creatures that they pass by without a second glance. While people may complain about how rushed and busy their lives are and how restrictive the rules imposed on them, it's still no excuse for their behaviour and had my dad been alive, he would have given them an earful.

My jungle jaunts accompanying Dad could be exhilarating to say the least. Often we would reach a *patti* where we would attempt to refill our water and get first-hand information about animal movements in the vicinity. The subsistence of the inhabitants was largely dependent on *ragi*, jungle greens, roots, and wild fruits which they never had enough of to give away. We knew that their meagre lives provided a hand to mouth existence for the few families that constituted the *patti* and never thought of asking for food. Our food hamper was a curious mix of meat curries like vindaloo, tinned butter, bread, pickle, condensed milk and chapattis. When we ate, we ate well, always justifying to ourselves that food was better inside our bodies than outside, where it could get spoilt. With that attitude, it wasn't surprising that we ran out of rations quite quickly. So, we hunted or trapped small game like jungle fowl, spur fowl, hare or mouse deer, which incidentally is exquisite, borderline venison. If we planned to provide meat for a village or settlement, we would look at larger game in our cross-hairs, wild boar and sambar being first choices. Of course, if the trip was planned better, we would attempt a father-son version of a vindaloo. Our cooking was quite like the way we moved in the jungles—by instinct—and the well-intended proportion of jeera, coriander, and chilli powder combined with copious amounts of ginger, garlic and whatever else the gunny bag held always seemed to blend into the most amazing dish although perhaps not as vindaloo-esque as originally hoped for.

In some of my dad's books, he mentions cooking game birds. In my opinion, there is nothing to surpass the taste of a well-cooked male red jungle fowl. He is a fine bird with a beautiful call that gets you ready for the day. He is extremely cunning and provides a real challenge to any hunter to bag him. The effort is definitely worth it, for although the meat is tougher than domestic fowl, with almost no fat, it is extremely tasty. A favourite of the Anderson family was smoked pork. Portions of the boar after the blood had been let out would be cured with spices and hung to dry in the pantry adjoining the kitchen in the bungalow. A similar process can be done for venison as well.

If you do not have the convenience of staying at a forest guest house and are in the open, you can still manage to do this. Create an enclosed structure and start a fire in the middle. As the intent is to cure it by smoke and not heat, the fire need not to be very big. The wood you choose must be carefully selected, and ideally wood that is slightly green is alright. The meat must be cut into thin slices and hung on horizontal sticks some distance above the fire. Canvas cloth works well as an enclosure to contain the smoke and direct it towards the meat. As a rule, meat cured this way for about a couple of hours will last you a week.

Food was always something that could be managed; if you ran out, you could manage to last a few days, but water was always a concern. We had to travel light, especially when we were walking, and it did not make sense to lug large containers of water. Thirst is the mother of all water-borne maladies in the jungles and the presence of water sources dictated the distance we covered walking when we were there. It could mean a rushing river or water reached by digging in the sands of a riverbed. If we had the equipment, we boiled water before consumption, but more often than not it meant lying down, filling the cup of your palm, and praying that the germs were minimal! Science trumped religion in those days, for I have contracted typhoid, dysentery, and black fever from jungle pools. These notches in my belt with other big hitters like malaria and painful tick bites whose effects last for months on end, were parts of my jungle adventures that were far from amusing.

Of course, that did not mean that we did not carry medicines. When we were out in the jungles, my dad would carry a mix of his own concoctions and the only ones that worked were Epsom salts, Easton's syrup, permanganate of potash, penicillin, and ammonia. This would be dependent on our mode of transport and how much walking had to be done. If it was a weekend trip and included a fair bit of walking, we would each carry just our canvas haversacks that held just the basic items.

By the mid-sixties, trips to the jungles had changed considerably. My dad no longer carried his gun, and our trips were less strenuous. Although I was still picky about the kind of people I took along, we— my friends Merwan, Wille Wollen, Dad and myself—had formed a clique. Merwan brought the car, petrol and food to the equation. My

Dad brought the contacts with the forest department and his knowledge of the area we were going to. There were still some jobs that had to be done and they were divided equally. Right up till a few months before he died, Dad continued to go his beloved jungles if he had the company of like-minded people. He mucked it up with us youngsters—he was in his sixties while we were in our thirties—but he got along with everyone and was a good sport on these trips.

The picture of Dad which hung in my room and became famous has an interesting story. In the early seventies when I was working at Binny's, Cordell was a rival brand and when they came out with a new shirting line, they were on the lookout for "inexpensive, and preferably free" brand ambassadors to be models. In those days, getting your name in the newspapers was a big deal and that's what their sales pitch was. This line of clothes was meant for the man who loved the outdoors and they wanted rugged men. I was a natural choice among the eligible men in Bangalore, but I refused as Cordell was a competitor to Binny's.

However, I managed to convince the people at Cordell to get my Dad as a model. Naturally, he was not happy about it as he was never one to dress up for any occasion, in fact he almost decided to come to June's wedding in a *lungi*, believing that no one had the right to decide what he should wear to any function, social propriety be damned. Only two buckets of tears provided by June at short notice managed to change his heart and more importantly his clothes. Luckily, I did not have to follow the same tactics, and practically speaking, it would have been impossible, but I massaged his ego and mentioned the fame he would get, and finally he agreed. However, when we landed up, we found out that they were keen on him wearing a white shirt, holding a rifle. He was already in a foul mood when we left home as it was unilaterally agreed that his .405 was too weather-beaten for this shoot, and my rifle would be used instead.

"You buggers, don't you know that only a complete idiot would venture into the jungle wearing white?" he bellowed when the second piece of bad news was shared with him. Unfortunately, all his ranting fell on deaf ears as they had decided what shirt they wanted, and poor Dad suffered the ignominy of falsely representing what a genuine hunter would look like. His scowling countenance is a true reflection of his mood on that day.

Cordell's brand ambassador

If ever someone needed proof of Dad's ability to sense things that others couldn't, he proved it by predicting his own death. A couple of month before he was diagnosed with cancer, he and I made a memorable trip to Javalagiri. It was supposed to be a weekend trip, with no expectations other than to spend the nights at our favourite waterhole. We reached on Friday night, and had finished the dinner that we had packed from home. Tinned meat, chapattis and of course a pudding to complete the feast! It was just about 9:00 p.m., and usually we both liked to have a small nap before we headed out to spend the night, but this time Dad seemed almost eager to get started. Grumbling under my breath, I put on my jacket. Neither of us had guns, so I checked my torch, ensured that I had spare batteries and left our hut trying to catch up with him. Just as we crossed the forest rest house and passed a patch where the land had been cleared for some cultivation work, out of the blue, three tuskers appeared in front of us. They were not particularly large, and I was sure that they had just wandered away from the herd they belonged to, but it was a most unusual sight to see three of them stand almost side by side. There was no wind, and though it was not a particularly dark night, I don't think they could feel our presence. We stood motionless, but after a couple of minutes, they seemed to get agitated. They were making small snorting sounds and flapping their ears. Not quite alarm signals but they were getting restless. Then, almost synchronised, they started raising their trunks, almost as if in salutation. It was not like a circus elephant's greeting, but an ear flap—trunk curl salutation and to see three of them do that, standing next to each other was a wondrous sight. Then they just turned away and melted into the shadows of the undergrowth. I felt exhilarated but it seemed to have the opposite effect on him.

"I want to go back," he quietly mentioned. I was curious but knew better than to open my mouth then. We trudged back, and he lay down on his rug on the floor of the hut, looking up.

"That's a sign Don, even the elephants know that my days are numbered." I scoffed at that remark, but he always had these premonitions or "sixth sense" as he writes in his books, and I had a horrid feeling in my gut that he was right.

Toward the latter half of the sixties, Dad realised that his phenomenal understanding of the Indian jungle could be used to make money. He was thus, one of the pioneers of wildlife tourism in Bangalore. He was quite finicky about the kind of people he took, they were usually foreigners, especially Americans, and he managed to have a small stream of income. This carried on for a few years, and suddenly one day towards the end of 1972, he was getting ready to go for a trip, but when he woke up that morning, he said that he didn't want to go. He just wouldn't explain it, but I've always believed in his "sixth sense" and knew that something was about to happen, something that none of us, not even he, could explain. He then inexplicably burst into tears. He was inconsolable and considering that he was never one who cried for anything, we were naturally upset as well. He never told me, and I never got the chance to ask him, but I am sure that he knew the very day the cancer cells started spreading. He was depressed for about a week, and then the symptoms started to appear. There was blood in his stool and urine (in those days we used to have dry latrines) and it was only a matter of time before he was diagnosed with cancer at St. Martha's Hospital in Bangalore. His doctor was Dr. Joseph Antony, one of Bangalore's premier urologists at that time. Through some aggressive treatment it was believed to have been brought under control, but in six months' time, the bleeding and the pain was back, and we were advised to take him to Vellore for radiation therapy where we believed the oncology department was superior.

I was working with Binny's at that time, and after a whole week of working on the shop floor, I would leave on Friday evening, reach Vellore in the middle of the night and sleep in my car as the hospital wouldn't let me in at that time. Then early in the morning, I would get medicines, test results, see the doctors and, of course, spend time with him. He would want to know about all the news he was missing out on. He rarely asked about people, he was only interested in his pets, and news from the jungles. Like all old people, and patients, he made it as difficult for me as possible. Once when I was there, he had a very high fever, and the doctor had asked me to wake him up every three hours to apply cold bandages and give him medicines. I would be so tired after working non-stop and driving, that I would miss a few instances. Of course, he wouldn't miss the opportunity. He would have the medicine and bandages ready, but instead of administering it himself, he would wake me up and ask me to do it!

The specialists in Vellore started treating him with cobalt radiation, exposing parts of the bladder where the cancer had spread, to kill the cells. Of course, this brought its own set of problems and he had started hemorrhaging profusely every night. The morning rays would fall on copious amounts of congealed blood—there would be blood on the sheets, the mattress, his clothes and of course on his body, a truly horrific sight. It was almost poetic that he would look like a victim that survived an attack from a man-eater, the very kind of people he had protected all his life.

It's not often that one will find staff at a hospital to be empathetic to patients and CMC was no different. The radiologist was extremely hostile and his attitude was aggravated by my dad's incessant questioning on his methods. The Andersons are no pushovers and after a couple of incidents where better sense prevailed, one-day Dad left in a huff over a trivial issue. He got into a taxi and turned up at home unannounced, refusing not just to go back to Vellore but to take any sort of treatment too. It took all of us over a week to convince him that he needed treatment, but I don't think deep in our hearts any of us were convinced that any treatment would be a permanent solution. He finally agreed to go to St. Philomina's but by then he was convinced that he could cure the cancer using his alternate stream of medicine. It was an eclectic array that had bits of homeopathy, good old jungle magic and everything else in between. He started reading even more voraciously about cures and about the afterlife. He made me get swamis and other religious men to bless him and fight the disease, but things didn't improve.

The cancer had been extremely aggressive and the doctors equally so in their treatment and that left the large part of his bladder burnt and ineffective. They realised this at Philomina's and had two suggestions— either connect the small intestine to the bladder through a tube or have a bag outside, which could be emptied at regular intervals. He preferred the latter despite the social embarrassment. However, the decision taken was to have the internal tube, and as he predicted, infection set in, and soon his kidneys were affected. He then begged us to take him home, beseeching us not to let him die in a hospital. Sometimes I think the fear of dying within four walls was worse than the fear of death itself. He said that he wanted to feel the sun on his skin and the wind on his face, he wanted to hear birdsong, and touch his pets. He no doubt loved all of us, but he would never admit it like the way he spoke about his love for nature. He was heartbroken that June couldn't come and see him, and as he swayed in and out of consciousness, he would be whimpering with pain and ask for June. Unfortunately, she couldn't come, and he passed away without her ever having to see him in that state.

The agony he went through because of the cancer and the radiation was unbearable to watch, but what terrified him most was the thought of suffocation, and I know that that that fear is something he has passed on to me. During the last operation, as he was going into the operation theatre he had an oxygen mask on, and couldn't speak, but his eyes had a terrified look. He had an imploring look, as if to say, "Don't let me suffocate in there", and all I could do was stand there helplessly. Tears welled in my eyes and I just knew that there was no hope for him. He then beckoned me with a finger. I knew I was a moment away from breaking down when he said, "You've been a brick, Don. You're my everything" and then they wheeled him away.

Looking back, I can think of so many things I should have spoken to him when I knew he was on his deathbed but the words wouldn't come. Instead I focused on taking care of things, the treatment, the finances, and the hundred other things he was involved in. I was a coward, I knew that I would break down if I talked either about his emotional state or mine, so I avoided it at all costs. I don't think he wanted to do that either, but one day after a particularly bad attack of pain, he motioned me close and said, "I want you to do two things for me. You have to stop killing yourself with your smoking and I need you to stop hunting."

I used to smoke about two packs of cigarettes a day, but I had no problem giving that up ... but hunting! How could I give up the most important thing in my life, something my entire life revolved around, something I had made so many sacrifices for?

I never shot another living creature ever again.

In the last couple of days, the pain was so excruciating that he had to be administered morphine for relief. This was done at St. Martha's, where he eventually breathed his last on 14 August 1974. His body was first brought to Prospect House and then taken to Hosur Road cemetery. I remember a point during the last days where we had a huge argument about how his epitaph should read. He was adamant and wanted to write something along the lines of "Here lies Kenneth Anderson, who was burnt and killed by radiation, thanks to the incompetent doctors at Vellore", but we ignored his rant and made something else that was far less inflammatory! For someone who never believed in God, he became extremely pious during his last days. He always believed in spirits and unexplained energy but he never could convince himself to attribute it to God. In fact, apart from the time when he was very young, he never went to church, but during the last few months of his life he accepted God as someone that was responsible for everything, including things he couldn't explain. For his tombstone I managed to get a huge red stone from his Secret River, a stone that was almost rectangular shape, smoothed over thousands of years and it made the grave looked grand. But sometime during the late 1980s, it was stolen.

Dad used to shoulder all the responsibilities of the house, and I was in shock when he died as I was suddenly left with so much to handle. June had gone to Australia and I had practically been an only child for more than twenty years. Only then, like all children who lose their parents, did I realise how much he had been doing, without a murmur. He worked full time, did all sorts of odd jobs around the house, and ran a well-oiled machine on the home front, especially finances, and only after he was gone, did it all dawn on me. Although I was never a believer in the afterlife, somewhere deep down I felt that having gone to the other side he would show himself to me through some form or manifestation, but that never happened. I wish I could have spent more time with him.

However, I was selfish to such an extent that whenever work didn't take up my time, I used to head to the jungles with my friends. Of course, he came occasionally as well, but looking back I know I should have spent more time with him. He was a most interesting person, had tremendous energy for anything he was involved in, and possessed a razor-sharp wit.

My mom died of pulmonary edema on 11 March 1987 at the age of seventy-seven at St. Martha's hospital, the same hospital where he spent his last days. Just as in the case of my dad, I would work all day at Binnys, then visit her at the hospital, spend the night in the car, drive to Whitefield in the morning, change and then drive to Hebbal for work. I would eat at the YMCA and this became my routine for a while. We had sold Prospect House by then and were living in Whitefield. A lot of Anglo Indian families had moved to Whitefield and my mom felt right at home, although it was a rude awakening to live in our humble two-bedroom dwelling after living in the palatial Prospect House. She didn't suffer as much as my dad, but after losing her, I started what would become my life long problem with depression. When you lose your first parent, the concept is so alien, that it breaks your spirit. Then when you lose the next one, you realise that you're an orphan, with no one to look up to, no one to ask for advice, and the fact quickly dawns upon you that you are well and truly alone in the world. Perhaps if I had married and maybe even had children, I may have stood a chance to a recovery, but then the folly of my actions struck me hard. My dad was the only child, so I had no relatives on his side. My mom's family had migrated to Australia and I was never very close to them. June had moved to Australia as well, and I felt so alone. I had no shortage of friends or female companionship but neither that nor, to my surprise, the lure of the jungles could wake me from my stupor. I was inconsolable, and for weeks I refused to talk to or see anyone. The only time I went out of the house was to visit the grave and I took white lilies that were her favourites. My parents were living separately, something that no child likes to see, so perhaps an illogical part of my brain thought that the only way I could get to see them together was for them to share a grave and that's what I did. I would sit there and I would almost fall into a trance—I would keep dreaming about the past, think about missed opportunities, lost chances, the creatures whose lives I had snuffed out, and all the mistakes I had made…there were so many. Sometimes too much introspection can be a bad thing, and in my case, one outcome was that I would never get so attached to anyone ever again.

I lived in Whitefield for years after that; I just could not imagine going back to the cantonment area and pass the place where my house used to once stand. It had been demolished and something else had come up. While it's not common nowadays, and perhaps I am one of the last to have experienced it, in earlier times, children would be born at home, and spend their growing years, and eventually die, in the same house. I had hoped for the same but things never work out the way you plan. I lived on rent in a few places in Whitefield, and although I never made any trouble for my landlord, each time when I was asked to move on, I would get into a terrible row and ensure that I never went away without a fight. Soon my infamous nature began to take its toll and no one wanted to rent out their property to me in Whitefield, and I had to come back into town. I was lucky to find a place in Eejipura, the back of beyond, and stayed there for a few years.

A few years later, the owners wanted me out, and this time I was hell bent on getting compensation for having to relocate again. I was paying my rent on time and did not create any trouble, and I knew that it was sheer greed that drove them to throw me out and get tenants who would pay more rent, and so I deserved to get adequately compensated. From a neutral perspective, it might have looked as though I was asking for too much, but the nightmare I faced getting the last tenants out of Prospect House was too deeply etched in my head and I wanted to pass on the same treatment I received. During my ill-tempered battle with the owners of the Eejipura property I was desperately looking out for a place to stay and I happened to learn that Mrs. Norris, an Anglo-Indian lady, was looking to let out part of her house on Richmond Road. I knew her quite well, although she was a decade or so older than me, and Richmond Road suited me very well. She was happy to let out a section of her house to me, in fact she had refused quite a few applicants. I think, deep down, she was waiting for an Anglo-Indian family to approach her. She was a quiet old bird, and mostly kept to herself. She didn't bother me or ask questions and I too kept to myself. She passed away in Australia when she went to visit her daughter and soon her heir, her niece, arrived on the scene. I could sense what her intentions were, but she behaved civilly and mentioned that she was happy to have me as a tenant. As she was leaving, she hinted that someday she would like to sell the property, and I could see numbers churning in her head. She was hoping that the market would appreciate, and she was willing to wait for a while. Neither she nor I realised how long a wait that would be. Considering the many illnesses I had, I was sure that I would die in this house, rather than in some apartment hundreds of feet above the ground. Imagine not being able to walk on grass or smell the wet earth after the rain. Imagine not being able to hear a ripe mango fall or the last drops of rain trickling into a puddle. I would rather die than live a day knowing that I could never experience those things again

No. 10 Serpentine Street became my address in 1999 and I handmade the small postbox on the gate that said DMSA (Donald Malcolm Stewart Anderson). My landlady would visit Bangalore every year and with every visit her intentions became more vocal. Of course, I wasn't the only tenant she had to deal with. To explain it better, the compound had four buildings. The middle section was the main house, which had a partition on the right side, and I occupied that. Then were the two servant outhouses on the extreme right and an old Coorg lady occupied the first section on the left as you entered the premises. Mrs. Norris and I occupied the middle section, she got about 80% and I got the rest, just a small room and a bathroom at the back. Outside lay a couple of buildings in a state of dilapidation for there had been no upkeep for many years. The landlady's greed had reached tipping point and she wanted to sell the property. Again, I was disciplined to pay rent on time, in fact I always paid advance rent for at least six months and she couldn't find a reason to ask me to leave, so one day during one of her visits, she brought up the topic of safety. I don't want you to stay in this terribly old building, she gushed, overflowing with concern for my welfare.

"Who knows what would happen if it collapsed one day." She could have tried that stunt with anyone else but not with Donald Anderson.

"Don't worry, I'll take my chances," I retorted.

Our relationship nosedived after that. To her credit, the building was in bad shape, and she tried to convince me that her intentions were noble—she apparently did not want me out of the compound, just out of the main house. So, I moved out and into one of the outhouses meant for hired help, decades earlier. I took up residence in the larger of the two sheds, while the smaller building housed a lot of my trunks and other material I had collected over the years. What a fall from grace! From Prospect House where I grew up with so many bedrooms and servants to wait on me, to a one-room, bathroom and kitchen, all of which would have fitted into a tiny corner of a room at Prospect House. The reality did not hit me till I had moved all my stuff in. As I lay down in my bed, I could practically reach out and touch all the walls. There was just enough space for a large bed, two almirahs and a television, all touching each other. The roof had leaks, the walls were crumbling, and the roof was broken in places. Cobwebs and filth had collected over decades, the room was dank and musty, years of dust and grime had taken its toll, and I knew this was where I would die one day.

Epilogue

The Last Days

DONALD MALCOLM STUART ANDERSON PASSED AWAY
on 12 June 2014. He was eighty. A life surviving on borrowed time came
to an end, motioning the end of a distinctive era. Eighty is a ripe old
number, but considering what the world was like at both ends of his
life, it translates into something unique. He was running around with
catapults and air guns during World War II, and he was a teenager when
India got Independence. At the end, he was a relic who had learned
not just how to survive in an ever changing, ever crumbling world but
to adapt incredibly well, fighting off poverty, loneliness, depression,
numerous afflictions and, of course, the painful loss of friends and
family.

This chapter is an attempt to capture a very small part of his life, the
years I was privy to, from 2008 till 2014.

I grew up in Cochin, and as a young boy, my shelves overflowed with
books by Enid Blyton. As I progressed to books written by Richmal
Crompton, and then Willard Price by the time I was ten, I noticed a
set of eight books written by Kenneth Anderson that my father had
purchased a few years earlier. I was at an impressionable age and the
combination of the photographs on the cover and the stirring titles got
me interested. I had not read any books of this kind, not even Corbett,
so I was enthralled to say the least. As the stories were set in south
India, I began to relate to a few areas and places mentioned in the books
and before I knew it I was hooked. I knew that Kenneth Anderson had

passed away but never for a moment did I imagine that Don would be alive, and at that young age I couldn't even comprehend the notion of meeting him. I was content with just reading the books.

I finished my schooling and went on to get my engineering degree in Bangalore. Again, for the four years that I was in the city, I never thought of looking for Donald, although I had brought along all my books and would read them regularly. I came back to Bangalore after my post-graduation in 2002, with a job in hand, and I began to think of ways to revisit the places that Anderson wrote about, spending a lot of time online.

During this time, I joined a thread on an online hunting forum called "The Jolly Roger" where someone was discussing Kenneth Anderson, and I added my comments. In a matter of a month, we had about six or seven interested people writing to each other, all die-hard Anderson fans. So, I created a yahoo e-group for Kenneth Anderson fans and someone mentioned that Don was still alive and not too far away either, and we decided that we would certainly go and meet him. A few of us—Praveen, Ravi and I—from the newly found Kenneth Anderson fan club visited places like Sangam, Anchetty, and Sivanipalli, to retrace the stories from the books. The e-group grew in strength and it helped bring together more than just armchair fans. We got a huge shot in the arm when Sandhya, one of the original members, managed to get June to join the group.

I first met Don in 2003. From various sources, I had heard that he was a recluse, shunning human company and always suspicious of strangers. Despite all the supposed fuss about how he was a loner and did not want to be contacted, he was listed in the telephone directory! To be absolutely sure, I called him.

"Am I speaking to Donald Anderson, at No.10, Serpentine Street?" The voice at the other end replied in the affirmative. That's all I needed to hear, so I disconnected the call without giving him a chance to ask me more questions.

The next day I reached Richmond Road and found my way to the address I had confirmed. Sure enough, the post box on the gate confirmed it, and as I stood there, contemplating my grand introduction that would floor him, make him invite me in and show me guns, trophies and photographs, I was interrupted from my reverie.

"Son, can I help you?"

It didn't sound like the voice on the phone, and the person in a floral nightdress looked a lot more feminine than the one I had seen in the books I had grown up reading.

"I'm looking for Donald Anderson," I blurted.

"Oh, let me get him for you," the old lady quipped. "Don, someone here to see you."

And then, there was Don Anderson walking up to me. The familiar, though slightly sun burnt face from the photographs I had seen in the books I had read, walked up to the gate, ever so slowly, with a surly chocolate brown Weimaraner by his side.

Polite, but suspicious. "Yes?"

I hadn't expected this response, for I mumbled something about Kenneth Anderson, thinking of something to say to impress him, but my brain refused to work. He made it easier for me. "I'm sorry, but I am very ill, and I don't want to talk to anyone," he proclaimed. It sounded like a well-rehearsed line, unlike my feeble attempt. I scurried away, feeling very embarrassed, and it was a whole year before I gathered courage and practised my lines before I attempted it again.

I attempted this twice more, and each time I got the same response. The last time his eyes held a faint flicker of recognition—mild acknowledgement of a familiar pest—but I didn't make any progress.

No. 10, Serpentine Street

Naveen, one of the founder members, and I, met friends of Don and were repeatedly reminded of his inclination to lead a private life and not be disturbed. All that changed in 2008. Kakarla Jayaraman, one of the group members, got to hear from someone that Don was in hospital for a surgery, and landed up at Santosh Nursing Home. While the bulk of the expenses at the hospital had been paid, Jayaraman paid the balance. There wasn't too much of a protest from Don and that act of kindness changed Don's attitude forever.

Initially Jayaraman, being the good samaritan, was given the sole privilege of speaking to Don. We couldn't wait for the first meeting to get over and to hear all the details, and Jayaraman with his amazing memory did not disappoint us. However, it wasn't enough; we didn't want to miss even a single word, and so we convinced Jayaraman to hide a voice recorder in his pocket and prepped up him with questions we needed answers to! Thus, began the first of our sting operations... exciting times indeed. He would keep the tiny recorder in his pocket and rattle off our mammoth list of queries meticulously, and when he came back we would all revel in the success of our secret exploits.

Then one day Jayaraman had a surprise for us. He, Naveen, and I had finished listening to the last recorded session when, as cool as a cucumber, he asked us, "Would you chaps like to go to the jungles with Don?"

"Of course, we would," we chorused. Was there a need to ask?

"Ok, then let's go 2 weeks from now."

I was dumbstruck. I had imagined it to be something in the distant future but here was Jay, grinning from ear-to-ear and practically bursting to tell us, doing it with such élan, it sounded almost rhetorical. The next couple of weeks were a blur and one early morning in Oct 2008 we set off to meet Don, armed with video cameras, books, hundreds of questions and of course our secret recorder. We hired a vehicle (no one wanted to drive and miss out on the conversation), pushed and shoved each other out of the way to occupy the seats behind Don (he sat in front), and poor Jayaraman realised that this was one occasion where his age did not merit any consideration. Don had a vast repertoire of jokes, rather crude and perhaps common in his circles, but he had us in splits right from the start.

He could have even read out the telephone directory and we would have found it rib tickling, for such was the mood he created. Although hesitant at first, we bombarded him with questions, and he patiently and skillfully answered only those he wanted to. Most of our questions were about the places and people mentioned in the books, and after a while he admitted that he was familiar with the stories, but clearly did not have the tenacity and borderline psychotic enthusiasm that we did. He mentioned that most of his father's hunting stories took place during the late thirties to the late fifties, so he was party to only some of those adventures. However, he told us about a whole different set of adventures, those that he experienced in the jungles, and we sat there, spellbound.

Don was a good storyteller, always hamming, and when he spoke Tamil, it was almost impossible to make out what language it was. The result was entertaining to say the least. Don had so many stories about the places we passed on the way to Bandipur. They were not always about hunting; there were stories about angling, girlfriends, fights, losing his way in the jungles, getting into trouble with the locals—he had such a vast array, we all looked on enviously at this man for having lived this colourful and extraordinary life.

It was way past lunchtime when we reached Bandipur, and Don had made arrangements for us to stay that night with his friend Sunita who was absolutely delighted to see him. We helped ourselves to some delicious minced meat and rice. As we were settling in for a siesta, Don stated, "Boys, don't think that I'm boasting, but I bring good luck to a lot of people who come out into the jungles with me. If things go well, we should get to see some big cats." I nodded in earnest, half asleep, but I smirked to myself. Good luck? I had been visiting these forests since I was a toddler and had never seen a tiger or panther. "Poor delusional old man," I said to myself.

We were keen to go for a safari but Don was reluctant, stating that he was a foreign national and did not want to go in a government jeep in case they asked him for proof of nationality. It was an absurd idea but that's what Don felt. It was a glimpse into a mind full of inherent suspicion, irrational fears, and above all a stubborn attitude that had no room to listen to anyone else's point of view. While the safari was the usual fare, as we were leaving the main area and heading off onto the Mangala Road, a small panther ran across the road and climbed a tree. We were very excited but it happened so fast that none of us got any photographs. We rushed back to tell Don the news. "What did I tell you?" was his casual response. I wanted to point out that we had seen the cat when his absence was notably conspicuous but I didn't want to be a kill-joy so I let his comment pass.

"Are you saying that you saw the tree that it had climbed, but you did nothing after that?"

It was a bizarre question, what did he expect us to do? Get down from the vehicle, walk up to the foot of the tree and look up? His expression seemed to suggest that.

We decided to go for dinner to the Masinagudi Log Hut some distance away. This was before the ban on vehicular traffic at night, so there was no restriction on moving about. At 7:00 p.m. a sharp downpour delayed our start from Mangala, and since the trip to dinner was an excuse to spot wildlife, we decided that we would wait for the showers to subside. By 7:40 the rain had practically stopped, and we decided to try our luck. We were hungry and did not arm ourselves with our usual arsenal of torches and cameras. I remember putting aside my video camera thinking that in pitch darkness, with chances of more rain, it would not be of any use. The drive up to the Ooty road proved uneventful, and just as we started noticing the lights on the right side of the road, from the huts that belonged to the forest officials, we saw that a jeep coming our way had stopped, pointing its headlights to the bushes that were to our left. Clearly, they had spotted something, and we concluded that whatever they were looking at was significant. It was still drizzling, and we couldn't make out what it was. We turned a slight corner and there was this incredible sight! Caught in the jeep's headlights was a chital stag struggling in a lantana bush, its throat caught in the jaws of a panther! The fact that we had never seen anything like this was proven with the staccato cry of "Kill. Kill. Kill." from one of my friends who clearly was overawed by this sight. The panther was quite unsettled with the headlights and tried hard to get the stag into the lantana bushes but the big antlers were stuck and the deer's struggles did not make it any easier. I cursed myself inwardly for not getting my camera, and we cursed each other quite vocally for not getting more torches, as the only one we had could barely throw light more than a few feet away. Minutes passed, and we sat transfixed watching the spectacle. Then the stag finally ceased to struggle and the panther found it easier to wrench it through the lantana. The jeep left once the action was over but we decided to stay on, hoping to see or hear something. Unfortunately, the light source that helped us was gone, and the drizzle drowned out any sounds we were hoping to hear. A disgruntled lot, we were resigned to the next inevitable step—to move on and head for dinner. Then Don spoke. "Are you guys done?"

Assuming he wanted to know if our interest levels had been satiated, we replied in the affirmative. I tapped the driver to move on when I heard a door open! The next few minutes will always remain etched in my memory. Don stepped out of the car with his tiny torch and hobbled towards the bushes. I'm not sure why but none of us asked him to get back. No words of discouragement, no words to "be careful", nothing. We froze and watched in horror as Don staggered over tufts of grass and small bushes, tottering towards the lantana bush into which the panther and its prey had disappeared. Surely, he would get mauled or, worse, killed. No cat likes to be scared off its meal, and I was sure that this panther was no exception. However, we did nothing; we were mute spectators to an inevitable gory end. Luckily, the terrain proved to be too difficult for Don to manoeuvre in the darkness despite his torch, and much to his consternation, he had to turn back before he reached the particular bush. "He got away," Don muttered in obvious disgust as he got back into the car.

"Guys, if I were five years younger…"

"Don, were you out of your mind!" we exploded, having regained our long-forgotten senses.

"Tchhhe," retorted Don, "I just wanted to show you guys that these things are like pussycats. I know panthers, and the moment it heard me walking towards it, it would have run away." Don added with a twinkle in his eye, "Another day, another time, and maybe I could have shown you how I would have dragged the carcass out." It sounded as though he had done that before. The next thirty minutes was a recap from each individual member in the car on how they felt while all this was happening; a cluster-catharsis of sorts. Don just sat quietly in the car. There was no display of pride for what was clearly a very brave, yet incredibly mindless, accomplishment.

We didn't see anything else that evening, so we hit the sack by eleven or so. If we were hoping for a blissful night's sleep, we were in for a rude shock. It was pitch dark when I heard a voice shouting "Time to get up boys". It sounded like Don, but I felt that it was my imagination till a few seconds later when I felt the full fury of a powerful torch on my eyes. Not the most pleasant way to be woken up, but this was Don and I really couldn't say much. There were multiple groans from the room as

Don went to each bed scorching the occupant's face and waking him up.

"Don, its only 4:30, let's sleep for a bit more."

"You buggers, if you want to sleep you shouldn't have come for the trip. Get up now!" he thundered.

We were not unaccustomed to waking up early to go for a drive and spot wildlife, but 4:30 was a stretch. This was typical Don; if he wanted to do something, everyone in the group had to follow, there was no room for individual consideration. We just followed the leader of the pack, something that would become the permanent undertone of all our trips in the years to come. After breakfast at the Masinagudi Log House, we found ourselves with nothing much to do for the rest of the morning. Naveen had a brainwave. "Why don't we visit Mark Davidar?" he queried.

A strange look came over Don's face, but he was a sport and said, "Ok, let's do that, I haven't been to that place in about thirty years."

So, we drove along the Ooty highway and turned left at Chadapatti. Don whispered something into Naveen's ear, and they both grinned at each other. We reached Mark's home and a familiar sight greeted us. Mark was in his verandah, smoking a cigarette and occasionally peering ahead with his binoculars. Naveen got out of the car first, Mark's mood being notoriously fickle. Luckily, he recognised Naveen and they spent a couple of minutes talking to each other. Naveen then motioned towards the car, which was our cue. We got out of the car and Don gingerly walked towards the duo. I could sense confusion on Mark's countenance; he apparently did not recognise Don but realised that this was not an ordinary visitor. Don settled down in a chair next to Mark and indulged in some idle chatter. I could see that Mark was curious and wanted to ask for introductions, but he wasn't making the first move.

"C'mon Mark, don't you recognise me? You've been telling these boys that you know me very well, surely I haven't changed that much," chortled Don.

After much hemming and hawing, accompanied by visible discomfort, something unusual for Mark, he professed that he did not know the occupant of the chair next to his.

"We go back a long way Mark, in fact our parents knew each other very well."

Poor Mark, he kept staring at Don but no answers would come.

Then Naveen jumped in. "Mark, this is Don Anderson, Kenneth

Anderson's son."

Mark jumped out of his chair as if he had been stung.

"Oh, Don Anderson," he kept repeating over and over again.

We were then privy to a most unusual sight. Mark started hugging Don repeatedly. "I thought you were in Bangalore and bed-ridden," he exclaimed as Don tried to extricate himself. It was a funny sight—puny, stick-like Mark trying to smother barrel-shaped Don who was trying to stop Mark as gently as possible. Mark was at his hospitable best, professing that it was his life-long dream to meet Don. Like any other visitor to Mark's place, Don was astounded with the wildlife he saw there, joining the esteemed company of many famous people who stayed with the Davidars including George Schaller.

We spent the afternoon there and headed back, but Mark had insisted that we come back again to stay with him and we did that on numerous occasions. Despite Mark's strict rules, it would be accurate to say that this was Don's favourite place in the wild, and he would often tell us how much he regretted not knowing about this spot earlier. He spoke with such authority on just about anything that was connected to the jungles, and we were so much in awe of his phenomenal knowledge, practically all of which had been based on real life experiences.

With Mark Davidar

"Guys, I know just a fraction of what my father knew. I'm not saying this because he was my dad, but the breadth and depth of the knowledge he possessed about the jungles . . . he was incomparable, and I wish you guys could have met him, he loved to talk to youngsters like you."

Mr. Jayaraman, who was sixty, and just fourteen years younger than Don at that time, swelled with pride!

That first trip to the jungles changed our equation with Don. At first, we would be allowed past the compound gate but would have to sit on the cement blocks outside his door. We weren't allowed to get closer and we would fantasise about what lay beyond those forbidden walls! Our progress was inversely proportional to his health, and there came a day when he could not get up from bed; he had a severe cough and Naveen had to get inside to help him. That marked another turning point in our relationship with him.

The first trip gave us a glimpse into his modus operandi. It's true that he was famous for his exploits and the fact that he was Kenneth Anderson's son brought him instant adoration. However, even ignoring these two factors, he had a certain charm in the way he spoke to people, and always managed to cement friendships very soon. His predilection for the barter system opened our eyes to how he had survived all these years. In his tiny eco system, with minimal investment, he helped to move the economy just by helping goods and services change hands. In return for his time and entertainment, we would take him around in our cars, and buy meals and medicines for him. The master of the swap still felt that the equation was one-sided, and so would offer to buy us meals at some of the places he frequented. They were extremely derelict places, like the small biriyani joint behind the mosque at Johnson market. Despite considering ourselves to be accommodative, we drew the line when it came to some of these. His life of penury had forced him to eat at these terribly unsanitary places and it's a miracle how he never got typhoid or dysentery. While he would protest about us picking up the tab when we took him to better restaurants, no meal was complete without the mandatory vanilla ice cream. He would always call "Bearer" if he needed something, and asked for "Tomato Sauce" as an accompaniment for everything that was brought, the type of cuisine did not matter! He would be horrified at a 10% tip, and always grumbled about what that could buy, forgetting the passage of time!

As we started to get involved in Don's life, he started to let down his defences. After having led a very secluded life for all these years, relying only on close friends, it was a remarkable turn-around, especially considering his age. Here was a man so set in his ways, so stubborn about the way he led his life, it was extraordinary that he opened his life up to strangers, and sadly, his physical condition was a major reason. As his health deteriorated, in the absence of friends and family who were no longer around to help, he had to find alternative ways to survive. He realised that his last days were no longer nebulous, but a harsh inevitable reality.

After a year or so, Don felt that he needed to reward us for all that we had done for him. He refused to divulge more information, but promised Naveen, Jayaraman and me that he would take us to a jungle, two hours from Bangalore. It sound too good to be true. We knew, of course, that no such place existed. But to humour him, we played along. We picked up Don at five in the morning, and drove past Jigani and then towards Hosur. He told us of how June and he would go cycling to Devarabetta on these same roads when they were young. Soon we reached Javalagiri, and the fact that Don had not visited the place in many years became evident as he could not figure out the landmarks. At Javalagiri we enquired about Muniyappa, Don's shikari guide. Alas, Muniyappa was no more, but we were guided to his home. As we drew up the car, a few members came forward and asked us what we were looking for. They confirmed that this indeed was Muniyappa's house, but he was no more.

"How about Venkat Swamy?" asked Don, referring to Muniyappa's son.

"Oh sir, he too is no more," lamented a lady.

Venkat Swamy's mother's eyes filled with tears as she explained that her son had passed away just a couple of months earlier. Fiercely dabbing her tears, she pointed to Don and stated,

"I remember that *Dorai*."

Don quietly nodded in acknowledgement as he mentioned how he used to spend a few hours at Muniyappa's house and how the lady used to serve him food back in the day. Don abruptly interrupted, "What about the trees I planted?"

She nodded in the affirmative, and although she was too ill to show us the way, asked another lady to do so. She led us to two big mango trees, and we noticed two graves under them. One belonged to Muniyappa and the other to Venkat Swamy. Obviously, they were buried there for a reason, and although we dared not ask why, it seemed to us that it was only fitting that they were buried under the same tree that they helped

Don to plant during his visits in the sixties. Don told us that he had brought saplings from Lalbagh during one of his visits, and his eyes filled up on seeing those lovely trees and realising the fact that both his shikari guide and his son were no more. It was evident that they had had some good times together. Don's memory was phenomenal, he kept bringing up names of people he knew at the village, but unfortunately they were no more. Don was feeling downbeat, so we asked him to take us to the spots in and around the village and that brightened him up. The first stop was the forest bungalow. It still stands today, and as Don mentioned, in almost the same condition since the late sixties. In those days it stood on the edge of the forest and Don pointed us to a room in the bungalow.

"Do you know that once I sat up from bed on hearing a panther calling? The sound was so close to the bungalow, I thought that perhaps I could see the panther from the window. Sure enough, there was a panther walking away from the bungalow, sawing. Without losing a minute, I shot it from behind, and it sank to its knees. It was not a very sporting shot, but that stands out as the only panther I shot, from practically the bed I was sleeping on!"

...And I let fly. With Jayaraman at Javalagiri Forest Bungalow

Don then mentioned two waterholes that were his favourite haunts when he visited Javalagiri. One was two furlongs from the main road, a muddy tank called Dassarachettycheruvu. It was mid-day by now, and so we had no chance of seeing any wildlife. However even while scouting around, we didn't come across any tracks or pug marks. We were later informed that despite the lush vegetation there was practically no wildlife in these parts, most of it was wiped out by poaching, save the occasional deer or wild boar. It was depressing for Don to hear because he remembered the area full of game, including tigers even in the early fifties.

Months passed and some of us started taking Don to a lot of the places he had frequented when he was younger, and while it was a wonderful experience just to have him narrate hundreds of stories on the journey, perhaps the most poignant moment was when Naveen took him to BR Hills. Although he was hesitant at first, he agreed to come along. He was his usual exuberant self all the way, but as we entered Mudiyanoor, he fell silent and as we got into the driveway to Moyar Valley Ranch, his eyes welled with tears. It was an emotional reunion for Don; it had been thirty years or more since he had set foot here, and he just couldn't hold back the sobbing. Luckily, the owner of the property, which is now called Tiger Farm, was a Kenneth Anderson fan, and was ecstatic to meet Don in the flesh. He promised Don that he could come and stay as often as he wanted and Don was very touched.

On their way to Honathatti, among other things, they came across fresh tiger scat on the road, and Don picked it up in a little plastic bag. It was a vital ingredient of his *mantram* and that act of his soon became a regular feature on all our trips. When he passed away, we discovered in his tiny abode, enough tiger scat, carefully wrapped in little tiny plastic bags, to attract all the thousand odd tigers that were alive in India at that time.

Despite his obvious attempts at being a freeloader, Don was always honest; his philosophy was "borrow from Peter to barter with Paul" but he never swindled anyone. He had a sharp eye to identify someone who had the potential to help him and he would go overboard, usually overcompensating with things which might have seemed excessive to him but were in fact trivial and cheap. Most were in return for favours that involved efforts like running errands or work that he was physically incapable of doing himself. If one took him to his bank at Shrungar

Complex on MG Road, it was considered a big deal because by then he couldn't ride his bike. The thought of travelling by autorickshaw was utterly alien and you would be surprised how he managed to survive for so long, till you realised that all his life Don managed to get people to do these sorts of chores for him. He was the undisputed master of getting people to do things and in his mind, a carton of double yolk eggs was adequate compensation for a morning of taking him around in one's car, while he did his "marketing". Giant bottles of jam from the wholesale market, cheap lighters from the footpath vendors, hats bought from peddlers at traffic signals, and rusty knives were the kinds of things he would give us in return for helping him. Despite his obvious dereliction of propriety, we would be constantly reminded about his hardship through random incidents. We used to take him out for lunch about once a week and halfway through his meal, he would declare that he was full, and would get the rest packed for his next meal. It was painful to watch. His pride would not let him admit that he was unsure where his next meal was coming from. Although he was quite uncomfortable when we took him to popular restaurants, he could still be choosy. Hyderabad House on Richmond Road and The Only Place where he knew the owner, Haroon, were two of his favourites.

The irony of Don's health was that for someone who had led an epicurean devil-may-care life, he was in relatively good shape for a seventy-four-year-old. He was as strong as an ox, had a ravenous appetite, perfect eyesight that could spot a movement in the jungles hundreds of yards away, and a razor-sharp mind and hearing. His only illness was a dry cough, extremely distressing to hear, that would precipitate during the summer. His body would be racked with convulsions, and his chest would sound like a hundred marbles being ground inside a mixer. Each fit would leave him breathless, and the listener, quite shaken. He had had it for years, but it was getting steadily worse, and we took him to every doctor recommended by his well-wishers. Taking turns, we visited hospitals of every kind; from Manipal and Mallya to the most obscure ones in shady alleys behind Kapali Theatre, we experimented with all, but none of them seemed to make a difference. Each doctor would ask Don to stop all the medicines that he was taking and prescribe a fresh set. Don's impatience made matters worse; he would never carry out a full course and expected instant results, and on most days that we met the doctor, I would get a call late at night stating how much petrol I had wasted by going all the way because there was absolutely no change in his condition. He would often mix and match various prescriptions, and was always clear in his head why some were discontinued while others remained on his roster. He had a certain irrefutable logic and by then we had realised that it was futile trying to get Don to change his mind once he had decided on something. It was also the first glimpse into his obsessive hoarding behaviour. He had prescriptions of the last twenty years or so, for all his ailments, carefully filed although in no particular order! I don't think he ever looked into the files, but he got some comfort from the fact that they existed. The bouts of coughing were worst when the weather got hot, and we tried everything from cleaning the cobwebs, dusting and fumigation his house and even re-laying the floor, but nothing worked. As always, Don found the solution himself—he placed his bed outside the house, tied a giant plastic sheet over it and slept in the open.

Soon, other symptoms started to surface, and the first was breathlessness. He always complained that he was not getting enough oxygen, and we would simper behind his back, exchanging glances; here was a hypochondriac who knew not just the exact diagnosis of his symptoms but the resolution as well. So, at night, a table fan was kept right next to his face, and if that wasn't enough, he felt that he needed a CPAP machine and an oxygen tank, just as back up. Thanks to the generosity of people like Ajit St John, Prashanth Sethi, Ashok Tendolkar, Darryl Ross, and Don's sister, there were always finances flowing in to take care of his medical condition.

I don't blame him, most of the doctors got the diagnosis wrong, prescribing medicines that never improved his ailments, but somewhere we got lucky and on further testing found out that he had aortic valve stenosis which was causing the shortness of breath. This got progressively worse, and during the last few months of his life, he could hardly walk a few paces before stopping to catch his breath. His doctor would advise him to walk as much as possible, but he had lost the motivation. Even when we took him to the jungles he would be content just sitting in the car, a huge change from the times when he was eager to get his feet on the ground and explore.

If all that didn't make his life tough, there was the constant fight with his landlady. She would come every year with the intention of checking the value of the property and finding a buyer if the price was right.

Property value was on the rise in Bangalore and she believed that if she waited a little while longer she would get a better price but the bigger challenge was getting Don to move out, for her to sell the estate. With every visit, the confrontations got uglier. In 2009, I was witness to one. At that time, I worked with TNT Express, a five-minute walk from Don's house, and during those years I spent a lot of time with him, visiting him almost every day after work, and hearing his stories, complaints, and discomforts, not necessarily in that order.

He called me over one morning, and said, "Josh, I want you to just stay inside my house. On my cue, come out and look very serious, don't say a word."

I did as I was told. As I sat in his house, he walked over to talk to the visitors and soon decibel levels were on the rise. There was so much anger in the conversation and the landlady was screeching her head off when Don said something and then called out to me. I reached the spot and Don pointed at me. "Do you know who this is? He is a top shot lawyer I have retained to sue you for distress caused to an old man. He specialises in cases like this, and has represented tenants like me who are being unfairly targeted."

I suppose they were taken aback by my neck-tie and the sheets of paper I had in my hand, so they didn't notice that my knees were knocking. I squinted and gave them a cold stare, with a nod to Don, as if to confirm his statement. It was a masterstroke because in a second, the volume of the conversation dropped. They were trying to size me up, and I looked back with what I hoped was an icy glower.

"You may be a hot shot lawyer, but I have other ways of handling this situation," she retorted. The anger and malice were gone and was replaced by a false bluster.

I suppose one of the reasons Don survived so long was his ability to foresee and mitigate potential disasters, and he was a marvel at that. Once, the landlady threatened to send *goondas* (thugs) to get him evicted. Don pre-empted it by going to the Ashok Nagar police station and filing a report that he was being threatened. While he had to pay a bribe to get the policeman to visit the premises, it worked when word got around that a policeman was visiting his house every evening. In all fairness, Don had no right to continue to live at No.10, Serpentine Street. He had been practically evicted from his house in Eejipura and faced the same situation here.

However, he was adamant that he would not give into threats, and refused to listen to our suggestion to move to a different locality. It was pride, it was stupidity, it was stubbornness, it was heart-breaking bravado, but this was his last stand

There was a smaller building adjacent to the one he lived in and this was Don's dumping ground. I had set my eyes on this place the first time I was invited in the compound, fantasising about the contents that lay inside. At some point, I asked Don if I could rummage through his hoard, and he didn't seem to mind. Over decades, he had managed to fill that room with an astounding number of things; things no one would touch even if you offered them money. From broken rubber bands and coconut shells from pre-Independence days to damaged rubber boots and receipts of telephone bills paid during the Emergency. Wallets held together by fungus-covered pieces of paper that upon closer inspection would prove to be a grocery list from shops that no longer existed. Broken plastic pots, pens that did not work, sheets of paper held together by rusty pins that crumbled upon touch, trunks filled with clothes soiled by water and dust, and a hundred thousand dead silverfish and cockroaches.

I saw this as an opportunity to touch, feel, and inhale history, and I knew that the secret treasure I was searching for was just another dust-filled trunk away. I knew that I wouldn't find guns or trophies, but I always kept searching, braving dust and sharp rusty metal parts as I dug deeper. There was absolutely no space to manoeuvre in that crowded room, so it meant lifting heavy boxes, twisting and turning, and getting my arms and legs scraped against corroded metal pieces, while enjoying frequent dust allergies.

He was always encouraging when I brought out trunks. I did not have the patience to look for the right key, so I would take a hammer or wrench and force upon the trunks, only to find yet another colossal amount of indisputable garbage in it.

"Don, can you please tell me what on earth you are going to do with this?"

I rolled my eyes at an eclectic mix of irreparable motorcycle tyre tubes, hardened cement mixture, parts of a lavatory flush system, thirty-seven empty tubs of Brylcream and three egg shells whose contents had been consumed when Don passed kindergarten.

"You never know when you might need them," pat came the answer.

"You youngsters won't understand. In my days, when something was broken we didn't throw it away, we tried to fix it, and if not, we kept it aside, for sometimes you never know when you will need the parts to fix something else."

"Does that apply to the eggshell too, Don?"

He burst into a false cough, clearly wanting to have the last word in that conversation.

Some days I would strike gold. Photographs of his relatives from Scotland from the late 1800s, to hundreds of negatives from his father's trips to the jungles, I slowly put together the life and times of a family that had all but disappeared. And holding phonographs that were more than a century old made me even more determined to bring this story to life, someday.

Don's health spiralled downwards dramatically from 2010, and it was painful to see the transformation happen so quickly, right before our eyes. The first time we had met him in 2008, he was recovering from an operation at Santosh Nursing Home after he had had his gall bladder removed, and also to correct his hernia, but for some reason the hernia procedure was not successful, and he walked around with a large belt to hold things together.

A few months before that, Don had called his friend Noel Peacock and complained to him about chest pains. Noel had rushed there in his autorickshaw and taken him to Santosh hospital again, where the doctors found that his body was limp, and he did not have a pulse; he had suffered a cardiac arrest. When he had arrived at the hospital, there was no room in the men's ward, so he had to be taken temporarily to the women's ward. The joke among his friends was that while it was not planned, that was got Don's heart to start beating again!

By 2010, his hernia had got worse, his movements were extremely limited. He had no choice but to have an operation. Don had a morbid fear of being subjected to anesthesia, as he felt that with his breathing trouble he would never recover. What compounded that was the fact that two of his friends had lost their lives on the operating table and hence he fought the decision to go under the knife till a point where he was in excruciating pain and could not even get up from his bed. In November, he was operated on by Dr. Kenneth D'Cruz at Philominas Hospital, the one place where Don did not want to get admitted as his mother had died there. A laparoscopy was done, and everyone believed that it was a success. He was warned by the doctors to be extremely careful with his diet, but to Don, who had never listened to anyone all his life, it was just one of the things that was meant to be ignored. In less than a week's time he started to feel acute discomfort in his stomach, and he was right in diagnosing that this was not like before; the pain became excruciating and painkillers did not seem to bring any relief. He was taken back to Philomina's where it was noticed that he had a case of intestine malrotation or a twist in the intestine. This time, there was no choice but to have a regular surgery and once again Dr. D'Cruz stepped up, and as before refused payment as he knew about Don's financial condition. The operation was successful, and they introduced a mesh to hold the intestine together. This brought relief to Don and he was warned to watch his diet, and go for walks regularly, but everyone knew that it would only fall on deaf ears. A few months later, the area started acting up again. This time there was fluid accumulation around the mesh that caused a portion of his stomach to bulge out. It was not painful like in the past, but it certainly was something to worry about, and we convinced Don to go back and get it fixed. Don had another operation, and Dr. Kenneth, who had clearly warned Don of something like this happening, aspirated the whole thing and fixed it. Another mesh was introduced, and for some reason, despite Don's total lack of restraint, it did not aggravate beyond a point.

During one of these surgeries, Don was lying in the general ward and had an IV tube connected to him. In the middle of the night, one of the nurses came to tend to him and change the IV bottle. After she was done, Don called out saying that something was wrong, and that the IV wasn't fixed properly. Being seasoned in her field, she nodded her head and confirmed that she would come back to fix it, and with typical apathy, left, leaving Don in a limbo. Once Don put his mind on something, he would never let it go till it was resolved, so he sat up, adamant that he would not sleep till the IV had been fixed properly. However, the medication he had taken left him drowsy and a couple of hours later, he woke up with a start. His pants and sheet were wet, and his immediate reaction was he had probably wet himself. So, he took out his torch and checked, and to his horror found that the entire bed was covered with blood. The IV needle had fallen off and he had been lying there bleeding for a while. He shouted for the nurse and she recoiled in shock when she switched on the light, for there was blood everywhere—on his body, his clothes, the sheets, even a bloody hand print on the table.

Although he was taken to many hospitals, during a check-up at Narayana Hrudayalaya it was discovered that he was suffering from Atrial Fibrillation and that there was a good chance that he would suffer a stroke at any point. However, surgery was ruled out as it was extremely risky considering his age and condition. His constant bouts of insomnia got worse and he began to look haggard. The only thing that kept him going were trips to the jungles. He was willing to meet and talk to anyone in exchange for an opportunity to be taken to the wilds. All he did was sit in the car, he could hardly walk, but he just wanted to breathe the air, and take in the sights and sounds. It was such a tragic change; from being a recluse who protected his privacy with such ardour, to a blubbering old man, willing to give people time and attention, telling them stories and jokes he had repeated so many times before, just to be invited for a drive to the forests. That too had consequences—he was often violently ill with shortness of breath, nausea and vomiting, and we feared that his premonition of dying in the wilderness would come true.

During one of the tests, an X-ray showed up something surprising, and it speaks volumes of the various doctors who had been looking at Don's lungs all those years. It appeared that Don had suffered a broken clavicle at some point, and the bones had eventually fixed, but at an odd angle as it had not been set right during the healing process. Don was as surprised as the doctor who pointed that out but could not remember when that had ever happened! His prostate had been constantly giving him trouble, and shortly, his kidneys started giving him trouble, causing his feet to swell to mammoth proportions. Don was deliriously happy that he had to pay the nephrologist just one consultation fee to treat two conditions!

In Dec 2013, he started accumulating phlegm in his lungs and was subsequently diagnosed with pneumonia. We were once again faced with a situation where Don would have to undergo surgery for his heart condition which had aggravated. In the past, Don would sign the papers before going in for surgery that absolved the hospital of liabilities, considering his age and health, but at Mallya hospital where he was last admitted, the doctors stated, for the first time, that surgery was not an option, as Don would not survive it. I can't even comprehend what goes on in someone's mind when the doctor confirms that there is no cure, not even an operation. It would crush the spirit of most people, but Don was different. He received the news with remarkable aplomb and his bravery during times like this often would overwhelm us.

On the other hand, he demonstrated time and again that he was not just a hypochondriac, but a manic worrier about everything. He was worried about treatments, the costs of operations, post-operative care, whether medicines were working, but his biggest fear was whether he would be allowed to be buried in Hosur Road Protestant Cemetery. For all his rants arguing about the existence of God and the role of the Church, in the end, it mattered to him where his final resting place would be, and he was adamant that he wanted to be united with his parents.

Somebody up there certainly liked Don for every time he found himself in a quagmire, someone would appear on the scene to bail him out, and often it used to be people who hardly knew him. Take the case of K.M. Srinivasa Murthy, an ardent Kenneth Anderson fan, who was astounded to learn that his hero's son was still alive. For the short time he knew Don, Mr. Murthy's generosity knew no bounds in taking care of most of Don's expenses.

I knew Don for just six years, and it's hard to credit one single person with Don's well-being during that time, but in my opinion Naveen Sathyanand exemplified selflessness and devotion to such a degree that most of Don's friends and well-wishers would be put to shame. From the first day we met Don till his funeral and everything in between, Naveen was the one constant in Don's life; the son Don never had. He was with Don for every hospital visit, however minor the procedure was. He tried to be available for practically all the trips that Don made to the jungles, doing most of Don's odd jobs, and most importantly, putting up with Don's hypochondria, stubbornness, and lack of consideration for other people's feelings. For Don, everything was an emergency and the time of day was immaterial. And to top that, he would keep repeating himself till the job was completed in the manner he felt right.

If I were to make a list of all the people whose efforts made a difference to Don, it would run into pages. However, it wouldn't be right if I did not mention two women, who've been with him through thick and thin. The first lady was diffident about having her name included in the book, but it would be a gross injustice if I didn't, so I'll refer to her as Khushi. She was always by Don's side; in fact, his only constant for the thirty-nine years they knew each other. She played many roles over time, but the most important one was that of a companion and a nurse, and Don was helpless without her. She, in turn, was totally devoted to Don but much to her distress, Don never wanted to marry her despite all she had done for him over the years.

The other is someone who's known him since the day he was born—his sister, June. Although she left home sixty years ago, as typical sisters are, she looked after him unconditionally. In the fifties and sixties, she was constantly trying to get Don to move abroad, but Don couldn't bear the thought of living far from the jungles of India. Despite all her troubles, she always looked after Don financially, sending him money that she had saved away.

During his last years, Don survived on handouts and the goodwill of people. He was not a charitable organisation or a good cause. No, this was different. To a large extent, this was the power of writing, the words of Kenneth Anderson, immortalised through the books he had written.

Those books had such a profound impact on people that when the time came, they felt that helping Don was their way of paying back. Of course, there were his old angling buddies like Jimmy, Sudhir, Prithvi, Meru, Sal, the incomparable Nader Mirza and so many others. Each of them had a role to play and their combined efforts always ensured that Don had just about enough to get by. It often defied logic how Don managed to get people to help him out at different times of his life. He was extremely cantankerous, finicky, stubborn, and would always take people for granted after a while. It's sad but true that the only constant thought in his mind was how to make friends with the next person who could be of some value to him, and he was not unduly worried if he burnt bridges with his friends from the past.

He had lived his life doing exactly what he wanted and was therefore used to everyone falling in line with his plans. To his credit, he was never ungrateful, and his appreciation was frequent, vocal, and always heartfelt. Despite his ability to understand how the world had changed, he would still hold on to ideals and beliefs that no longer applied. He was amazingly bright to understand how the internet worked, especially "Googly", but he still believed that a one-rupee tip was good enough at a restaurant. He understood how bills could be paid online but expected someone from the telephone or electricity department to be there in ten minutes after he made a complaint. He understood MRI scans, and video conferencing, but would never complete a course of medication, as he fussed about the lack of results after a day or two. He expected us to pick up his calls whenever he called whether it was the middle of the day while in office, or the middle of the night, at home. He would eat meat in the company of vegetarians, he would make sexist and racist jokes, and generally be oblivious to the fact that the world had changed.

Even his jokes that included references to money had paise as the default denomination!

Don the fixer, called us excitedly saying that he had made friends with a certain gentleman who owned a huge property in the Nilgiris, and had got permission for all of us to visit that place.

"You can hear tigers and panthers from the bloody window," boasted Don.

Although we knew that he never exaggerated about stuff like this, it seemed too good to be true. We expressed our disbelief, having frequented those parts for years. Then Don revealed that we were going to a place called Anaikadu, which was past the Singara check post at Masinagudi. We had heard about this place but knew that it was impossible to get past the check post controlled by the state electricity board. Don's benefactor, Darryl Ross, knew the owners and had managed to get a free pass for Don and a couple of his friends, as it was not a commercial resort and access was only given to select people. We could hardly contain ourselves, and each of us pacified relevant stakeholders at office and home and ensured that we did not miss this trip. Unfortunately, I had some other commitments and hence had to withdraw. Naveen, Don, and a few others had an unforgettable time at this unique abode.

Months later, I got a chance to visit Anaikadu with Don, who by then had made friends with everyone who worked there, especially Raju, the superintendent of the property. This is a massive estate that borders the forest and in the middle is a very charming house, built in typical Kerala style but on huge stilts. The first evening we were out in two jeeps, Raju driving one, while our friend Ravi was driving the other. We had spent thirty minutes driving around and hadn't seen much, so we stopped for a bit and Don got out to relieve himself. Almost on cue, we heard a deep moan from beyond the bushes. We all froze, too excited to believe what we had heard.

"Tiger, tiger," whispered Don, with a twinkle in his eye.

I was too excited to wait for Don. I asked Raju to follow the sound of the tiger, and we sped past. The moans were getting louder but it was too dense to see the cat. In a while, the other car arrived with Don, and he saw us peering intently.

"Boys, let me try something," he muttered as he got out of the car.

I expected him to clap his hands or make some noise, but instead he came up to the jeep and asked Naveen for his camera. He snatched it out of Naveen's hands while Naveen was still weighing the pros and cons. "Drive ahead and wait at the fire line," he suggested.

I had no idea what he was talking about, but I motioned to Raju to drive on. As I turned back, I noticed that Don had disappeared into the undergrowth, hobbling with his walking stick in one hand and the camera in the other. We couldn't see anything, but the sound of twigs breaking and the occasional distinct sound of Don's hoarse cough reassured us that he was still alive. If we could hear Don, the tiger could as well, and suddenly, it was déjà vu. I had a knot in my stomach, knowing that this time, it was going to end badly. Then, right in front of us, breaking cover at the fire line stood the tiger, almost sheepishly, having been drawn out by Don! Naveen, who had no expectations from Don's charade, had got down and was caught between the safety of the jeep and the tiger. His lifelong dream of seeing a tiger on foot had been fulfilled, but he didn't look particularly ecstatic when the tiger stared at him! However, it lasted just a few seconds and then it moved off. We were so elated that we forgot about Don. Huffing and panting, he walked up to our jeep.

"Hope you boys got a good sighting because I couldn't get any pictures."

Apparently, while stalking the tiger through the bushes, it had turned back and looked at Don a couple of times, but by the time he got the camera ready to click a picture, it had taken off.

"These things are harmless," muttered Don as he tried to catch his breath. "Nine times out of ten, they are more scared of you than you are of them. It's so safe, you can chase any of them."

Back at Anaikadu, the excitement of Don chasing the tiger had built such a feeling of euphoria that we refused to just sit back and enjoy the evening. We quickly gulped down our dinner, eager to try our luck again. We hopped into our vehicles and spent the next hour driving around.

During the journey Don suddenly asked, "How many of you have caught nightjars?" A puerile question really; he might have as well asked how many of us had tickled tigers!

"Let me show you how it's done," he added.

All along the property was a barbed wire fence and often we would catch the glowing eyes of these birds as we drove along flashing our torches. "Hold it right there," he said. The piercing beam of my torch had found the eyes of a nightjar as it sat on a post, and the bird stood still, mesmerised.

"Don't move a muscle," he warned, as he got down from the car ensuring that he didn't block the beam. In a quick motion he grabbed the bird, who still sat hypnotised by the headlights.

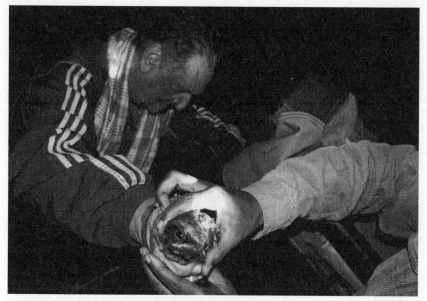

A nightjar in hand…

With Don, there was never a dull moment. However, a visit to the jungles meant that he dictated the entire trip—the timing of each activity, the places we visited, what provisions to take, it was all planned down to the last detail. He would be up-to-date on the weather forecast and even try and coincide the trip with a full moon.

Every shikari has his own superstitions and beliefs, and Don was no different. While he no longer had to carry five cartridges when he was in the jungles, there were a lot of other oddities that he would demonstrate. His prized possession was a good luck charm, which was a small piece of bamboo sealed with beeswax on both ends, and trapped inside was the spirit of "a wild animal" whose sounds or vibrations would entice any big cat to come out from wherever it was hiding. However, the more elaborate subject was his *mantram*. This magic spell was guaranteed to get us a viewing of a tiger when we were out in the jungle. It had been taught to him by a Sholaga and despite relentless begging, he would not repeat it in front of us, or even allow me to record it. He was, however, generous enough to chant and bless any man-made object, thus ensuring that in the next few days a tiger would come within its sights. He assured me with all seriousness that it worked equally on cameras, as it did on guns, and having listened to my complaint of how I had never seen tigers in the wild assured me that after the *mantram* incantation, things would change.

261

"Josh, you need to bring me your camera close to your date of travel, for like my prepaid mobile recharge, this too has a validity," he said, giving me an analogy I could understand! I nodded earnestly and although I was flooded with derision, I agreed to humour him. The ingredients of his spell included seeds from the coral tree locally known as *kundumani*, tiger scat, camphor, a half-lit candle, the gun/camera of course, and the spell that he would chant. The first time we took Don to the Nilgiris, he sent Muthu, Mark Davidar's hired help, into the jungles to collect some of the ingredients, an act he would repeat at every opportunity he got. It was another classic Don move. It wasn't a sham, he truly believed that the *mantram* worked magic, and was eager to bestow its powers on to the camera of the next person he would meet—in the hope of getting a favour in return!

The second time we were at Mark's place, Muthu came back exceptionally quick, which surprised Don.

"I hope you haven't brought me the wrong animals' scat," he warned Muthu.

"No point luring Mark in front of the camera, is there?" he winked.

Forget seeing, none of us even heard Don during the incantation. He never shared the *mantram* as he had taken an oath never to share it, and the punishment for breaking it was death. "So, you see, in the interest of self-preservation, that secret can never be repeated to another living soul." Sometimes, during his bouts of lamentation of how his end was near, I would dishonourably sneak in a request for him to teach me the *mantram* - as he was going to die anyway, but he was old-fashioned that way, and took that secret to his grave.

Well, did it work?

I visited Tadoba immediately after my video camera had been blessed and I saw six tigers on that trip. I then saw two tigers in Bandipur, a couple more with Don in Segur, and although I never truly believed it, I couldn't shake off the feeling that somehow it had made a difference. There are others for whom the *mantram* did absolutely nothing at all, and Don's face would contort into a scowl when someone dismissed the *mantram* as rubbish.

"You should believe in it," he would tell me. "The *mantram* will not work on people who do not believe in its power."

"Of course, Don." I said, looking away, hoping he didn't notice the guilty look on my face.

Despite his obvious contempt for the supernatural, there were instances that led us to believe that perhaps deep down he believed in it, maybe subconsciously, and this became more evident during the last year of his life. There was a time when his breathing was getting so laborious that he put a bed outside the house with a makeshift roof made of plastic to protect him from rain. At night he would stay indoors and hardly sleep, but during the day he would lie in his bed outside. Late one evening, I was with him indoors, talking, when suddenly he interrupted.

"Don't look now, but there is someone sitting on my bed outside."

I immediately turned around for I thought it may have been some vagrant who had accidentally wandered into the property, but I could see no one.

"Nice joke, Don," I retorted, but Don's face was frozen, staring intently at the bed outside.

I realised that it was no joke and I felt the hairs at the back of my neck standing up. I just couldn't explain it. After a minute, he woke up from his reverie and renewed the conversation as though nothing had happened.

When I visited him a week later, I could see the change in him. He had a heavy stick that he kept by the side of his bed for protection and he had a couple of torches by his side. When I asked him about it, he mentioned something about people wandering in. I thought it may have been people sent by the landlady to oust him from the property, but she was still in Australia. If these were people out to rob him, they wouldn't let themselves be seen. I concluded that they were just a figment of his imagination and I told him so.

"Josh, do you think I believe in ghosts? Contrary to your perceptions that ghosts are moaning apparitions, these are regular people, who look like you and me."

I think that he wrestled with this ghost/non-ghost theory for a while and came to his own conclusion. "I think my end is near," he confided in me. "This is a sign from beyond."

Maybe it was the lack of sleep, but whatever the cause, it began to have an impact. He started losing weight, and began to look gaunt. On a couple of occasions, Naveen caught him uttering unintelligible curses from his room, looking into the darkness.

Then came the oddest incident of all. Early one morning I got a call from Don, "It's urgent, come fast." Short, and very precise; that was his style. Having listened to this old man who had cried wolf so many times, I knew that it was possibly nothing, so I took my time. I didn't notice anything odd as I walked into his room. He looked ashen and visibly upset. "Go look outside, I finally caught them."

"What do you mean, Don?" I asked incredulously as I rushed out to look.

No, there was no one lying dead, but I stopped in my tracks when I noticed the blood splatter on the wall. It was at about my height and looked fresh. That was not all. There were drops of blood on the ground, leading away from the door on to the stone slabs, suddenly ceasing beyond that. It was very odd, and I never found an explanation and he wouldn't speak more about it

For weeks after that Don slept with a heavy stick kept within touching distance and a black toy pistol that would not have fooled a three-year-old. However, it seemed to give some level of comfort and who was I to mock him?

If I had thought that that was the last such incident, I was wrong. Once Naveen and Don were going to Bandipur early in the morning and it was still dark when they were leaving Don's room. This was during the time when Don slept outdoors during the day and inside his room at night. Suddenly Don froze and then without warning, started yelling "Haji boko! Haji boko!" over and over again, gesticulating with his arms. Then he stopped and walked off, leaving Naveen startled. As they got in the car, Naveen couldn't control his curiosity.

"What on earth was that, Don?" he whispered, still shaken from the incident.

"I didn't want to upset you, Naveen, but as you were walking into my house, I saw a human form with long hair sitting on my bed outside. I couldn't make out whether it was male or female, but it had a definite form. When I heard your car, I switched on the light, and that's when the person disappeared. I have been seeing that form for some time now, and it means only one thing; my end is near. However, I did not want you in its sights and that's why I uttered the incantation to protect you. It was taught to me by a formidable Sholaga priest, and I have known it to be extremely powerful."

Naveen did not sleep peacefully for many days after that!

Despite his education, and the competence to rely on logic and common sense on most occasions, deep down Don's beliefs were irrevocably steeped in myth and superstition like the people from the jungles he spent time with. For someone who used to mock his father's belief in the occult, in his last days his mind succumbed to quiescent influences that perhaps had made a deeper bearing on his mind than he would have liked to believe. Don was in effect, a paradox of epic proportions. While he was proud of his hunting exploits and loved to narrate them, he was often racked with guilt, and suffered bouts of depression, lamenting on the lives he took. Though he loved company and could be very charming to a captive audience, he was quite often lonely. The only respite from gloom for him were the visits to the jungles when his eyes would sparkle, and every minute of the outing would be crammed, leaving no opportunity for wasted time—it was almost as though he knew that he wouldn't come back again.

The story of Donald Malcolm Stewart Anderson ends here. Unlike his father, who left behind a legacy through the books he wrote, Don will fade into obscurity in a few years. At best, he may come up in passing conversation, as a vestige of a time and place that we wistfully reminisce, without ever truly knowing or understanding. He won't be mourned by more than a handful of people because most of what he did was for selfish reasons. But he didn't really care, he did it anyway and in his own indomitable way. The world will never see someone like him again, for he represented not just the last generation of those who bestrode British and Independent India but also the archetypal great white hunter. The last of his breed who literally walked the jungles of south India, he learnt about its creatures and their behaviour not from books or television, but by observing them at close quarters. Reading about his exploits, armchair detractors will perhaps pass judgement on his actions, but he exemplified freedom and represented adventure in its truest sense.

Who will blink first?

About the Author

After much contemplation (and mostly lack of ideas), Joshua has decided that this will be his last book.

He lives in Bangalore with his beautiful wife (he only writes non-fiction) and two superheroes masquerading as his sons.

For more information about the book visit his website www.thelastwhitehunter.com. Scan the QR code printed below to link directly to the author's website.

Note from the Publisher

Dear Reader,

This is a *reSource*+ book!

In order to enhance your reading experience we have provided online Digital Resources, which you can access via the QR code given below. See video clips, photographs, and additional information related to this book via the QR code.

How to use the QR code:
If your phone does not have an inbuilt scanner, download any QR code scanner app from your app store on your mobile and scan the QR code given below.

Thank you for choosing this book! We would love to hear from you—do write to us with your feedback at info@indussource.com.

About Indus Source Books

Indus Source Books is a niche, independent book publisher in Mumbai passionately committed to publishing good and relevant literature. We believe that books are one of the most important mediums of communication and we seek to bring out publications that help to serve the community and the world we live in.

At Indus Source Books, we celebrate the diverse spiritual traditions, culture, and history of the world and present it to our readers in a contemporary format that retains its essential flavour: "Indian Spirit, Universal Wisdom."

Use the QR code below to visit our website www.indussource.com.

Indus Source Books
PO Box 6194
Malabar Hill PO
Mumbai 400006
India
www.indussource.com
info@indussource.com